ACCLAIM FOR
Shakespeare's Holy Grail

Shakespeare's Holy Grail reveals something momentous: insights, spiritual awareness and divine truths that have been hiding in plain sight for 400+ years. With a deft hand and astute turn of phrase, Paul takes us beyond dogmatic religiosity into the true meaning of religion that Shakespeare well understood — awakening and reconnecting to the depth of our own spiritual Being. Paul has discovered the true meaning behind Shakespeare's many works: to help us awaken to profound depths of spiritual attunement and see into our own souls..

—Dr. Russell Bishop, Best-selling Author, Transformational Change Coach, and Creator of Insight Seminars.

A powerhouse of a book, refreshing, invigorating and iconoclastic. With extraordinary scholarship and rapier insight, Paul Hunting takes us on a wild ride into the hitherto veiled spiritual mysteries of Shakespeare's work. For this ride, you will need to hold onto your beliefs, because they will be challenged at every turn. Hunting will open up areas that are thought-provoking, paradigm-shifting and will awaken your consciousness to new possibilities.

This book is truly ground-breaking. There are no other books that have addressed Shakespeare's hidden spiritual mysteries with such unabashed courage and bravado. Courage because Hunting speaks from the heart with a passion and intellectual rigor that is startlingly original. A great contribution to mystical literature.

—Rev. Dr. Paul Kaye, President, Church of the Movement of Spiritual Inner Awareness

I love paradox. Who'd have thought Paul Hunting could pull off a work of such outrageous importance? On the other hand, who else but Paul could have done it? He jolts us out of the religion-induced coma of our Judaeo-Christian culture. His has been a prodigious undertaking. His devotion, dedication and tenacious perseverance to the process has been impressive.

—Terry Tillman, Bestselling Author, World-
Class Leadership Coach and Facilitator

A brilliant gem of metaphorical, spiritual connections between William Shakespeare, the Bible, and Spiritual Psychology. In thoroughly exploring the plays with wisdom, clarity, and wit, Paul Hunting masterfully demonstrates why Shakespeare is still so relevant in reminding us of our true spiritual nature and our connection to each other as loving spiritual beings.

—Dr. H. Ronald Hulnick, President, University of Santa Monica

Brilliant and beautifully written. I could not put it down. William himself would be proud of you. It reminds me of the *Jewel Net of Indra*.

— Anton Lesser, Leading Actor, Royal Shakespeare
Company, Film and TV, *Game of Thrones*, *Endeavour*

Profound, insightful and thought-provoking. Despite my knowing little about Shakespeare and the Bible, Paul's quirky humour helped me feast on many essential spiritual revelations.

— Will Skaskiw

As a Catholic turned Buddhist, I found this brilliant piece of work by Paul Hunting opened my eyes to the universal truth underpinning all religions.

— Dr. Vijith Kannangara, Medical doctor
turned CEO based in Sri Lanka

A remarkable work of art. Insightfully written and enjoyable. In order to access the deeper mystical teachings of the gospels as revealed in Shakespeare,

Paul Hunting entices us to search within and find authentic attunement with our own truth. No mean feat. Truly a pearl of great price.

— Dr. Kinka Gerke, Consultant and Politico-Economic Strategist

Thanks to books like this, the luxury of knowledge and deeper understanding is no longer just in the grasp of academics. It is in its rightful place in society.

— Seton Spenser, Philosopher and Next-door Neighbour

Praise for Paul's Presentations

- Your presentation for our Transcendent Leadership gathering today was stellar and marvellous.
- Thank-you unbelievably Thank-you
- I always knew the Bible was coded, and you've confirmed the confirmation — opened it right up. I could see the connection between Shakespeare and what was going on in the Bible –
- OK, yes, Christ did WAY more than we were told. We've only been given an infinitesimal bit about why Christ came and what he did.
- I'm super grateful
- Totally enjoyed your presentation — Thank-you.
- Had initial resistance. But as soon as you started talking I pulled out my 16 year-old copy of the Complete works of Shakespeare. Tried to find the passages. My mind was very active, as I listened I STARTED GESTALTING IT just as you mentioned you had done! KA-BOOM!
- I'm now very excited — will re-read Hamlet and watch the presentation again. There were 2 or 3 moments when I went 'aaaah', I get it!' opens up a whole bunch of stuff.
- I love working with metaphor and simile with my own writing — a whole inspiration! Thank-you.
- Thank-you — fascinating

- This has been most extraordinary — we are really grateful for opening our eyes to your passion and those hidden deeper meanings. Thank-you.

- I had no knowledge of this other than what you presented — then BOOM! It hit me. I got it Thank-you, Thank-you, Thank-you

- I love what you've done. Got everything I needed — and more as it unfolds. Thank-you very much.

- I studied Shakespeare for my MA — even saw Laurence Olivier in Othello at The Old Vic. You've opened a gateway to a new knowing — accepting Shakespeare at a totally different level. I'll have to re-read the plays now — literally opened the floodgates to an awareness that is mind-blowing — where's this going to go?

- Wonderful Thank-you, Thank-you , Thank-you — this is a gift from heaven. Thank-you it's , aaah, breathtaking! The hidden messages, Paul, Thank-you. I shall go hunting.

- You've touched my heart — it brings out the joy.

Shakespeare's HOLY GRAIL

THE ANCIENT SECRET REVEALED

VOLUME I: THE POISONED CHALICE

FROM #1 BEST-SELLING AUTHOR
PAUL HUNTING

BARDASS
BOOKS

'This even-handed justice commends th'ingredients of
our poisoned chalice to our own lips.'
Macbeth, Act 1, Scene 7

What if Macbeth's 'poisoned chalice' is a veiled
reference to the cup of the Last Supper?

What if Shakespeare has encrypted the ancient
secrets of the Holy Grail into his verse?

What if knowing this forbidden truth has the power to
resurrect the sleeping soul within us? And, what if awakening
the soul, will (in Hamlet's words) end the heartache and
the thousand natural shocks that flesh is heir to?

As you'll soon realise, this book has two momentous revelations emerging in parallel: a new and profound understanding of Shakespeare's plots, poetic imagery, and process that illuminate never before realised depths to the Bard himself; and astonishing insight into the ancient, universal, mystical teachings of Jesus the Christ and the line of masters preceding him.

Published by Bardass Books

BARDASS

BOOKS

Cover Design, Text Design, and Composition by Victoria Wolf, wolfdesignandmarketing.com
Edited by Sophie Bradshaw, MA (Cantab.)
Proofread by Bublish
Produced by GMK Writing and Editing, Inc.
Managing Editor: Katie Benoit

Visit the author at: www.paulhunting.com

Printed by IngramSpark

Print ISBN: 979-8-9861737-2-6
Ebook EISN: 979-8-9861737-3-3

Note: *This publication is presented solely for informational, educational, and entertainment purposes. To the maximum extent permitted by international law, the publisher and the author and their affiliated entities and individuals disclaim any and all liability in the event any information contained in this book proves to be inaccurate, incomplete, or unreliable.*

For John Morton, spiritual giant and *Fisher King*. I once asked him to help me write this book, because no way did I feel worthy or capable of the task ahead. His deceptively helpful answer was: 'why ask me when you can go to the source?' I have never felt so empowered — ever. I hope you enjoy the fruits of what he bade me do.

Contents

Preface:

SOMETHING IS ROTTEN IN THE STATE OF DENMARK

Something is rotten in the state of Denmark.

Hamlet, Act I Scene IV

I'd like this to be the beginning of a conversation. A conversation about something 'rotten' that's gotten into mankind and something priceless and life transforming that's been kept secret for over two thousand years

Towards the end of 2014, I fell into a dark place of despair. My work life seemed to be crumbling away. All my attempts to resurrect my business failed miserably. All I had was an idea for a book. Just the title, really: *the forgotten self.* I suppose that was me, my soul, my true self, locked away in the oubliette. Against all my protestations, my coach insisted I write said book. To kick start it, I wrote down one of my favourite quotes from *Hamlet.* Six weeks and fifty thousand words later I began to review my splurge. I got no further than those few lines of verse. Like in the famous *Golden Buddha* story where yon peasant catches a glimpse of the golden Buddha glinting through the crack in its clay camouflage, I saw flashes of gold glinting at me from behind the familiar words of the Bard.

I knew that to really expose the full glory of what I sensed, I needed to crack open the status quo within which the treasure was protected. Not with a wrecking ball. With some piercing questions. Questions that broke all the rules. Questions that only an outsider with nothing to lose would dare ask. Questions that could lead nowhere — or maybe everywhere.

What if Shakespeare were far more than just 'the Bard' — perhaps a spiritual master with a direct line to the divine? What if all the plays were connected together by a single golden thread? What if all the great characters were not just characters, but also characterisations of the core archetypes of human consciousness? What if all the plots were not so much about the outer world of matter and material, but the inner world of spirit? What if his final play, *The Tempest*, was placed first in the folio because it was both a foreshadowing and a denouement that summed up the subtext of all the other plays? What if Shakespeare was part of that great covert underground movement of artists and sages that knew there was something rotten in the religions, and did all they could subliminally to (a) subvert and undermine the authority, corruption, and tyranny of Church and Crown and (b) reveal the truth those in power do not wish us to know?

As I continued this quest, the key question burning a hole in my doublet and hose became: could this add up to the Holy Grail? Was this the forbidden hidden knowledge about Jesus the Christ that makes the Grail so sought after, so hard to find, so precious? Is Shakespeare's oeuvre the solution to the world's greatest mystery? Is this the secret Shakespeare devoted his entire body of works to both hide and simultaneously reveal?

As I present the evidence and my personal interpretations I shall not restrain my excitement. Please do not confuse this passion with a desire to convince you or have you believe me. Au contraire, I encourage you to find your own meanings. Go even deeper than I did. Share what you discover with me and all of us in search of truth.

The Ancient Context

Imagine what it must be like living under the rule of the Taliban or Isis today. That's how England would have been for Shakespeare. That's how the Holy Land was for Jesus. No freethinking, spiritually aware, creative genius was safe to express themselves. Any spontaneous remark or innocent spark of inspiration could result in the grimmest of lingering deaths for you and your loved ones. To express himself, live and ensure the survival of his works, Shakespeare also had to apply his skill as a creative genius to the encryption of his subtext. He had to disguise his deeper purpose.

The legacy of mediaeval religious terror still lives in our DNA. It still inhabits our laws and our mores. It still inhibits our freedom to express and be who we really are.

In late 2014, when all I could see ahead was a long, dark tunnel, my life coach urged me to do something I really did not want to do: write a new book about my soul-centred work with horses. All I had was a pinprick of light: a title. And a laptop. The title was *The Forgotten Self* (short for 'me'). The laptop was called Mac (short for Macbeth). Seven years on, I have a book that I had absolutely no inkling, let alone intention, of writing. A book that took me on an inner Grail quest that has totally transformed my life.

I've had the most amazing time putting it together. I hope you enjoy it. I hope you get value from it. If you do, tell everyone. If you don't, tell no one. The more I think I understand, the more I realise I don't know. So, if you'd like to join in this conversation, if you have questions, further insights to contribute, deeper understanding than I can fathom, if you think this quirky way of seeing things might help you fulfil your life purpose, then let me know.

Jesus Christ's Divine Heresy

Between 30 and 33 CE, Jesus Christ said, did and taught hundreds of things that violated the prevailing law. He was tried and executed for several counts of heresy and blasphemy. Looking around the war-torn planet today, it might appear that his death prevented him from completing his divine mission to bring peace and goodwill to all mankind. However, it seems the details of Jesus's true teachings were grossly misunderstood. They were not only *omitted* from the early Christian narrative but also declared *heresy*.

At the Council of Nicaea in 325 CE, under the aegis of the Roman emperor Constantine, the genesis of the orthodox dogma of what became the Christian narrative was agreed by consensus of the bishops. Known still as *the faith,* anyone challenging it was brutally silenced under the laws of heresy and blasphemy.

Unfortunately, what went missing, presumed dead, was the inconvenient truth about what Jesus Christ actually accomplished for all mankind. The very reason the Messiah had to come and what he really did was eradicated from the orthodox doctrine of the Church and the narrative that has impregnated our DNA.

One of Shakespeare's most subtle and most dangerous heresies is to assert that not only was Jesus not the one and only Christ, but that the Christ dwells in and as every man, woman and child born on this earth. For sure, we are not all equally aware, but we are all equally blessed, equally anointed. Christ is simply another word for king, soul or true self (its literal meaning is 'anointed one') — called many different things throughout the ages and throughout the globe. Could our most noble quest, the enterprise of great pith and moment, be to awaken to this universal, spiritual, inner awareness?

Is it perhaps the deletions, distortions and generalisations — the tools of the ego, mind and personality — that have contaminated our lives and been referred to by Shakespeare as *something rotten in the state of Denmark* (the state of mankind)?

The way out of the dilemma and torture chamber of man's mind — his emotions and ego-personality (the false self) — rather than being shared with us and facilitated for us, was withheld, *extirpated*, declared heresy and cruelly punished.

The hubris and tyranny of religion, science and rationalism, starve us of the life force. They sever the arteries delivering the true nourishment of spiritual succour passed on to us from the ancients. Dogma, belief and sense-based perception form the meagre tip of a mammoth iceberg filled with knowledge cryogenically preserved in symbols, myths, parables and poetry. Knowledge that cannot be expressed in words. Knowledge that precedes language and thought. Knowledge that lies outside, above, and beyond creation. No wonder 'self-loathing' is the planetary master pandemic that causes all our ills. We feel lost in space, abandoned, cut off from the roots of the tree of life.

As the early Church grew in power and control, so grew the gap between the peace, love and forgiveness promised by Jesus and the terror and suffering inflicted by the Church in his name. The distortions of Christian narrative that still influence our lives, moral values and laws have, over time, become more seemingly 'true' than the original truth Jesus Christ taught. To this day, the real teachings of Jesus are still dangerous, still forbidden, still very strange sounding to our modern ears and still condemned as heresy.

So, what was Jesus really here to achieve?

This is surely the 'Who wants to be a millionaire?' question. For one million pounds, was it:

1. to forgive the Original Sin,
2. to fulfil the law of Moses,
3. to reopen access to the Tree of Life, or
4. to breach the seven seals?

If you're confused about what each of these even means, let alone which is the correct, life-changing, final answer, you're in pretty good company. But by the time you reach the last page, with Shakespeare's invaluable help, you should be a whole lot clearer.

This book has no ending. It is a continuous journey of questions and answers, a conversation between those of us who share a hunger for truth and a thirst for adventure.

The Original Holy Grail

In time, freethinking poets and writers who were attuned to their own soul consciousness began creating poems, myths, stories and deeply convoluted legends to counteract and undermine the tyranny of the Church and keep the truth alive in the hearts of men. As you'll see, one of them turns out to be William Shakespeare.

But before that, in the twelfth century, to protect this crucial wisdom from total extinction, the secret 'heresy' of Jesus was camouflaged as the legend of the Holy Grail.

The legend of the Holy Grail is one of the most enduring in Western European literature and art. The Grail is said to be the cup that was shared at the Last Supper and, at the Crucifixion, the vessel that received the blood flowing from Christ's side. It was supposedly brought to Britain by Joseph of Arimathea, then lost and laid hidden here for centuries. The Grail, serving as an important motif in Arthurian literature, is still believed by many to be a treasure with miraculous powers that provides happiness, eternal youth or sustenance in infinite abundance. Different traditions describe it as a cup, dish or stone, often in the custody of the Fisher King. The Fisher King, also known as the Wounded King, is said to be the last in a long line of gatekeepers to be charged with keeping the Holy Grail.

In 1983, three new heroes came on the scene. Baigent, Leigh and Lincoln caused an international sensation with their book *The Holy Blood and the Holy Grail*. Fictionalised by Dan Brown in his blockbuster *The Da Vinci Code*, they presented compelling theories and evidence that the term *Holy Grail* derives from the old French *sang real*, pronounced *sang graal,* meaning 'royal blood'.

From here, it was a short step to infer that this 'royal blood' is actually the *royal bloodline* of Jesus Christ, and thence a giant leap to postulate that Jesus had survived the Crucifixion, married Mary Magdalene and sired a royal dynasty of children, descendants of whom are alive to this day. This certainly rattled a few paradigms.

But what does Jesus himself tell us about the blood in the cup, symbolised by the wine? In Matthew 26:28, he's very specific: "This is my blood of the New Testament which is shed for all for the remission of sin."

When I say specific, I also mean inscrutable. In fact, until I figured out what this really means, I was just as flummoxed as the billions of Christians worldwide. Even though they were historians using Leonardo da Vinci's *Last Supper* as their Rosetta Stone, could the three amigos nevertheless shed more light on the blood Jesus shed?

When I read *The Holy Blood and the Holy Grail* about twenty years ago, one particular paragraph jumped out and grabbed me by the throat. I found it the other day, underlined in red:

> *There seems little question that on one level the Grail is **an
> initiatory experience** which in modern terminology would be
> described as a 'transformation' or 'altered state of consciousness'.
> Alternatively it might be described as a 'Gnostic experience', a
> 'mystical experience', 'illumination' or 'union with God'.*
> The Holy Blood and the Holy Grail, p. 318

Years before my Shakespeare revelations, I had the pleasure of having lunch with Richard Leigh a few times, shortly before he died. He had a mind as fertile as the Nile valley and a wit as dry and prickly as a cactus in the Nag Hammadi desert. I tried to prod him into opening up about what he had meant about the

Grail's being *an initiatory experience.* Was it not a seismically glib understatement to juxtapose *altered state of consciousness* with *union with God*? After all, drinking a glass of red wine can lead to an *altered state* but can hardly be the pith and moment of a *union with God*! His eyes glazed over as he lit up yet another cigarette. Then he grinned (or was it a tobacco smoke-induced squint? Depends who's drinking the wine!) and confessed that, as a historical researcher, he didn't personally care that much about the *initiatory experience* angle.

But this mystical idea of the Grail turned out to be quite a gem for me. As a stubborn truth junkie from way back, I've always seen the entire scripture as a quagmire of symbols. Since the Grail was inextricably linked to the blood of Christ, I was far more interested in the possible trail of spiritual, mystical and initiatory symbols leading to an absolute truth than a possible literal or physical bloodline leading nowhere.

Could the *Holy Grail* be another of those spiritual metaphors that get taken literally and morph into a red herring? Is the chalice itself a red herring — not unlike the fruit of the tree of the knowledge of good and evil, which got taken literally and morphed into a red apple?

Is it the ingredients in the chalice that also got lost that really matter? Is the Fisher King also the one who has the keys to this *initiatory experience*?

In the Arthurian legend, the only knight to find the Grail was Galahad (which, in my mind at least, sounds like 'Godhead'). As soon as he did, he was enlightened and ascended to heaven like Jesus. An initiatory experience? A union with God? The mystery to me is why so many people are obsessed with the literality of the supposed holy relic. Why are they so fixated on the chalice or the womb of the Magdalene if even the ancient, original Grail legend itself makes it obvious they should be seeking an inner experience of soul-self-awareness? So what if Jesus the man married Mary the Magdalene? So what if he sired children? It may put a few pious noses out of joint. It may even be true. It may also be irrelevant. And it may also be another red herring. It is a physical world event that may have nothing whatsoever to do with the mystical events foreshadowed throughout the Old Testament and at the Last Supper.

Whichever Grail myth resonates with you, they all have the same starting point: the Last Supper, that immortal cup of wine, the blessing of the New Testament, the remission of sin and the sop Jesus gave to Judas. But rather than speculate on da Vinci's somewhat dubious symbols, I'd rather take my chances by going to the source: the Bible.

We know how the dogma interprets the gospels — and the hell on earth that follows. But what would Jesus himself say if he came back speaking English?

Maybe he did.

The premise of this book is that encrypted throughout the drama and poetry of William Shakespeare's works is the forbidden, universal knowledge about Jesus Christ's mission on Earth. This knowledge was excluded from the early Christian dogma, deemed heretical and later symbolised as the legend of the Holy Grail. These revelations about why Jesus had to come and what he *actually* did, said and meant go a significant way towards filling the Grand Canyon–sized gap between the truth and the predigested narrative force-fed to the masses as 'Christianity' for two thousand years.

But how did I come across this wisdom? Neither academic nor avid reader, my primary research technique is watching Shakespeare's plays as DVDs with my intuition on full volume. While so doing with Orson Welles's incredible 1948 noir *Macbeth* movie, I suddenly had what for me was an 'inconvenient hunch'. There is a scene — a fleeting, blink-and-you-miss-it scene that is often omitted as irrelevant by directors — just before Macbeth betrays and murders King Duncan. In it, Banquo passes a diamond to Macbeth; he says it is a gift from Duncan to be given to Lady Macbeth. Here it is in all its glory:

BANQUO

What, sir, not yet at rest? The King's abed.
He hath been in unusual pleasure, and

Sent forth great largess to your offices.
*This **diamond** he greets your wife withal,*
By the name of most kind hostess, and shut up
In measureless content.
Macbeth, Act II Scene I

When I say 'hunch', I really mean the shivers. A diamond is a potent spiritual symbol. I hit pause and replay a few times and asked myself what on earth could this diamond possibly symbolise? Something deep down in my self replied: 'The Holy Grail'.

Rather than use the infamously devious, symbol-laden fresco of Leonardo da Vinci's *Last Supper* as my enigma-decryption reference, I was drawn to the source: the key passages in the gospel. Here, I began where the Grail trail should always begin — with the accounts of the cup of the Last Supper. Then I went back to the play for more clues. And this is where this whole new deeper level of revelation began for me.

I found that Shakespeare connects the seminal words from the Last Supper with some of the famous last words in the Bible to compose one of his most profoundly inscrutable verses. Here it is, where Macbeth weighs the pros and cons of his forthcoming regicide:

MACBETH
If 't were done, when 'tis done, then 'twere well
It were done quickly. If th' assassination
Could trammel up the consequence and catch
With his surcease success, that but this blow
Might be the be-all and the end-all here,
But here, upon this bank and shoal of time,
We'd jump the life to come. But in these cases
We still have judgment here, that we but teach

Bloody instructions, which, being taught, return
To plague th' inventor. This even-handed justice
*Commends th' ingredients of our **poisoned chalice***
To our own lips.
Macbeth, Act I Scene VII

I was mesmerised.

First, look at the first line of text:

If't were done, when 'tis done, then 'twere well It were done quickly.

Now remind yourself of what Jesus says in the gospel when he passes the sop to Judas at the Last Supper:

*That thou doest, **do quickly.***
John 13:27

Ring any bells? These two lines are expressing the exact same sentiment: do this deed quickly. The only difference is that one is a line from the Gospel of John and the other is from *Macbeth* as our antihero contemplates the imminent betrayal and murder of his own king.

It's no exaggeration to say that this moment of enlightenment totally transformed the way I read and understood Shakespeare's symbology. In the diamond scene, Banquo — Macbeth's closest comrade and father to a line of kings — passes to Macbeth the gift of a diamond from Duncan, the king Macbeth is about to murder. But what we really have is a scene where the traitor, the one who is about to betray his king, is handed a precious jewel from the father to a line of kings. Could this delineation itself be alluding to Banquo representing the Christ? Given Banquo's destiny as the play unfolds, it would seem so.

Said fleeting diamond is to be *passed down a line* from the king, Duncan, through Banquo and Macbeth, and on to Lady Macbeth. But it fails to reach its destination. At the Last Supper, Jesus tells Peter that the one to whom he gives a sop (bread dipped in wine) will betray him. He then passes the sop to none other than Judas Iscariot (meaning: assassin).

Now consider these complementary lines again, as there's another level of meaning to them:

> *And after the sop Satan entered into him. And*
> *he sayeth,* **that thou doest, do quickly***.*
> John 13:27

And in *Macbeth,* Macbeth is contemplating his impending betrayal and murder of King Duncan and says to himself a sure paraphrase of what Jesus said to Judas:

> *If 't were done, when 'tis done, tis well it were* **done quickly***.*

This is more than a mere allusion to the first biblical reference in the Bible to the ritual of the Eucharist. It's more than a paraphrase — it's a spotlight indicating something momentous. Is the cup of the Last Supper the *poisoned chalice* foretold by Macbeth?

It was with this small, seemingly insignificant yet seminal scene that this book really began. How on earth could I check out this hunch and validate it? This book is my answer to that very question.

I'll reveal the true depths of the incredible truth I discovered that day later in the book. But suffice to say, suddenly it was as if a portal in my consciousness swung open and I could see the most exquisite patterns appear in the text, just like those magic eye puzzles that became so popular a few years ago. You don't just see them; a whole new part of your perceptive process opens up. I quickly began to see dozens of these subtle allusions popping up, not just in *Macbeth*, but relentlessly, exquisitely, in all the plays. It was as if a window into all the biblical motifs of Shakespeare's plays had opened to me.

To the orthodoxy, it is heresy to suggest that the Bible is also written in code, that it contains metaphors, symbols, parables and poetic imagery. But taking the Bible literally can easily end up as a travesty of the truth. What if what's in the Bible is not so much an account of what happened and what was said but a revelation of only those things we really need to know? After all, it only contains a few hours from Jesus's thirty-three-year life. As it turned out for me that day, Shakespeare is using the exact same code the Bible uses to hide the truth from those who would reject it and to reveal it to those ready to hear it.

To this day, despite volumes of literature and countless quests to find it, the Holy Grail remains shrouded in mystery and seemingly lost forever. But what if it's only lost because we do not have the eyes to see it nor the ears to hear it? What if it's not lost at all? What if it is we who are lost? What if we can find ourselves, not by changing the world, but by changing our perceptions of the world? What if Shakespeare has taken timeless wisdom — wisdom that very few in this age know about — and transformed it into the sublime poetry and gripping drama adored by millions for four hundred years? What if Shakespeare's subtext, his purpose, was to share with us the knowledge of these ancient, universal, mystical teachings? Timeless teachings that sit behind and unite all the major religions? Teachings banned and discredited by the orthodoxy — perhaps since time began? Teachings those in power will still stop at nothing to stop us knowing?

When I had my last lunch with Rich, little did we realise that Shakespeare had beaten us all to possibly the ultimate solution to the Grail mystery. That William Shakespeare, affectionately known as 'the Bard', deserves also to be dubbed 'Spiritual Master'. That, as it turns out, all his plays can be seen as parables that express the deep, mystical, arcane teachings of the line of masters and sages through the ages. That, in *Macbeth*, for example, Shakespeare actually took the same metaphor of the royal blood and, in a nexus of symbols so iconic, so subtle, so sublime they make your eyes water, followed the blood trail in a very different direction.

Rather than assume that 'royal blood' infers the genetic bloodline of Jesus the man, and thus follow the sperm into history, Shakespeare took the original symbolism of the blood of the Last Supper and followed the inner, mystical blood trail into our own story: the evolution of the soul.

For this is my blood of the new testament,
which is shed for all for the remission of sin.
Matthew 26:28

Transcending the tyranny of sin

It's hard for us in the west today to understand how insidiously oppressive the law is — a modern-day law based on the prehistoric laws of Moses. We are only just beginning to regain personal freedoms lost from thousands of years of religious tyranny — a nexus of outmoded moral strictures that, whether we like it or not, is still running amok inside our heads.

The knowledge Shakespeare has woven into his tapestry is still deemed 'heretical'. But what's so important about it is that it is not just the Bard's homespun philosophy — it is abundantly present in the Bible. But only those who are willing to look at the scripture from a paradigm, a world view, very different from the restricted way the narrative views it and the life-limiting way it interprets the surface structure of the words can see it. This wonderful, liberating truth has been right under our noses for thousands of years — it was just rendered invisible by the ego-centred narrative. It is only made visible from a soul-centred viewing point. Our winter of discontent is made glorious summer by this son of Stratford.

What Shakespeare seems to have done is reinterpret key biblical passages from the Old and New Testament in a soul-centred way and transform these unorthodox interpretations into his plays and poetry. Thus, the subtext of his entire works is this deeply 'heretical' version of the very words of God Himself.

The purpose of this conversation

I want to do two things. I want to reveal what I am convinced Shakespeare is telling us is the absolute last word on the mystery of the Holy Grail. And I want to show how, through his insight, wisdom, courage and cryptographic genius, he secretes the secret truth about the misrepresentation that has been (unwittingly, perhaps) committed in the name of Jesus Christ. Not so that we can be outraged and punish the perpetrators, but so we can enter into the grace that comes through forgiveness and find the essence the Grail myth promises us all: union with God or, more prosaically, peace, joy and happiness unbridled.

This could be an expression of the deeper purpose of us all: to remember the forgotten soul and to re-establish it as the centre of consciousness within ourselves. This action has already been done by Jesus Christ; he has opened up the possibility for us to do it. But he cannot do it for us. We have to do it for ourselves in our own unique way. We are each responsible for our own karma. Jesus (and possibly other mystical masters from other traditions) has shown us all how to do it — how to resurrect our own true selves. Our job here on earth is perhaps to find out how to do this for ourselves — how to liberate ourselves from the darkness, ignorance and suffering caused by the rampaging, off-course ego-personality.

The original meaning of sin: key to the Grail secret

Since the Grail, the blood of the new testament, is inextricably linked theologically with the remission of sin, let's challenge our beliefs about what is and what is not a sin. The truth about sin could be the key to the secret of the Grail — and the key to why it has been missing presumed dead for over two thousand years.

My friend and personal theological oracle, author David Elkington tells me that in the older faith of Israel, the Hebrew (as opposed to the later Jewish) faith, there was Noel one sin — ignorance — it was seen as a crime against Wisdom, the feminine presence of God.

As well we know, the current meaning of a word is oft not so much determined by its original, deep, semantic structure, but corrupted by common usage. So it is with sin.

One is pressed to find a definition of sin that varies from, say, dictionary. com:

- transgression of divine law: *the sin of Adam.*
- any act regarded as such a transgression, especially a wilful or deliberate violation of some religious or moral principle.
- any reprehensible or regrettable action, behaviour, lapse, etc.; great fault or offense:

However, I found this gem in my old and trusted Penguin Dictionary. In parenthesis, underneath the well-worn standard definition of sin, the editor adds:

Usually taken to refer to moral (and especially sexual) misconduct, the term 'sin' implies a state in which a person has chosen to separate themselves from God. Since breaking religious or moral rules is believed to be a sign of such separation, sin has come to refer more generally to the action rather than the spiritual state.
Dr. Mel Thompson, The Penguin English
Dictionary, 2nd Edition, 2003

What if to disobey God's law is not a sin, per se? But feeling guilty about it is? What if the inner state of guilt is the sin, not the act itself. The something rotten in the state of mankind: does the Bard mean sin? In *Measure for Measure,*

Isabella (the soul archetype) tries to prevent Angelo (the Lucifer archetype) from raping her by threatening to expose his impending crime. Chillingly, he boasts, 'Say what you can, my false o'erweighs your true.' Could the master be telling us that those in the Church that interpret what they believe to be God's law have themselves been beguiled? That religious truths are false? That the true truth seems like lies? That what has been passed down through the generations as God's truth was in fact corrupted at source? Perhaps through that misunderstood concept of original sin? That the meaning of sin desperately needs an upgrade and a reboot?

Traditionally, for religious deployment, 'sin' been weaponised to strike terror and guilt into men's hearts. Could the irony be that to accuse someone of committing a sin, and causing them to feel guilty, thus becomes the true sin?

The big question now is: why would Jesus, the son of God, openly and repeatedly violate the laws of the land? Why would he repeatedly 'sin', commit blasphemy, and heresy — knowing he would be executed for his crimes?

Either he was not the son of God. Or the laws he broke were not God, his father's!

And if not his father's, then whose?

Forgiveness: the mother of all paradigm shifts

If sin is not an act, but a state, then it follows that forgiveness, too, must be a state. If sin is defined as breaking or disobeying God's law, it defines sin as doing something wrong or evil. But what if the whole state of being called 'good and evil' has nothing whatsoever to do with God? What if morality itself is not God-made but man-made? Ego-made? What if right and wrong is a delusion? Hamlet said, 'There is nothing either good or bad but thinking makes it so'. The mind makes things 'right or wrong' not God. What if guilt itself is the sin: the inner state of self-judgment that cuts us off from God? Forgiveness therefore is a transcendent state: a state above and beyond the prison of the mind and its compulsive need to judge.

Deeper: how could the blood shed by a man called Jesus 'forgive' the sin of the world? Applying the mind with its logic and reasoning power led the three amigos away from the scripture into a rational-sounding secular hypothesis: he must have survived the crucifixion and sired a dynasty! And then — so what? Are you experiencing Ananda through contemplating the womb of Mary Magdalene?

So let us apply our transcendent powers. Let us look within and ask the master Shakespeare to guide us. Let's open ourselves to a mystical revelation. A state of heightened awareness. A way that leads to the bliss of letting go of all guilt: absolute absolution.

Can you even begin to imagine a world without sin, without guilt, without resentment, without judgement? Dare you visit that world deep inside where all is forgiveness?

The Grail Quest

The reason why Jesus was vilified, hated, and executed goes far deeper that what is said in the gospels. He was one of the Essenes. The Essenes were savvy with the ancient mystical teachings going back to Hermes Trismegistus and beyond. These teachings were deemed heretical because they liberated mankind from the tyranny of the priesthood. When they executed Jesus, to maintain their stranglehold, the priesthood also had to extirpate the teachings from all sources and from all people who spoke of them.

Could the knowledge Shakespeare has woven into his tapestry therefore be the very 'heresy' of Jesus himself? The 'heresy' the Church cut out of the dogma? What's so important about what's hidden in Shakespeare is that it is not just the Bard's homespun philosophy — it is abundantly present in 'code' in the subtext of the Bible. The irony being that because the mind and its prosaic mindset cannot grasp the deeper meanings, the translators unwittingly left all the clues to Jesus's true teaching in the text. Our job is to follow the Grail trail and dive down below the surface.

But only those who are willing to look at it from a paradigm, a world view, very different from the restricted way the narrative views the scripture and the life-limiting way it interprets the surface structure of the words can see it. This wonderful, liberating truth has been right under our noses for thousands of years — it was just rendered invisible by the ego-centred narrative. It is only made visible from a soul-centred viewing point. Our winter of discontent is made glorious summer by this son of Stratford.

What Shakespeare seems to have done is reinterpret key biblical passages from the Old and New Testament in a soul-centred way and transform these unorthodox interpretations into his plays and poetry. Thus, the subtext of his entire works is this deeply 'heretical' version of what could be the very words of God Himself.

HOW TO READ THIS BOOK

Therein the patient must minister to himself.

Macbeth, Act V Scene III

You can read this book in many ways: preferably with your inner eyes open. Believe nothing. Be open to anything. Validate everything. The value of this book is much more about attuning with the heart than analysing with the mind. As Einstein said, 'Logic gets you from A to B, intuition gets you everywhere'. The secret of how the Grail has been hidden for so long is that its truth is not accessible to reason alone. Words point the way but you will need to transcend your rational, logical mind to grasp it. Shakespeare's entire oeuvre seems to be an homage to what some western mystics call *the sound current*. This may sound new and inscrutable to you. But it is the key spoken of by sages throughout the ages that opens the gate to the infinite possibility through which those in power do not want us to pass.

For me, writing this book was (and still is) a thrilling journey of personal revelation. I am not a scholar, nor restrained by academic conventions. I am a very ordinary person who just happens to have seen the invisible ink in which Shakespeare writes the sub-text for his inner play. I have attempted to balance sharing my passion and enthusiasm with not forcing on you my own interpretations of Shakespeare's cryptic message. As I keep emphasising, this is the beginning of a dialogue — your unique interpretations are just as vital as mine or anyone else's.

You can read this for information, for intellectual stimulation, and/or for spiritual succour. I say 'spiritual' advisedly as — as soon you'll see — Shakespeare was far more than 'the Bard'. He was surely a spiritual teacher whose cryptic, divine revelations are merciless in challenging the dubious values, moral imperatives and sacred cows that characterise religious doctrines. His insight is as ruthless as an inquisitor drilling down through the quagmire of time for a truth upon which we can build a life that really works — one filled with love, joy, fulfilment and happiness unbridled.

As you'll see when you arrive at the last word in this book, it's not the end, but the beginning. It's the beginning of a conversation, an endless discussion about the biggest question in life: Who on earth are we and why the hell are we here?

The thing about understanding the Grail truth is it requires much more than mere logical or mental comprehension. To find the Grail, we need to shift our level of consciousness to look within. This existential game of cosmic hide-and-seek is just the beginning of a continually, infinitely expanding experience. It becomes a relationship, an interaction that grows, or rather blossoms like a flower inside us. Perhaps this is what the mystics call the 'eight-petaled lotus', the higher state of Ananda — the intense, ecstatic bliss, happiness and joy arrived at in deep meditation.

I can give you as much information-level stuff as possible, I can throw you the ball, but you have to catch it yourself. If you want to knock it for six, that's fine. You win. And thus, you lose. But if you choose to catch it, you might want to think about what you would ask of the Grail when you find it. What might you wish to heal or let go of? What might you want in its place? Joy, happiness, wealth, awareness, understanding?

Last week, during one of my Q&A sessions, a participant asked me if I had read Leo Tolstoy's *The Gospel in Brief*. Who? What? I ordered it immediately. Highlighter working overtime, I picked out this amazing passage:

> *Never, since the time of Arius, has the affirmation of any dogma arisen from any other cause than the desire to condemn a contrary belief as false. It is the supreme degree of pride and ill will [Malvolio] to others to assert that a particular dogma is a divine revelation proceeding from the Holy Ghost: the highest presumption because nothing more arrogant can be said than that the words spoken by me are uttered through me by God; and the greatest ill will because the avowal of oneself as in possession of the sole indubitable truth implies an assertion of the falsity of all who disagree. Yet that is just what all the Churches say, and from this alone flows and has flowed all the evil which has been committed and still is committed in the world in the name of religion.*
> Tolstoy, *The Gospel in Brief*, Page 10

The purpose of *Shakespeare's Holy Grail* is partly about revealing how Shakespeare is putting to rights the misunderstanding and injustice done in Christ's name. This tract of protestation from Count Lev Nikolayevich Tolstoy, usually referred to in English as Leo Tolstoy, is truly a vote of empathy and support for this very same cause.

Tolstoy was a Russian writer who, like Shakespeare, is regarded as one of the greatest authors of all time. Unlike Shakespeare, Tolstoy received nominations for the Nobel Prize in Literature every year from 1902 to 1906 and for the Nobel Peace Prize in 1901, 1902 and 1909. Also, unlike Shakespeare's more covertly heretical works, *The Gospel in Brief* was banned in Tolstoy's native Russia.

Also unlike Shakespeare, as far as I can tell, Tolstoy sought the truth mainly in the Gospels. Shakespeare, as you'll soon see, extracted the juice of the whole fruit from the core of Genesis to the outer skin of Revelation. Indeed, how can we understand what Jesus really did until we understand why he had to come in the first place?

To do that, you have to be ready. As Hamlet said, 'The readiness is all.' But all are not ready. Are you? Are you ready to go on a quest for the Holy Grail? Are you ready to be blissfully happy?

From Frogs to Princes

Like in the fairy tale, the frog is waiting for the kiss of the beautiful princess to transform him into the prince he really is. But the princess must kiss the frog, trusting that he is not what he seems. She must view him differently to how he appears.

Are you ready to kiss that frog? Are you ready to look at familiar things in new ways that may initially seem distasteful? Are you ready to embrace perspectives that challenge your beliefs, kill your sacred cows, take you out of your comfort zones? Are you willing to consider ancient spiritual and mystical precepts that may sound strange to your modern ears? Have you the inner strength to transcend the primal instincts to fight for and defend your social, religious, a-religious and cultural programming regardless of what may be the truth?

Of course not!

Let me make it easier for you.

Do not believe a word I say. And do not *dis*believe either. I will bend over backwards to explain how the mind, the ego-personality, the false self, acts like a prison. But there is a way out. A door. It may be closed, but it's not locked. Here is the key. You can open it if you're willing to take the risk. Once open, it will set you free. The true, deeper secrets of the Grail are held in a place in consciousness to which the ego-mind-personality has no access. That's the adventure. What happens, where do you go, when you transcend your ego?

From Mindset to Mind-Boggle

We hear so much these days about *mindset* — how we must change our mindset in order to get what we want. But what if we already have everything we really want? What if we already are who we want to be? What if we already are blissfully happy? What if we already are in heaven, paradise, nirvana or whatever you want to call it? What if we already are blessed by God beyond all measure? What if we already are absolutely, totally, unconditionally forgiven for all the sins, crimes, mistakes, errors and cock-ups we've ever made or ever will make?

Is that a mindset? I don't think so. More of a mind-boggle.

Baruch Bashan: An Ancient Mind-Boggle

Hebrew: The blessings already are.

Baruch Bashan could be described as a quasi-Hebrew affirmation that means 'The blessings already are.' It's a mind-boggling idea that is far too big to fit in anyone's mind. It's an idea that's anathema to the mind and its right/wrong-making ego-personality. This doesn't require a new mindset as much as an intention to awaken the sleeping soul within. If we've forgotten who we really are, then it behoves us to remember who we really are, does it not? To do this, to know our own divine nature as a living reality, the masters say we must transcend the mind and the ego. We must listen to our soul with our soul. The soul is the self that is above and beyond the mind, perceiving and interpreting what is placed before it. The soul is the neutral observer that simply notices without judgement what we, the ego-personality, says, does, thinks and feels. They are like two separate people within us — one the fake self, and the other the true self. Their opposition, their conflict, is the source of all our ills.

What have we lost: that is so hard to find?

So, are we searching for something we already have? If we ask, 'What is the Grail? Where is the Grail?' we become lost in the mists of Avalon. But if we ask the same question from a different altitude: 'What of priceless value did we, humanity, lose (that would be worth any price to find again)?' we begin to open ourselves up to a range of very different answers. The most prosaic answer could be: humanity lost its humanity. We lost our soul-self-awareness and everything that goes with it. Something rotten, as it were, usurped us, and the right order was lost. When I first checked this latter question with Google, it sent up posts and websites about God, Christ and the soul! Try it yourself!

Baigent, Leigh and Lincoln, the authors of *The Holy Blood and the Holy Grail,* were historians. For their answers, they asked history and art, specifically Leonardo da Vinci, the symbolism in his mural *The Last Supper* and the frescos in the chapel at Rennes-le-Château in France (where I also met Henry Lincoln).

Myself, I'm much more of a maverick theologian. I contemplate the Bible — taking great care to ignore the orthodox interpretations. And what does the Bible say that mankind has lost? Access to the Tree of Life.

Access to the Tree of Life Was Cut Off and Then Reopened

Without wishing to sound facetious, I recently realised that to understand what the entire Bible is really about, all you need are the following two key verses — one from Genesis, the other from Revelation. These two verses give great insight into what humanity actually *lost* in the beginning, and what was finally *found* in the end: access to the Tree of Life.

So he drove out the man; and he placed at the east of the
garden of Eden Cherubim, and a flaming sword which
*turned every way, to **keep the way of the tree of life**.*
Genesis 3:24

*Blessed are they that do his commandments, **that they may have right***
***to the tree of life**, and may enter in through the gates into the city.*
Revelation 22:14

In the very beginning, as above, in Genesis, the Bible says mankind was banished from Eden (meaning 'heart of God') and lost access to the Tree of Life. In Revelation, at the very end, it says access to the Tree of Life was restored. In between is an account of how this reopening came to be. In other words, the entire scripture is devoted to telling us this one saga, and I am going to show you how to shift your viewing point so you can see that Shakespeare encapsulates that same entire saga in the subtext (the poetic symbols and imagery) of every single one of his plays.

What Is the Tree of Life?

Clearly, the Tree of Life is an important metaphor. It's no more a tree than the Garden of Eden is a garden. It is an aspect of consciousness — and a crucial one at that. Think about the symbology: *Tree of Life*. The source of everything. In John 1, he says the Word was the source of everything. *In the beginning was the Word*. In the beginning, the Tree of Life, the Word, the voice, the sound, the name of God, was 'planted' in the Garden, in the heart of God, in the soul of man.

Could it be that the symbol of the Holy Grail is simply another symbol for the Tree of Life? It neatly answers our question: What of priceless value was lost? If so, why? Why would a whole new legend and mythology have arisen to preserve and camouflage something that is mentioned so specifically and already has its own vast tomes of deep study? No, there's more to it. Something else of priceless value that we cannot yet fathom must also have been lost. A clay cup transformed into a golden chalice? Hardly! But what about what that cup symbolises? Could it be simply a metaphor for the priceless lost inner treasure that transforms our consciousness from something rotten — a fear, guilt and depression machine — into a fully aware, abundant self? Is this the native hue of resolution that was sicklied o'er by the pale caste of thought?

That's what I'm hunting.

But before we consider the *what* of the so-called Shakespeare Code, let's consider the *how*. How does he divulge the Grail secrets right under the noses of the inquisitors without being noticed?

The answer: *Invisible ink.*

Chapter 1:

INVISIBLE INK: SHAKESPEARE REVEALS HIS CODE

There are more things in heaven and earth, Horatio,
than are dreamt of in your philosophy.

Hamlet, Act I Scene V

Since biblical times, writers have been using invisible ink — parables, metaphors, fables, symbols, symbols of symbols, secret codes, misdirection, hidden clues — to encode their meaning in language. The entire armoury of today's cryptic crossword setter is as old as the rock of ages. As a species, we revel in them. We love nothing more than a mind-boggling mystery or a fiendish puzzle. The cryptic genius of the Master, Shakespeare, is now about to be showcased like never before. Not just for fun, but also so that the great secret of the Holy Grail can have the life-transforming impact on you that it so rightly deserves. We're about to take a look into the mind of God Himself.

The Elizabethan/Shakespearean era, spearheaded by the dreaded spymaster Francis Walsingham, was a vipers' nest of cryptic communications and misdirection. According to the Folger Shakespeare Library, it has been proven unfounded that, say, Sir Francis Bacon (or anyone) left secret codes in Shakespeare's plays. However, ironically, Bacon is credited for providing the first English summary of the science of ciphers in his famous work *The Advancement of Learning*. If Bacon was a genius at ciphers, then of course it would have taken four hundred years and a mystically attuned mindset to crack them! When you begin to see these codes disgorge their secrets before your eyes, you'll understand the levels of hubris that feed the academic mind and block the advancement of truth — *if I cannot see or understand it, it cannot possibly exist.*

Now it's your turn to see for yourself and decide.

If Shakespeare had been as brazen as Tolstoy, we'd never have heard of him or his works. When he started writing, the subject matter beneath his subtext had been ruthlessly extirpated for fifteen hundred years. Now, the sleeping beauty within has had to wait another four hundred years for her prince.

It verges on the crass to use 'code' to define how Shakespeare protects universal, mystical secrets from extirpation. It's an inadequate description for the way he simultaneously hides and flaunts his dangerous heresies, blasphemies and sacrileges, how he flips the finger to the authorities and tyrants who remain oblivious to his sedition. It demeans the fecund genius of how he transforms the very Word of God Himself into thirty-two iterations of the forbidden truth of the Grail, like an ancient palimpsest where the original truth is overwritten by an innocuous fabrication. But 'code' it is, in some ways, although the word doesn't do justice to his plethora of cryptic devices. Whatever we want to call it, the myriad wordplays, double entendres, puns, anagrams and homonyms that I am about to reveal suggest the very hand of the divine at play.

These vignettes, pastiches, tableaux, parodies — whatever you want to call them — are so subtle and so prolific they are virtually impossible to count. But, like grains of sand on a beach, they make the subtext, and thus the oomph of the play, what it is. My way of discerning them is to ask inwardly for what or who a scene or character represents, listen to whatever the answer is and, however unlikely it seems, keep asking, listening to and following the inner directives. In so doing, I have discovered seven 'tools' in Shakespeare's toolkit — seven ways in which he hides true meaning ready for us to discover.

As far as I can tell, these tools — the patterns and symbolism I was beginning to recognise pretty much everywhere in the plays — have not been recorded by any previous scholar or writer in all the four hundred years of study of the texts. The species of symbolism I am about to share were all incredibly subtle, creatively reimagined motifs of a heretical version of the story of Jesus the Christ — and the line of the Christs going back to Adam.

A Little Help from Dante

Ironically, Dante Alighieri, the wild Catholic poet famous for his fantastical representation of the levels of hell in *The Divine Comedy*, now comes to the aid of us heretics. He asserts that all great art and scripture can be interpreted on four interrelated but distinct levels — an immensely useful categorisation as we discover Shakespeare's seven tools.

Literal — The story acted out on the surface, e.g., Jack and Jill went up the hill to fetch a pail of water. Jack fell down and broke his crown, and Jill came tumbling after.

Allegorical — The hidden story just below the surface, e.g., Jack and Jill were an overambitious couple who already had a plentiful supply of pure water.

Moral — The life lesson inherent in the story, e.g., greed goes before a fall.

Anagogical — The spiritual, mystical, or soul-centred meaning, e.g., Jack and Jill are metaphors for Adam and Eve. 'Adam and Eve' is itself a metaphor for the male-female polarity of the soul, the emanation of God that is who we all really are. Adam and Eve were warned by God that the water at the top of the hill would kill them. They were beguiled by a snake telling them it would not kill them but instead give them magical powers and turn them into gods. The snake lied. They did metaphorically 'die'. The water was poisoned with a powerful hallucinogenic. They drank, became deluded into believing they were 'as gods'; they believed they could now tell right from wrong. Jack lost his true crown. They both fell down into a living hell, bringing the whole of mankind tumbling down with them into the nightmare of 'good-and-evil'.

Of course, the outer literal level of Shakespeare is wonderful, gripping and enthralling. People are also constantly drawing understanding and modern-day relevance from the allegorical and moral levels. But my interest is exclusively on how the literal level is a vehicle for the *anagogical* level of interpretation. To *get* this level, you have to let go of your attachment to the surface structure and any investment you may have in what it means. For it is from here, deep down at the wellspring of the spiritual and mystical level, that what the orthodoxy (if they had the wit to see it) would decry as his (subtextual) heresy, blasphemy and sacrilege draws its power and poignancy. If you're not ready to be open to this deep structure, you're not ready to receive the Grail. It's protected. Your own inner tyrant, inner prison guards, inner threshold guardians are still keeping the sacred Grail truth safe. You may get to stay *right* and feel *safe,* but the price you pay for submitting to them is darkness and ignorance.

Wittgenstein: Transforming Rabbits into Ducks

Did God create the universe? Or was it Darwin? Perhaps Stephen Hawking? The answer is 'yes'. Because we *all* create the universe. You, me and the girl next door, we are all creating the universe — from subatomic particle to farthest galaxy — every nanosecond of every breath, every blink, every wink. As Prospero says in *The Tempest*, 'We are such stuff as dreams are made on.' That's the fundamental premise of soul-centred coaching — we have the very power of God Himself within us. How to be all that we really are, or not to be

— that is the question. And that power is given to us as the extraordinary ability to shift paradigms. We don't need Trident missiles to get peace on earth; we need to use something far more powerful and far less polluting — free choice.

As a soul-centred coach, I know that the key to great results is not in giving advice, opinions and answers to a client, but in asking intuitively led questions, validating them together and facilitating soul shifts. This is what I am doing throughout this book — conducting a series of radical thought experiments in seeing things right under our nose in transformational different ways.

Wittgenstein's Rabbit-Duck

What do you see in this image, known as Wittgenstein's Rabbit-Duck? A rabbit? A duck? Or both?

See, the exact same information on the page and at the retina gives rise to two totally different interpretations, both equally valid. But suppose those in power decreed the very idea of ducks was heresy? Suppose it was made a sin to acknowledge ducks' very existence? That to see or talk about ducks was a crime? And anyone found to practice 'duckism' would be tortured and executed in the cruellest possible way?

Now what do you see? Rabbit or duck?

However, if you were a mystic, poet or troubadour who knew the truth about ducks and the crucial importance of ducks in living a meaningful, fulfilling life, you might camouflage it in poems, songs, myths, and legends that seem harmless to the enforcers of the dogma. You could then keep the duck alive and quacking until it's safe to unveil the truth.

The primary promise of the premise is that, throughout his works, Shakespeare has been presenting us with rabbits on the surface that are also ducks in the subtext — not just your ordinary mallard, but the dangerous, heretical, forbidden secrets of the Holy Grail. From my extensive research, I have identified seven interrelated ways in which he does so — seven 'tools' in his toolkit that, if we dare, we can take up and use to uncover the truth. They are:

Inner World vs Outer World

Just as Dante describes, there are two readings of all of Shakespeare's plays — the outer 'plot' and the inner view that presents us with the anagogical meaning or subtext.

All the plots and players in the outer world of the plays are metaphors of our own inner world of consciousness.

Three Core Archetypes

Once we understand the outer play versus the inner play, we begin to see Shakespeare's subtextual underthought as not pertaining to the characters of the outer world but to the archetypes of consciousness in our inner world. Our inner world is composed of three, fundamental, existential, polar-opposite archetypes:

1. God-Satan
2. Adam-Eve (the true self)
3. Cain-Abel (the ego-personality)

This goes even further. Suppose the book of Genesis is not a poetic mythology about the creation of the outer world, but of the creation of the inner world of man. It is our inner process of perception that creates our inner experience of what appears to be the outer world of time and space. If we can show that Shakespeare is encrypting his works in the same way the Bible was encrypted and that Shakespeare is really dramatising those archetypes, it follows that the characters and stories in the Bible are also metaphors of our inner consciousness.

As a transformational spiritual psychologist and soul-centred coach who works with horses to mirror my clients' shifting states of being, I have been using the term 'the three circles' to describe the model of consciousness I use to help us navigate the way out of the illusions of the ego-personality and into the authenticity of the true self. In this model, the inner circle represents the true self, and the two outer circles represent the twin false selves. Crucially, this model shows the way those egoic impostors drive us, through fear and shame, to cover up our true self, project a phoney self-image and try in vain to make ourselves happy while ending up making ourselves miserable.

Ten or fifteen years ago, when watching a Shakespeare play, I suddenly *felt* his characters were personifying the same qualities as the 'true self' and 'false selves' in the three-circles model I was using every day. Little did I know then how critically important this little insight would become. What's important here is simply to see the single pattern emerging. Here's how we use this three-circles/three-archetypes model in soul-centred coaching:

THE 3 SELVES OF SPIRITUAL PSYCHOLOGY

"Ontogeny recapitulates phylogeny"

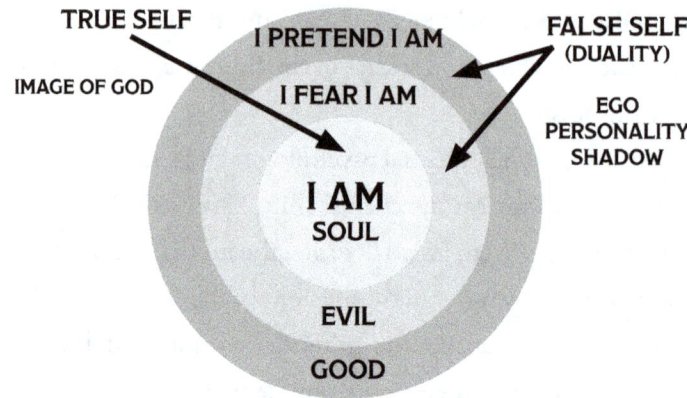

The two selves of spiritual psychology

And here's how Shakespeare uses this in his 'theology':

ADAM AND EVE

*"And the serpent said unto the woman, Ye shall not sure-
ly die: For God doth know that in the day ye eat thereof, then your eyes
shall be opened, and ye shall be as gods, knowing good and evil"*

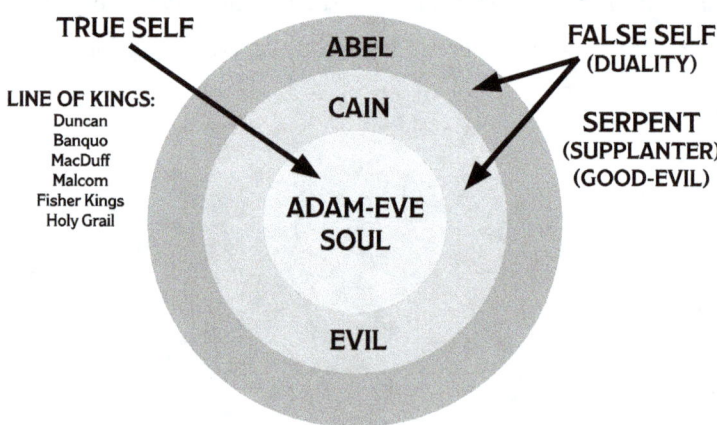

The archetypes of Shakespeare's theology

So, the Adam-Eve polarity represents the soul, which is the true self. The Cain-Abel polarity — the 'monstrous birth' referred to in *Othello* — represents the false self or ego-personality. Even deeper insight into how Shakespeare uses Cain-Abel as an archetype is developed in *Volume II*, where we examine the evolution of the soul through the lives of Richard II, Henry IV and Henry V.

Thus, we all have two very distinct purposes in life — one for each 'self'. The soul has a fundamental, existential purpose, a destiny, a divine mission. The ego also has a purpose, a destination, a desperate need to prove itself. When these two purposes are aligned, we feel happy, fulfilled, joyful and abundant. When we do not experience deep, abiding happiness, chances are it's because we are out of alignment with our soul's purpose; our two selves are at war.

With his signature irony, Shakespeare uses Romeo's priest and mentor, Friar Lawrence, as a 'mole' to deliver this concept.

> *Two such opposèd kings encamp them still in man as well*
> *as herbs — grace and rude will. And where the worser is*
> *predominant, full soon the canker death eats up that plant.*
> *Romeo and Juliet,* Act II Scene III

The *two opposèd kings* living inside mankind's skull — the true self and the ego-personality (false self) — would only be understood by one who knows the essence of his spiritual psychology. As ever, Shakespeare's encryption technique conceals the forbidden truth from the uninitiated whilst revealing it to those who are ready.

So, one of the reasons I felt this close attunement with Shakespeare is that the model of consciousness I had been using for working with clients and horses is the same triune structure the Master uses to structure his plays. The mind leap is to consider that, instead of using *characters* to populate his plays, he is using *characterisations* of the same three core, opposite-energy pairs of archetypes: God-Satan, Adam-Eve, Cain-Abel.

Friar Lawrence's opposèd kings begin with the God-Satan archetype. When individualised in man as the soul, God adopts the male-female polarity, Adam-Eve, to rule the inner kingdom of heaven. The Adam (male) would be drawn more to the higher spiritual worlds, while the Eve (female) is more attracted to the earth plane. Together, they balance heaven and earth. Hence the serpent (Satan) went first to lure the female and use the earth-drawn polarity to seduce the male energy into its trap.

After the serpent had raped and contaminated Eve and Adam (the soul) with the consciousness of good-and-evil, their issue (Cain-Abel) was part soul (God) and part Satan. The monstrous birth. It must surely be this terrible hybrid that is the *something rotten* that got into the state of mankind and usurped the kingdom of heaven inside us. And it is surely this something rotten that is the opposèd kings referred to by Friar Lawrence.

Characterisations vs Characters

Once we understand that the key characters throughout the works of Shakespeare are representations of the three archetypes, we see Shakespeare's characters not as characters but as characterisations. Macbeth and Lady Macbeth play the monstrous role of Cain-Abel in *Macbeth*, Claudius ('the serpent that now wears my crown') and Gertrude play it in Hamlet, and so on and so on.

One Inner Play, Thirty-two Iterations

Again, once we fathom the deep subtext of Shakespeare's work, see the characters as one of the three archetypes and view each plot as a representation of our inner world of consciousness, we start to see that there are not thirty-two independent plays (counting the two Henry sagas as two plays rather than seven) at all, but *one play* with thirty-two iterations on the surface. The fall of man, the cutting off of the sound current, the forgiveness of sin, the reunion with God and the attainment of Ananda is the subplot of all thirty-two plays. In the same way, the restoration of order that must correct the 'something rotten' is the subtext not only of *Hamlet* but of every single one of Shakespeare's plays — and to the state of mankind. It is Friar Lawrence's *two opposèd kings* in thirty-two iterations. It follows that, if there is only one inner play in the subtext with thirty-two outer iterations, we cannot fully understand any individual play without reference to one or more of the others. As an example, *Macbeth* metaphorically introduces the concept of the poisoned chalice as incepted by Jesus himself in the Garden of Gethsemane, but it is fulfilled literally in the finale of *Hamlet*.

NameAlchemy and Wordsmithery

Shakespeare was notorious for making up words and phrases that have now become enshrined in the vernacular, so it's no surprise he flouts all conventions to make his unique ciphers. It is often through subtle use of anagrams, part anagram part homonym, look-alike combos and other befuddling wordplay that Shakespeare codes his hidden messages.

I believe that what I call 'NameAlchemy' (funny-sounding names) is one of Shakespeare's simplest yet foremost Rosetta Stones. Understanding NameAlchemy is crucial in decrypting and enjoying the profound significance of his 'funny names' with poignant hidden meanings. When I first discovered the sublime beauty of Shakespeare's funny names, I was in a dilemma: What on earth do I call them? NameAlchemy came after many incarnations. I knew they deserved something special, because they transform the base lead of surface sounds into golden, multidimensional revelations. Code? If you must.

Consider this sublime example of NameAlchemy from *King Lear* that you'll need when we arrive at Prospero's magical isle in *The Tempest*.

In Act I Scene I of *King Lear*, Lear declares, 'Know that we have divided in three our kingdom.' In the outer play, this would mean his outer kingdom — ancient Britain. Exquisitely, this could metamorphose directly in the inner play as, '*We have divided into three archetypes our inner world of consciousness.*'

But how do we know this is the Master's intention? How do we know we're not just making all this inner stuff up?

NameAlchemy.

Each of Lear's three portions (of land) are destined for each of his three daughters: Goneril, Regan and Cordelia. The best, most opulent portion is reserved for his most beloved child, Cordelia. To get their inheritance, all his daughters must do is convince Lear of their love for him.

Waiting to betray him as soon as they have their property, Goneril and Regan ply their father with a barrel load of sycophantic goose fat — lying through their teeth about how much they love the old man. Cordelia, in contrast, tells him the truth: she loves him according to her bond — nothing more, nothing less.

Lear falls for the lure of false-self love. In a fit of anger, he banishes Cordelia and divides everything up between the two scheming sisters. How does the Master tell us this is a metaphor for how the soul, our spiritual heart, is banished from birth and we define ourselves as the two polarities of our false self (Cain and Abel)?

Anagrams.

Remarkably:

REGAN is an anagram of ANGER.

GONERIL is an anagram of RELIGON (looks like RELIGION).

CORDELIA is an anagram of... LEAD, LEAR? Only partly so.

What could CORDELIA be an anagram of? It's not. It's even more exquisite than that. As we shall see with the name Fortinbras in *Hamlet*, the clue is given if we listen to the *sound of the name* (the sound of the hallowed name that opens the *ear of man*).

CORDELIA sounds like... COR-DE-LIA... COEUR DE LEAR (the heart of Lear, the heart of the king, the soul of man).

Thus, in one fell swoop, we have not just seen signs of a secret code that may well apply to key names in other plays but gained more insight into what

Shakespeare is telling us in his subtext. We've also seen that he uses puns, anagrams, homonyms and, let's see what else, to charge his quill with invisible ink.

And here's the triune pattern again — this time with very little doubt about his intention:

KING LEAR — REAL KING

"I am made of that self-metal as my sister is"

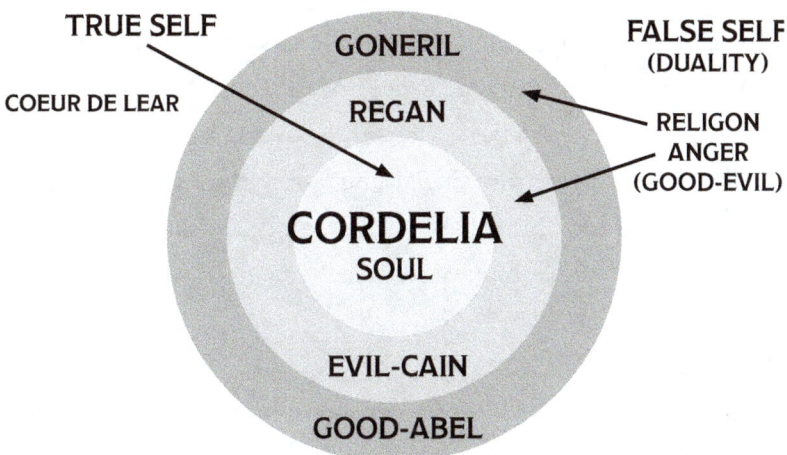

The archetypes in *King Lear*

Biblical Motifs

Just as this NameAlchemy uses code to reveal the subtext of the play, Shakespeare's use of biblical symbolism is key to unravelling the inner plot. It seems that usually, somewhere in the first act, scene, or even line, he colludes with the inner sleuth by cryptically foreshadowing the key to the entire play. Just as with NameAlchemy, I struggled to know what to call these incredible references. As they are sometimes throwaway, but unimaginably significant, I settled on 'biblical motifs'. To whet your appetite and open the door a crack on what we are about to discover, here's a brief example of a

Shakespearean-Wittgensteinian rabbit that's also a duck. All that's required is that you shift your viewing point.

In the eerie opening scene of *Hamlet*, Horatio tells of the crowing of a cock.

> *The cock, that is the trumpet to the morn,*
> *Doth with his lofty and shrill-sounding throat*
> *Awake the god of day.*
> *Hamlet,* Act I Scene I

Specifically, the verse alludes to when Jesus says to Peter, 'before the cock crow twice, thou shalt deny me thrice' (Mark 14: 30). But as we'll discover when we look at *Hamlet*, these three lines of verse are a portal to the entire biblical story of Christ, from the Last Supper to the Agony in Gethsemane, to the arrest, trial and death of Jesus. All the plots (the single plot) of the plays are composed of familiar biblical passages reimagined with a heretical slant.

Sound Current Allusions

Last but also very much first is Shakespeare's utter devotion to the sound current. The what? I hear you say. The sound current, I repeat. I would venture to assert that the sound current is the ultimate pinnacle of what's important to understand; yet the knowledge of which lies buried in the quagmire of misunderstood and forbidden mystical treasures. The sound current is who we really are, and the very stuff of the creation. It is seminal to Sufi, many Eastern mystical teachings (and the secret of the Holy Grail). Myriad symbols of the sound current totally dominate the verse of Shakespeare.

Understanding Shakespeare's allusions to the sound current is the sine qua non to understanding the Grail — and reaping the rich rewards it promises us all. It's one of those existential truths that belong to us all, that empower us all — and for this reason is withheld by the few that want all the power for themselves.

If you finish this book with no more than a hunger to hear and experience the sound current for yourself, then you will have the best quest possible on this planet.

Hang in there as your beliefs, paradigms, and mind-sets collide with each other and with the ultimate truth of the universal teachings that underpin all religion, philosophy, psychology, and theology.

Shakespeare's subtext abounds with ubiquitous, poetic allusions to the sound current — the sound of God that in the Gospel of John is called 'the Word', the sound and Name of God out of which everything that is made was made. It is truly our connection with our soul and our creator. In every play I've looked at, there is at least one poetically camouflaged reference to this eternal jewel, the sound current of all creation.

I want to give you a sense of how this invisible thread of symbols of the sound current sweeps us through the oeuvre.

1000 violins

The wind from heaven

Body bread humming

the waters **RIVER** **SURF**

bells Sound Current **STREAM**

Name of God THE WORD **SEA**

storm buzzing

Hue

Word made flesh **SHABDH** **Breath of Life**

Tide Music Stone **BROOK**

Tree of Life

Some of the myriad mystical symbols for the sound current.

In *The Merchant of Venice*, Lorenzo treats us to a perfect description of how the sound of God sleeps within, unheard, until we chant the sacred name that kisses it awake.

LORENZO

Such harmony is in immortal souls,
But whilst this muddy vesture of decay
Doth grossly close it in, we cannot hear it.
Come, ho! and wake Diana with a hymn.
With sweetest touches pierce your mistress' ear,
And draw her home with music.
The Merchant of Venice, Act V Scene I

In *Othello,* Cassio tells us how the soul, the divine Desdemona, is transported safely home by the mysterious wind from heaven.

CASSIO

'Has had most favourable and happy speed!
*Tempests themselves, **high seas, and howling winds,***
The guttered rocks and congregated sands
(Traitors ensteeped to clog the guiltless keel),
As having sense of beauty, do omit
Their mortal natures, letting go safely by
The divine Desdemona.
Othello, Act II Scene I

King Lear famously rails against the religions, blasting them with God's fury and alluding to the coming of the comforter (in tongues of fire on his head, Acts 2:2).

LEAR

*Blow winds, and crack your cheeks! **Rage, blow!***
You cataracts and hurricanoes, spout
Till you have drenched our steeples, drowned the
cocks.
You sulph'rous and thought-executing fires,
Vaunt-couriers of oak-cleaving thunderbolts,
***Singe my white head.** And thou, all-shaking*
thunder,
Strike flat the thick rotundity o' th' world.
Crack nature's molds, all germens spill at once
That makes ingrateful man.
King Lear, Act III Scene II

Macbeth echoes Lear in this gusty tirade against the tyranny of the Church.

MACBETH
*Though you **untie the winds** and let them fight*
Against the churches, though the yeasty waves
Confound and swallow navigation up,
Though bladed corn be lodged and trees blown down,
Though castles topple on their warders' heads,
Though palaces and pyramids do slope
Their heads to their foundations, though the treasure
Of nature's germens tumble all together
Even till destruction sicken, answer me
To what I ask you.
Macbeth, Act IV Scene II

Prior to his coronation, Henry V pays homage to the sound current that he has come to liberate at Agincourt (Vol II).

PRINCE HENRY
The tide of blood in me
Hath proudly flowed in vanity till now.
Now doth it turn and ebb back to the sea,
Where it shall mingle with the state of floods
And flow henceforth in formal majesty.
Henry IV, Part II Act V Scene II

In *Romeo and Juliet*, Capulet here ushers forth a feast of sound current sound bites that delineate the divinity that is Juliet. Notice multiple reference to a *bark* — a kind of three-masted sail ship. Hold that thought.

CAPULET

When the sun sets, the earth doth drizzle dew,
But for the sunset of my brother's son
It rains downright.
How now, a conduit, girl? What, still in tears?
Evermore show'ring? In one little body
*Thou counterfeits **a bark, a sea, a wind.***
*For still thy eyes, which I may call **the sea,***
*Do **ebb and flow** with **tears**; the **bark** thy body is,*
*Sailing in this salt flood; the **winds** thy sighs,*
*Who, raging with thy **tears** and they with them,*
Without a sudden calm, will overset
*Thy **tempest-tossèd** body. —How now, wife?*
Have you delivered to her our decree?
Romeo and Juliet, Act III Scene V

Back now to *Macbeth*, Act I, where the witches use the same phrase as Capulet.

*Though his **bark** cannot be lost,*
*Yet it shall be **tempest-tossed**.*
Macbeth, Act I Scene III

The astonishing focus of this weird allusion will be revealed later.

Then, the immortal opening line of *Twelfth Night* kicks off with a multidimensional allusion to the sound current, manna from heaven, the daily bread, and the manger of the epiphany foreshadowing the cup of the Last Supper — both containers of the body and blood of Christ.

ORSINO

If music be the food of love, play on.
Twelfth Night, Act I Scene I

Keeping up the 'food of love' metaphor, these examples are just an appetizer. You're soon to discover many more rare and precious morsels of nourishment embedded in the poetry. But these tools will test you. You will be challenged to be open and agile, to see ducks where previously you have seen only rabbits. In taking up this toolkit, in understanding the invisible ink Shakespeare uses to hide the truth, you will discover the true subtext in all his plays.

Beginning with *Macbeth,* I'd like to invite you to join me on a true Grail quest into the forbidden, secret world of Shakespeare's subterranean subtext. As with any true quest, this is not for the faint-hearted. This truly is *double, double toil and trouble* as we let the fire burn and the cauldron bubble. I plan to show you how Shakespeare has devoted his entire oeuvre to answering the most important questions for the sincere spiritual warrior, the sincere seeker of truth, health, wealth and the deep, lasting happiness of Ananda. I know that's what I want; I want the profound, blissful, inner experience the Grail promises. What on earth would I do with a golden chalice if I found it? Let alone the putrefying corpse of Mary Magdalene? Yes, 'union with God' sounds like a much better quest.

As we take apart the three plays in the following three parts, the inner workings of Shakespeare's story engine will come clear.

Part One:

MACBETH: THE PASSION OF THE SATAN

*This even-handed justice commends th'ingredients
of the poisoned chalice to my own lips.*

Macbeth, Act I Scene VII

Here in the West, we live in a culture that's predicated on so-called Christian values. We celebrate all the major gospel events with a holiday. We baptize our babies in the futile hope it will prevent them falling prey to the 'original sin' — a concept we do not understand. Our laws are built on the ancient Jewish laws: the ten commandments and selected sins curated from Leviticus. We're all reasonably familiar with the sentimentalised events surrounding Christmas, Lent, Easter and Whitsun. We sort of know what Christ did and that he died and resurrected — even if we don't believe a word of it.

But what about Satan? Maybe we've read Milton's *Paradise Lost* and gained some empathy with Satan's hostile takeover of God's foremost creation. But how did it feel for Satan to have pulled off this awesome coup, made a monkey out of God, only to have his milksop of a son come to earth and ruin everything?

Imagine, if you will, the mind of Satan.

Even when I kill this brat by nailing him to a cross for three days, he rises again, breaks my seven seals cutting off God's Tree of Life and, without so much as a 'by your leave' opens up paradise for anyone who asks to come in. I did all this to rule heaven my way, to make everyone scared and grovel before me in supplication and worship. I even mock, ridicule and scourge the lily-livered, love-your-neighbor wimp only to find that it's me they're laughing at. Me! Me wearing the crown of thorns. Me dressed up like Guy Fawkes on the bonfire and burning in my own hell.

If you chunk down the quote at the start of this part of the book from Shakespeare's version of Satan (Macbeth) into its component parts, it gets really interesting.

This even-handed justice commends th'ingredients
of the poisoned chalice to my own lips.

'Even-Handed Justice'

There is a high spiritual law that says we reap what we sow — what we put out is returned to us. It also seems like one of the Old Testament prophecies was that, for Satan's laws and iron grip on mankind's soul to be vanquished, he had to be defeated by his own hand — not exactly suicide but 'hoist by his own petard'. When the Christ confronts Satan's distortion of God's laws with the truth, and his response is an attempt to kill the Christ, he destroys himself. This is a running theme throughout Shakespeare's oeuvre.

'Th'ingredients of the Poisoned Chalice'

The cup (of the Last Supper) was a metaphor incepted by Jesus himself in Gethsemane. The 'ingredients' included the trial and Crucifixion — about this he was clear. But they also included the wine and the bread, his blood and his body. To mankind, they brought the way, the truth and the life. To Satan, they brought the end. Hence from Satan's/Macbeth's perspective, the ingredients were poison. Is it then the ingredients of the poisoned chalice that are the Holy Grail? The ingredients, not the cup itself?

'To My Own Lips'

This is the aforementioned hoisting of his own petard — another piece of vocabulary created by the Master himself.

Of course, nothing comes out of Shakespeare in a straightforward, easy-to-comprehend manner. He leaps back and forth across the centuries in the blink of an eye. Several characters might represent one archetype, or one character several. If you embrace the same agility while you come on this journey, you should enjoy the wee ride up to bonny Scotland — and beyond.

Chapter 2:

THE OUTER AND INNER MACBETHS

The Outer Play

Before we go backstage and into the soul of the author, let's quickly review what is acted out on stage in *Macbeth,* as the vehicle for the Master's spiritual and mystical genius starts to unfold.

Macbeth, set primarily in Scotland, mixes witchcraft, prophecy and murder. While returning home, victorious after a battle, Macbeth, Thane of Glamis, and his comrade Banquo encounter three Weird Sisters. They prophesy that Macbeth will be king and that Banquo will be father to a line of kings. When Macbeth arrives at his castle, Lady Macbeth lures him into a plot to assassinate King Duncan, soon to be their guest, so that Macbeth can become king.

After Macbeth murders Duncan, the king's two sons, Malcolm and Donalbain, flee, and Macbeth is crowned. Fearing that his crown is threatened by Banquo's descendants, Macbeth has Banquo assassinated. At a royal banquet that evening, Macbeth alone sees Banquo's ghost appear, covered in blood. Macbeth determines to consult the Weird Sisters, and again they warn him to beware Macduff, another nobleman, and reassure him he cannot be harmed by any man of woman born nor until the seemingly impossible event that Burnham Wood comes to high Dunsinane Hill.

Macduff joins forces with Malcolm, so Macbeth has Macduff's wife and children murdered. Malcolm and Macduff lead an army against Macbeth, while Lady Macbeth goes insane with guilt and kills herself.

At his castle in Dunsinane, Macbeth, with his false sense of security based on the Weird Sisters' ambiguous prophecies, confronts Malcolm's army, which is shrouded by trees hewn from Burnham Wood. He learns too late that his fate is sealed but continues to fight. Macduff, born by caesarean, kills Macbeth, and Malcolm becomes Scotland's king.

The Inner Play

Now we continue the Grail quest, seeking 'what was lost'. Consider that the ultimate 'hero's journey', the original quest, was the one undertaken by Jesus the Christ to liberate mankind from the tyranny of Satan's diabolical consciousness — good-and-evil. Are you open to a paradigm shift, where you see how *Macbeth* represents this quest not from the point of view of Jesus but from the perspective of Satan, the one whom Jesus came to vanquish? What happens to your understanding of the play when Satan is disguised as Macbeth and plays the archetypal anti-hero?

Remember that it was to Macbeth, the traitor, the one who murders the king, that Banquo gave the diamond. And remember that the diamond represents the sop given by Jesus to Judas, the one about to betray him. Shakespeare is implying that Macbeth is representing all of those who betrayed the soul: Satan, Cain, Judas — perhaps even Adam too, in his own way.

Archetypes in Macbeth

As we've learnt, instead of using characters to populate his plays, Shakespeare uses *characterisations* of the same three core, opposite-energy pairs of archetypes: God-Satan (serpent), Adam-Eve (soul), Cain-Abel (false selves).

It's important to understand and love the Satan archetype because, whatever it is, it is part of God's creation and part of our expression of who we are. Paradoxically, to know who we really are, we must first know who we are really not. We really are a perfect spark of God's great light, but we tend to believe we're the shadow, Satan. If we don't understand Satan, we can so easily end up hating ourselves. The forgotten truth of Satan is that he is not just evil — he is both good *and* evil. Dressing himself up as the devil, with horns and cloven hoof, is his highly successful propaganda campaign to keep us in constant conflict within and between ourselves.

Thus, for their first scene, let Macbeth, Thane of Glamis, and Lady Macbeth represent Adam and Eve. Let them in turn be a metaphor of the male-female polarity of the first soul within all mankind — including you. Make it about your deep, evolutionary history.

As the scene rolls on, the pair rapidly transform into the Cain-Abel archetype, where they remain until their demise.

MACBETH

"Look like the innocent flower, but be the serpent under't"

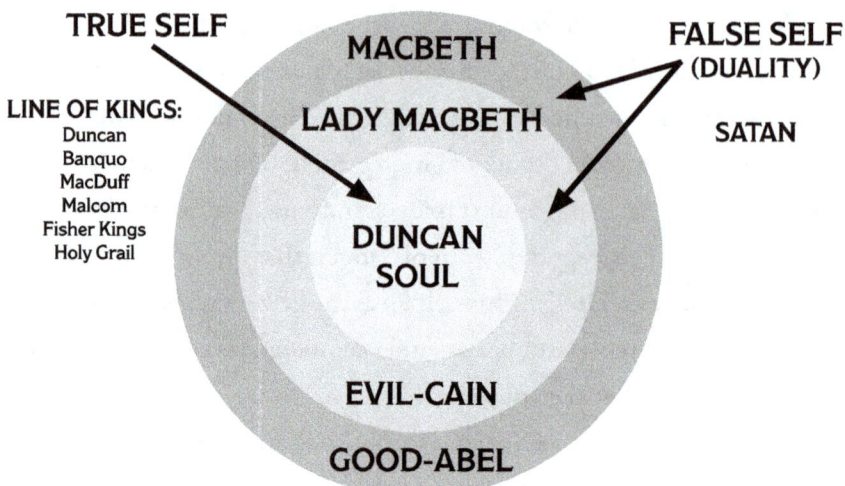

TRUE SELF

LINE OF KINGS:
Duncan
Banquo
MacDuff
Malcom
Fisher Kings
Holy Grail

MACBETH

LADY MACBETH

FALSE SELF
(DUALITY)

SATAN

DUNCAN
SOUL

EVIL-CAIN

GOOD-ABEL

The archetypes in *Macbeth*

Remember the diagram of the two selves in chapter 1? It's a fairly basic representation of the inner dynamics of who we are, but, crucially, Shakespeare is using a structure similar to this in all his plays. This is how the players in *Macbeth* are used to delineate the archetypes within us, how they interact and what drives them. In the centre of our being is the soul, the true self. Here, it is represented initially by Duncan, the king Macbeth betrays by murdering and deposing his crown. In so doing, he and Lady Macbeth 'fall'. As they absorb the contagion of good-and-evil into their energy fields, their roles shape-shift from the original Adam-Eve archetype to the hybrid 'sons' of Eve and the serpent: Cain and Abel — what Shakespeare calls (in *Othello*) 'the monstrous birth'.

As the play plays out, it recounts the story of the evolution of the soul and its quest to vanquish the tyranny of Satan through Cain and Abel.

In a letter, Macbeth tells Lady Macbeth that he met three weird women, prophet-like witches, who made the unlikely prophecy that he would not only be promoted to Thane of Cawdor but also king. His friend Banquo was told he would not be king, but his bloodline would be kings. Immediately confirming the prophecy, Macbeth was surprisingly promoted to Thane of Cawdor. He was now on his way home with Duncan, the incumbent king, burning with the tempting thought that it might now be possible for even he himself to become king.

By the time Macbeth gets home, Lady Macbeth is even more intoxicated with the ambition fired by the contagion of good-and-evil than he is. She has been well and truly ravaged by the serpent. One of Shakespeare's running themes is that the serpent raped Eve in the garden. If you allow your imagination to soar, her prayer to Satan (Night), 'Come thick Night... unsex me here' is already withering the love and bliss of the Tree of Life within her.

On one level, she's asking that all her gentle, feminine, soul-like qualities would be extirpated so she could be cold-blooded enough to murder the king and have her husband claim the crown, the 'golden round'. On another deeper, more subtle level, it is her cries of lust-fuelled rapture as the serpent penetrates and inseminates her with the consciousness of good-and-evil (Cain and Abel).

At first, Macbeth is too 'full of the milk of human kindness' to contemplate murdering the king. But she browbeats, mocks, humiliates and manipulates him till he agrees to the murder. They, just as did Adam and Eve, both have now 'fallen' into the duality of good-and-evil.

Duncan, on the other hand, is described as no ordinary king, but a deity. He represents the very soul of man, the breath of God, the source of life that feeds the soul of all mankind. When Macduff discovers the murder, whose loss could possibly evoke such an inconsolable wailing? A mere mortal king? No chance. The loss of the life within the Lord's anointed Temple (the soul)? Absolutely.

O horror, horror, horror,
tongue nor heart cannot conceive or name thee...
...Confusion now hath made his masterpiece:
most sacrilegious murther
hath broke ope
The Lord's anointed Temple
and stole thence
The life of the building.
Macbeth, Act II Scene III

It is indeed a dangerous, daring slice of heresy to suggest the body (not the church building) is the anointed temple of the Christ — even today.

When he kills Duncan, Macbeth finds he has banished his very soul, bringing darkness and despair to the whole of Scotland. Scotland here represents the consciousness of mankind, just as in *Hamlet* it is Denmark and in *King Lear* it is ancient Britain. Order is lost; something is rotten.

Here Macbeth has become as Cain, the son of Perdition. Scotland, the whole world of our consciousness, is now shrouded in darkness and stained with Macbeth's shame. Macbeth has given 'the eternal jewel to the common enemy of man'. The crown he stole has become hollow, fruitless and worthless. But having lost his soul, like Cain, he cannot stop himself from compulsively murdering anyone who might threaten his empty throne. Even his almost-brother Banquo.

Malcolm the son of Duncan, the rightful heir to the throne, one of four characterisations of the archetype of the true self in the play (Duncan, Malcolm, Banquo, Macduff) flees the scene. With Macduff's aid, as a parable of how the murdered soul is restored to its rightful place in our inner world, they prepare an army to restore the crown that is rightfully his.

Meanwhile, Macbeth (Satan) begins his mad killing spree. First, he murders Banquo, dubbed by the witches as father to a line of kings. The witches' prophecy comes true again. Macbeth entreats Banquo to 'fail not our feast' — and rues the moment he tempts fate so. Banquo, the Christ, resurrects. He rises from the dead and sits in his place at the feast celebrating Macbeth's pseudo-coronation. Macbeth becomes totally unhinged — imagine how maybe Satan felt when he knew his end was nigh.

The three witches warn Macbeth to beware Macduff. They also say that 'none of woman born' can harm Macbeth. Neither can Macbeth be vanquished till (the impossible occurrence that) Burnham Wood comes to high Dunsinane Hill. Then, Macbeth slaughters the innocent wife and children of Macduff.

Malcolm, Macduff and their spiritual warriors advance on Dunsinane to vanquish 'Satan'. En route, they cut down branches from Burnham Wood and bear them in the fore to camouflage their presence.

They storm Dunsinane. Macduff duels with Macbeth. Macbeth taunts Macduff with the witches' prophecy that 'none of woman born' could harm him. Macduff reveals that from his mother's womb he was 'untimely ripped' — and thus was 'not of woman born'. He kills Macbeth, cuts off his head, the crown of the serpent, reclaims the lost crown and hands the throne to Malcolm. The true self, the soul of mankind, once again rules the inner kingdom of mankind as the centre of consciousness. And Scotland has its well-deserved moment of paradisical glory.

Chapter 3:

BIBLICAL MOTIFS
IN MACBETH

O
f course, it was fascinating to realise that Shakespeare was using the mythic story of Jesus the Christ as his subtext. But my question was why? Why go to such lengths to keep it secret? Some individual motifs have been recorded by scholars, but never have they been linked together in this greater context. My answer was that these biblical motifs are more than mere biblical events; they are the key tests, tasks and trials Jesus was destined to fulfil in order to fulfil the scripture and vanquish Satan. Why this was declared 'heresy' is the key to understanding the Grail.

When you're cooking up a casserole, it often makes very little difference in what order you add many of the ingredients, seasoning, herbs and spices. Likewise with Shakespeare, when he tosses in his biblical motifs. Perhaps, as you'll begin to see, simply in order to have the energy, the vibratory frequency these events produce in our consciousness, he will allude to, say, the virgin birth, several acts after the resurrection.

To give some sense of order and logic, I have roughly followed the biblical chronology of the events. This means that, unless it is absurd, I shall be hopping around the plays like a jackrabbit looking for ducks in the undergrowth.

Biblical Motifs in Macbeth

BIBLICAL EVENT	SHAKESPEARE CODE
The fall of man: Eve is beguiled by the lies of the serpent	Lady Macbeth is beguiled by Macbeth's letter
The tree of life is cut off	King Duncan is murdered. The fountain of your (Royal) blood is stopped
Adam & Eve banished from paradise	Macbeth gives away 'the eternal jewel'
Cain and Abel born after the banishing	Macbeth's reign of terror
The Virgin Birth	Macduff not of woman born
Herod's slaughter of the innocents	Macbeth slaughters Macduff's babies
Jesus casts out devils	Siward casts out 'the evil'
God sacrifices his son	Siward's son is killed by Macbeth
The cup of the last supper (a)	The poisoned chalice
The cup of the last supper (b)	The witches' cauldron
My blood of the new testament	The ingredients in the cauldron
Jesus passes the sop to Judas	Banquo passes the diamond to Macbeth
Jesus crucified for blasphemy	Liver of blaspheming Jew
Pilate symbolically washes his hands	Lady Macbeth obsessively washes her hands
Jesus mocked with crown of thorns and wooden sceptre	Macbeth given fruitless crown and barren sceptre
Jesus bears his cross to High Calvary Hill	Burnham Wood comes to high Dunsinane Hill
The Epiphany, Baby Jesus Laid in a Manger and Shown to the Shepherds and Kings	A Baby in a Cauldron with a Crown Shown to Macbeth

Biblical motifs in Macbeth

Consider this chapter as a thought experiment. Are the cryptic codes Shakespeare uses to camouflage his subtext the same devices used by the original scribes of the Bible to protect divine wisdom from being extirpated or abused? Above is a table summarising the most important biblical motifs in *Macbeth*. What follows is a brief discussion of each. Although the other layers of coding discussed fully in chapter 1, Invisible Ink, take our understanding of Shakespeare's cryptic message to an even deeper level, it is the biblical motifs that are his keystones. To add in more confusion, Shakespeare's subtext story does not follow biblical chronology; it seems to be almost randomly sprinkled into the cauldron of the play like herbs and spices. Yet it is the invisible gossamer thread connecting everything in the body of works together, like the fascia of the human body. The table is to help you see some of the key motifs in the familiar biblical chronology. The discussion is more about the story of how I managed to make sense of things.

Three Witches: Three Wise Men?

> *When shall we three meet again?*
> *In thunder lightning or in rain?*
> *Macbeth,* Act I Scene I

That said, I must start with the first line of the play. The prophet-like three witches, their cauldron, spells and prophecies are the core drivers of both the outer and inner plays. What biblical characters might they represent, one wonders? Could the three witches be the twisted way Satan (Macbeth) experiences the Maji who foiled Herod's plan to kill the baby Jesus? Remember, Macbeth-as-Satan is the protagonist, and it is the witches' double-double entendre that makes not just Macbeth toil and trouble but also the Church. Mocking the orthodox belief in the second coming, the infamous opening line is a cryptic allusion to the endgame in the Christ mission — to restore access to the Tree of Life (the wind from heaven, the sound current) to its rightful place in the centre of our consciousness. This can only happen if and when the usurping, murderous Satan has himself been deposed.

The Fall of Man: Lady Macbeth Bites First

As we've discussed, we, mankind, did not fall — we forgot. The original GuiltSin was not, nor could not have been 'disobedience'. The parable in Genesis shows Adam and Eve given a *choice* and being warned of the *consequences*. Remember that Adam and Eve were not people. Nor was it an apple they ate. Nor was it a serpent. Nor was it a garden. They are all metaphors, symbols, *motifs* of impossible-to-put-words-on events deep inside our consciousness. They/we were told that if we ate or even touched the fruit of the tree of the knowledge of good and evil, we will die. Die, not as a punishment, but as a consequence. And did we die? No/yes. It depends how you interpret 'die'. As Romeo says, 'banishment is death'. We were banished. We were cut off from the Tree of Life. We died to the awareness of the soul that we truly are. Man did not fall — we forgot. Forgot who we really are. We died metaphorically. Why? What was the sin if not disobedience? Guilt, shame, lies, covering up, hiding. That was the original GuiltSin. That is the only sin. It's the guilt that cuts us off from the awareness of God. How can God, the supreme intelligence that created everything, including you and me, issue a commandment that cannot be obeyed? Absurd!

In *Macbeth,* in the beginning (as in Genesis) would be the temptation of power and glory (the crown), given (prophet-like) to Macbeth by the witches. In the back story and opening scene, Macbeth and Lady Macbeth are in their originally innocent stage, representing Adam-Eve in Eden. The witches' prophesy that Macbeth is to become Thane of Cawdor (something highly unlikely which immediately comes true). And they tempt him with the diabolical promise that he could also be king. To Banquo, they tell him he himself will not be king but, inscrutably, he is 'father to a line of kings'. What could this mean?

On his journey home, Macbeth writes to tell Lady Macbeth his good news. The letter is a vehicle for the serpent's venom. As did Eve, on hearing the voice of pride, Lady Macbeth immediately becomes intoxicated with lust for the power and glory of being queen, in other words, with *the knowledge of good and evil*: the very stuff the ego is formed with. She acts as an agent for the serpent to undermine Macbeth's/Adam's originally innocent nature (the milk of human kindness). She prays to Satan in the biblical code Shakespeare uses liberally throughout the plays (Night). She summons up the satanic power to kill the loving instincts of a mother, to 'unsex' herself, banish all conscience and apply the emotional crowbar to Macbeth to 'look like the innocent flower, but be the serpent under't'. As ever, here's the signature nod and wink that confirms he's referring to Satan. Just like in *Othello,* Shakespeare pairs 'night and hell', and just like in Genesis 3, through Lady Macbeth as the Eve archetype, the serpent has the pair murder the king and gain the golden round — the hollow crown.

LADY MACBETH
*Come, thick **night,***
*And pall thee in the dunnest smoke of **hell,***
That my keen knife see not the wound it makes,
Nor heaven peep through the blanket of the dark
To cry "Hold, hold!"
Macbeth, Act I Scene V

To go deeper still, one of Shakespeare's running themes is how the serpent raped Eve and sired Cain and Abel, the monstrous hybrid birth. Of course, he doesn't say this out loud; it's in the imagery when you look at it through those eyes of his that see the greater truth. Connecting these two darker-than-night speeches, can you not feel the carnal rapture as the diabolical metaphor takes root in the soul of man?

LADY MACBETH
Come, you spirits
That tend on mortal thoughts, unsex me here,
And fill me from the crown to the toe topful
Of direst cruelty!
Macbeth, Act I Scene V

The serpent, the god of this physical, psychic-material world, goes to the female/negative polarity because it is of the mother-earth nature. Through this magnetic attraction, the male/positive polarity, the father-God aspect, is thus contaminated with the delusion of good-and-evil and the addiction to judgement — the original GuiltSin of placing the ego's opinion above the will of God.

Cutting Off the Tree of Life

It's now as if Shakespeare is using Macbeth's voice to tell us how the Tree of Life was cut off in Genesis and simultaneously foreshadow its reopening in the Revelation.

Remember how, in the book *The Holy Blood and the Holy Grail*, the core premise of both this research and the novel based on it, *The Da Vinci Code*, was that the term 'Holy Grail' derives from the Old French *sang graal* meaning 'royal blood'?

Immediately after he has committed the murder most foul, Macbeth laments to Malcolm and Donalbain, the sons and heirs of the dead Duncan, that the royal blood that flows from their father (God, the fountain, the source) has been cut off. Macbeth is torn between feigning innocence and suffering the visceral effects of shock at the inner consequences of what he has just done. In verse, deliciously invoking both the wine and the blood of the Eucharist, in consecutive lines, he's again using, as a metaphor for something even higher than just any earthly king, 'Royal Father'. Is this yet another allusion to the Last Supper and also the Father in Heaven?

Here's what Macbeth tells the sons of the king he just murdered. Even though he feigns innocence, he is nevertheless apoplectic over what he has done and how he now feels.

MACBETH

*Renown and **Grace** is dead,*
***the wine of life** is drawn*
*The spring, the head, **the fountain of your blood** is stopped*
*The **very source** of it is stopped...'*
*...Your **Royal Father's** murdered.*
Macbeth, Act II Scene III

In the first of two hair's-breadth-close allusions to the word Grail (*sang graal*), is Shakespeare using his verse to evoke a deep, subliminal sense of a momentous event in the past of all of us — an event that cut off the very source of our life blood, the energy vibration through which everything was created: the Tree of Life, the Word of God Himself? It is an event deep in the story of our spiritual evolution that rendered us blind and deaf in the beginning, and blinds and deafens us, to this day, to the songs of the soul and the ultimate truth of who we really are.

Note also the resonance this verse has with the idea of the Grail as the *sang graal*, the Royal Blood, and his confirmatory allusion to 'the wine of life' — the very symbol introduced by Jesus himself at the Last Supper. Intone the resonance of Macbeth's reference to the 'fountain of your blood' with a passage from Revelation Shakespeare plunders over and over again.

*And he said unto me, **It is done**. I am Alpha and*
Omega, the beginning and the end. I will give unto him
*that is athirst of **the fountain of the water of life** freely.*
Revelation 21:6

41

Adam and Eve Banished from Paradise

Consider again that Adam and Eve were not the first two people to roam the planet but a metaphor representing the male-female polarity of the original soul created by God in the beginning. Putting these two verses from Genesis together, what do they tell you?

> *So God created man in his own image, in the image of God*
> *created he him; **male and female** created he them.*
> Genesis 1:27

> *And the Lord God formed man of the dust of the ground, and breathed*
> *into his nostrils the breath of life; and man became a **living soul**.*
> Genesis 2:7

Remember that the price we pay for shame and GuiltSin, for being addicted to good-and-evil, is darkness, ignorance, anguish, abandonment and despair. Hamlet refers to it as 'the heartache and the thousand natural shocks that flesh is heir to'. In *Macbeth*, Ross, a kind of narrator, again personifying Night, puts it this way. The consequence of the murder of Duncan, the rightful King (the soul) was:

> ROSS
> *Thou seest the Heavens, as troubled with man's act,*
> *Threatens his bloody stage: by th' clock 'tis day,*
> *And yet dark **Night** strangles the travelling lamp:*
> *Is't **Night's** predominance or the Day's **shame**,*
> *That Darkness does the face of Earth entomb*
> *When living light should kiss it.*
> *Macbeth*, Act II Scene IV

Before he murders Duncan, Macbeth himself quakes at the heinous act he is about to undertake. Remember, this is no mortal king he is to kill, it is a deity. The very God within mankind is being extinguished.

MACBETH

Besides, this Duncan
Hath borne his faculties so meek, hath been
So clear in his great office, that his virtues
Will plead like angels, trumpet-tongued, against
The deep damnation of his taking-off;
And pity, like a naked newborn babe
Striding the blast, or heaven's cherubin horsed
Upon the sightless couriers of the air,
Shall blow the horrid deed in every eye,
That tears shall drown the wind.
Macbeth, Act I Scene VII

Imagine the depth of sadness and misery implied by 'tears that drown the wind'. Imagine the pain that we as mankind must endure and find ways to cope with because the wind from heaven, the Tree of Life, the sound current, the unconditional love of God can no longer be heard and felt within.

As is his wont, Shakespeare drops in a passing allusion to Revelation, completing the circle by giving us the backstory, as it were, to this most poignant verse.

God shall wipe away all tears from their eyes.
Revelation 21:4

The Virgin Birth: Macduff Not of Woman Born

Hopping now to the final scene, Shakespeare has already alluded to the 'line of kings' (Fisher Kings?) through Banquo. And the role seems to be fulfilled by four characters: Duncan, the rightful king first murdered; Banquo himself, the martyr, who is also murdered; Malcolm, the rightful heir to the crown; and, interestingly, Macduff, the spiritual warrior. Just as Jesus as the Christ personified many different human qualities, so are some of these personified by this line of 'kings'.

Shakespeare pays no heed to biblical chronology; he's using the component parts of scripture as building blocks for his drama. It's only in the final showdown between Macduff and Macbeth that the Old Testament duck of the virgin birth glints through the clay rabbit.

Behold, a virgin will be with child and bear a son,
and she will call His name Immanuel.
Isaiah 7:14

The witches have given Macbeth a false sense of security by warning him to fear Macduff and simultaneously prophesying that 'none of woman born' could vanquish Macbeth. So, what's to fear about Macduff? He was surely from woman born. Or was he?

Be bloody, bold, and resolute. Laugh to scorn
*The power of man, for **none of woman born***
Shall harm Macbeth.
Macbeth, Act IV Scene I

Feeling invulnerable, Macbeth is upbeat about his victory. However, the witches, as well as acting as harbingers of Satan's dark destiny, are also part of the plot to vanquish Macbeth by luring him into his own pride-intoxicated trap. As the swollen-egoed Macbeth taunts him, Macduff reveals he was 'from his mother's womb untimely ripped'. This (loosely) implies he was *not of woman born*. Macduff now steps into the role of spiritual warrior, the only one who can vanquish Macbeth.

As an aside, note that, in the annunciation, Mary was told of her divine impregnation by an angel. Typically, Shakespeare drops in an additional cryptic, biblical corroboration.

MACDUFF

Despair thy charm,
*And let **the angel** whom thou still hast served*
Tell thee Macduff was from his mother's womb
Untimely ripped.
Macbeth, Act V Scene VIII

A Baby in a Cauldron with a Crown Shown to Macbeth

Due to the dire penalty of not taking biblical events literally, the meaning behind the intricate labyrinths of symbolism has been lost in a quagmire of superstition — up until Shakespeare. He has taken a wrecking ball to the laws of heresy and waited four hundred years for the superstitions to begin to crumble and fall.

In *Twelfth Night*, which represents the Epiphany, Shakespeare cues us in with 'If music be the food of love...'. The epiphany is when the baby Jesus is laid in a manger and shown to the shepherds and the three kings. Dwelling on this, one can see how the manger (a container for food) is *literally* said to hold the body and blood of Christ. This foreshadows the Eucharist, where the chalice (another container for food) is *symbolically* said to hold the body and blood of Christ. Here in *Macbeth,* the cauldron (another container for food) reveals apparitions of a bloody child and a baby wearing a king's crown. It is these baby kings who deliver the double-double entendre to Macbeth that brings about his downfall.

What is this, that rises like the issue of a King,
And wears upon his baby brow, the round
And top of sovereignty?

Macbeth, Act IV Scene I

I think we can guess the answer to that question, O false king Macbeth: it is the true king, the Christ, the sweet oblivious antidote to sin and guilt coming to take back his crown. Through Satan's eyes, all is twisted, shrouded in darkness, backwards facing. The chalice, filled with love, life and forgiveness for us, is poison to Satan. To us, the baby Jesus comes to liberate. To Satan, he comes to cast him into the bottomless pit. Only when we understand this perspective do we begin to understand *Macbeth*. Only then do we understand what really happened at the trial and crucifixion.

Herod's Slaughter of the Innocents: Macbeth's Slaughter of Macduff's Babies

The conundrum the babies in the cauldron give Macbeth is to fear Macduff but also that none of woman born shall harm him. Despite this, Macbeth decides to kill Macduff's entire family and retinue. During the harrowing scene where the wife, children and all in the line of Macduff are callously slaughtered, I got a powerful feeling. Up came an image of the story in the Gospel known as *The Slaughter of the Innocents.*

MACBETH
The castle of Macduff I will surprise,
Seize upon Fife, give to th' edge o' th' sword
His wife, his babes, and all unfortunate souls
That trace him in his line.
Macbeth, Act IV Scene I

What I didn't originally realise is that not only was this horror recounted in Matthew, but it was prophesied centuries before in Jeremiah. It puts Macduff's hasty flight from Dunsinane with Malcolm immediately after Duncan's death is discovered into a greater perspective. Macduff's wife is distraught at her husband's abandonment, and Ross suggests it might have been prompted by wisdom rather than fear. Indeed.

It looks like a motif of the flight to Egypt taken by Mary and Joseph with the baby Jesus on hearing of Herod's impending slaughter, and a mirror of the biblical event in the Old Testament this slaughter might be symbolising. When Moses was born, in order to control the rising population of Jewish slaves, the Pharaoh had begun a campaign of slaughtering the firstborn children of Israel. Moses was hidden in the bulrushes, found and adopted by the Pharaoh's daughter, and brought up as a prince of Egypt. It was subsequently the slaughter of the firstborns of Egypt that resulted in the release of the children of Israel from bondage. Maybe mankind, like God himself, had to sacrifice the innocent so as to let the children of God, all souls held in the bondage of Mosaic Law, go free.

Then Herod, when he saw that he was mocked of the wise men, was
exceeding wroth, and sent forth, and slew all the children that were in
Bethlehem, and in all the coasts thereof, from two years old and under,
according to the time which he had diligently inquired of the wise men.

Then was fulfilled that which was spoken
by Jeremiah the prophet, saying,

In Rama was there a voice heard, lamentation, and weeping,
and great mourning, Rachel weeping for her children,
and would not be comforted, because they are not.
Matthew 2:16-18

Would you not agree that this juxtaposition not only nails the cauldron as the Grail chalice, but also the three witches as the three Maji?

Shakespeare again uses this harrowing biblical motif in *Henry V.* We'll get another look at it in *Volume II.*

Jesus Takes All Sin from the World: Malcolm Confesses Wanton Debauchery

When in church as a little boy, I always deeply resented being told I was a sinner. Why? What had I done wrong? Those in power tell us we are all, without exception, sinners. This is a deeply damaging lie. The truth is we are all, without exception, divine. And the Old Testament law and its litany of so-called sins has been rescinded by the action of Jesus the Christ. So, we now have a new freedom of choice: grace. If we so desire, we can choose to live under the law and be bound by it, to succumb to our addiction to GuiltSin, the knowledge of good and evil. Or we can choose to live as our true self, in grace, enjoying health, wealth and happiness unbridled. To be, or not to be. And to choose grace, we must be merciful. When we forgive ourselves, forgive others and transcend the compulsively judgemental ego-personality of the false self, we experience grace. It's here, now, in the present moment. The blessings already are.

The kingdom of heaven is at hand.
Matthew 4:17

Think not that I am come to destroy the law, or the prophets:
I am not come to destroy, but to fulfil.
Matthew 5:17

In another bizarre, confusing scene that directors often cut, young Malcolm, rightful heir to the throne, before the final reckoning with Macbeth, confesses to Macduff that he is less fit to rule than even the devil Macbeth, because of his own litany of sins of insatiable lust.

MALCOLM
It is myself I mean, in whom I know
All the particulars of vice so grafted
That, when they shall be opened, black Macbeth
Will seem as pure as snow, and the poor state
Esteem him as a lamb, being compared
With my confineless harms.

MACDUFF
Not in the legions
Of horrid hell can come a devil more damned
In evils to top Macbeth.

MALCOLM
I grant him bloody,
Luxurious, avaricious, false, deceitful,
Sudden, malicious, smacking of every sin
That has a name. But there's no bottom, none,
In my voluptuousness. Your wives, your daughters,
Your matrons, and your maids could not fill up
The cistern of my lust, and my desire
All continent impediments would o'erbear
That did oppose my will. Better Macbeth
Than such an one to reign.
Macbeth, Act IV Scene III

Could this be Malcolm's 'to be or not to be' moment? Is this a cunningly disguised motif of Jesus's agony of decision in Gethsemane? Is this his Armageddon — the battle between the two opposèd kings raging within him? Would Shakespeare really dig down this deep into the theology?

Macduff is duly shocked, dismayed and on the verge of quitting his mission... but then Malcolm explains that he didn't mean what he said, he was just being tempted by 'Devilish Macbeth'.

MALCOLM

Devilish Macbeth
By many of these trains hath sought to win me
Into his power, and modest wisdom plucks me
From overcredulous haste.
Macbeth, Act IV scene III

Now, Malcolm has overcome Satan's temptations, taken away the sin of the world; the two aspects of Christ are now free to join forces to defeat the tyrant and restore the crown.

Jesus Casts Out 'Devils' and God Sacrifices His Son: Siward Casts Out 'the Evil' and Sacrifices His Son to Macbeth's Sword

These two motifs are entwined in one short scene near the end. Siward is the old English king who comes to Scotland's rescue — rather like Fortinbras in *Hamlet* — a God-like archetype, he adds yet another couple of ingredients to our already overflowing cauldron. Not only is he described as having miraculous, divine healing powers over a disease called 'the evil', but he then proudly sacrifices his young son in mortal combat with Macbeth. Listen here to the way divine Siward is portrayed.

MACDUFF
What's the disease he means?

MALCOLM
'Tis called the evil:
A most miraculous work in this good king,
Which often since my here-remain in England
I have seen him do. How he solicits heaven
Himself best knows, but strangely visited people
All swoll'n and ulcerous, pitiful to the eye,
The mere despair of surgery, he cures,
Hanging a golden stamp about their necks,
Put on with holy prayers; and, 'tis spoken,
To the succeeding royalty he leaves
The healing benediction. With this strange virtue,
He hath a heavenly gift of prophecy,
And sundry blessings hang about his throne
That speak him full of grace.
Macbeth, Act IV Scene III

The Cup of the Last Supper (a): The Poisoned Chalice

Dare I suggest that what Macbeth refers to as 'the poisoned chalice' is actually the cup of the Last Supper, known for centuries as the Holy Grail?

Yes. But why? How?

The key to the truth lies in not swallowing whole the predigested orthodox narrative but reading the scriptures with your eyes wide open.

Jesus Passes the Sop to Judas: Banquo
Passes a Diamond to Macbeth

As we saw in the introduction, in having Banquo pass a diamond to Macbeth, Shakespeare refers to the sop Jesus passed to Judas at the Last Supper.

BANQUO

What, sir, not yet at rest? The King's abed.

He hath been in unusual pleasure, and

Sent forth great largess to your offices.

*This **diamond** he greets your wife withal,*

By the name of most kind hostess, and shut up

In measureless content.

Macbeth, Act II Scene I

But, as is Shakespeare's wont, just as we're gasping for breath, begging it to stop, he gives us more. These biblical motifs may look like small actions here in the physical world, but often something truly momentous is happening in the Spirit world — Armageddon, for example.

Amazingly, in the sop of Judas passage in John, there's another vital ingredient, a subtle ambiguity. See if you can spot it.

Verily, verily, I say unto you, that one of you shall betray me...

He then lying on Jesus' breast saith unto him, Lord, who is it?

Jesus answered, He it is, to whom I shall give a sop, when I have

dipped it. And when he had dipped the sop, he gave it to Judas

Iscariot, the son of Simon. And after the sop Satan entered into

him. Then said Jesus unto him, That thou doest, do quickly.

John 13:21-27

Yes, it's the line: 'And after the sop Satan entered into him.' Satan entered whom? It's easy to assume Satan entered Judas (because he was about to betray the Christ). But Luke 22:3 has already said that Satan entered Judas when he took the thirty pieces of silver. Could the gospel be suggesting that Satan now entered not Judas but Jesus? This interpretation makes a lot more sense. Why else would Jesus want to get the Crucifixion done quickly? He now had the consciousness of Satan in his energy field. In Gethsemane, when he was praying for God's help, he would have been fighting the battle of Armageddon inside himself. No wonder he was sweating blood. Did Jesus then take Satan (the sin of the world) into his own body and consciousness so that Satan, not the Christ, would die on the cross? Yes, surely, only this makes absolute sense of it all.

In fact, the very first person ever to receive the blessing of the Eucharist was Judas. Judas, the so-called betrayer of Christ, was first blessed by Jesus himself and forgiven by God before his apparent act of betrayal — with a kiss. Imagine the blessing inherent in kissing Jesus Christ!

In *Hamlet,* the Master delves exquisitely into the greater detail of this in Gethsemane. But is he using *Macbeth* to foreshadow what is to come?

In the inner world of Spirit, Satan has entered the consciousness of Jesus, and inside mankind, the final battle begins: the battle between Friar Lawrence's two opposèd kings. Not the red herring, misdirection, distraction of the prosaic, self-righteous battle of 'good versus evil' — the real battle between the entire Satan consciousness of good-and-evil (that we, the egos, believe to be reality) and the forgotten Self, the God consciousness of the Christ (soul). This is the battle also known as Armageddon, commonly believed to be a future event. On the physical level, we cannot imagine the agony that ensues for Jesus the man as he absorbs the consciousness of Satan (good-and-evil) i.e., all the sin of the world. We cannot imagine the agony that caused him to sweat drops of blood in Gethsemane as he was battling inside himself to vanquish Satan's tyranny over the soul.

Thus, it is Jesus himself who first invoked the concept of the poisoned chalice. Is he destined to drink it not so much to poison himself but, through his self-sacrifice, to poison Satan, who has now entered into him?

By Macbeth also invoking this concept, yes, it is beginning to confirm this: the chalice of the Grail filled with the royal blood is prepared for Satan's lips, the ingredients destined to poison Satan. Later in Gethsemane, when Peter fights off those arresting Jesus, he chides Peter saying, 'The cup which my father hath given me, shall I not drink it?'

Before we move on to the next course, let us finish this. There's another delicious morsel of divine heresy on our dish. Compare this now-familiar, Macbeth tongue-twister with one of Jesus's crackers from Revelation.

MACBETH
*If 't were **done**, when 'tis **done**, then 'twere well*
***It were done** quickly.*
Macbeth, Act I Scene VII

*And he said unto me, **It is done**. I am Alpha and
Omega, the beginning and the end. I will give unto him
that is athirst of **the fountain of the water of life** freely.*
Revelation 21:6

Shakespeare has forged a union of these two crucial New Testament verses. I know it's subtle, but given the current context and, as you'll see, how he uses some form of this crucial biblical phrase 'It is done' throughout the plays, I have to point it out and offer it to you on the smorgasbord. The question is: What is the 'it' that is done? Is this the answer? Is this what those in power do not wish us to know? Is this the very key that opens the mystery of the Holy Grail?

Let it soak in. IT IS DONE. The final words of Jesus to John in the Spirit. Can you not feel the whole earth quake? Does he mean most of 'it' is done and he'll come back sometime and finish things off? Not to me, he doesn't. He means what he says. And he says what he means.

IT IS DONE. EVERYTHING HE CAME TO DO IS DONE.

And another reminder, this time from Lady Macbeth, 'What's done is done...and cannot be undone'(5.1). The New Testament promise is done — for all eternity.

And here's another crucial revelation at the Last Supper. The blessing of the remission of sins.

> *And as they were eating, Jesus took bread, and blessed it, and brake it, and gave it to the disciples, and said, Take, eat; this is my body. And he took the cup, and gave thanks, and gave it to them, saying, Drink ye all of it; For this is my blood of the new testament, which is shed for all for the **remission of sin**.*
> Matthew 26:26-28

What does this really mean? Absolution? Absolutely! Do those in power tell us what it means? Do they even realise? Absolutely not! In Jesus Code (lest it be extirpated and lost), he tells us that when what he is about to do is done, there will be *no more sin — and no more guilt*. The law of Moses that distorts every natural human action from mastication to masturbation into a sin is over, it is done! No longer does anyone have the right to judge themselves or any other. Every one of us is accountable directly to God through our own soul, our own true self in the spirit.

It is right here that Jesus foretells the promise of the Holy Communion, the new commandment, the New Testament sealed in his blood. And it is in Revelation where he confirms 'it is done'. What once was lost, now is found. But Constantine decided not to tell us, but rather to make it illegal, heretical and blasphemous to know or speak the truth.

If these interpretations of the symbology of the Last Supper are what

Shakespeare wants to give us, and if he is true to form, he will confirm it, and we will feel fulfilled. If they are not, we will be left hungry and thirsty.

Before we question the symbology of the trial and Crucifixion, there's one major symbol we must first confront: the cauldron.

The Cup of the Last Supper (b): The Witches' Cauldron

Remember Macbeth's foreboding about the poisoned chalice? It is *the ingredients* that he feared. At the Last Supper, the two ingredients were both symbols — bread and wine, symbolising the body and blood of Christ. This symbolic marriage union was to bring life to the soul of man, but death to the Satan aspect.

Consider the iconic witches' cauldron is the Master's ironic genius at work.

A cauldron is a large, chalice-shaped cooking pot (another vessel for food). It is the ingredients in the cauldron (*the charmèd pot*) that enable the three weird sisters to gain their prophetic sight and cast their spells. If the cauldron represents the chalice of the Grail, why would its ingredients be poisonous?

It behoves us to examine the entire list of ingredients that go into that cauldron. See what jumps out of the fatal cocktail and bites you in the place of natural knowing. If we're on the right track, the Master will always confirm with a nod or a wink. I've put in **bold** those that spring out at me.

For me, it resonates with the same energy as the curse visited upon Adam in Genesis, plus various allusions to fire and hell. *Double, double* speaks of the impervious nature of original sin, how it both cuts us off from God and turns truth to lies and lies to truth — Satan's masterstroke in the mind of man.

If you want to concoct your own witches' brew, here's the recipe. Don't forget to sing, cackle, dance and generally cavort with god-intoxicated abandon. For the *amuse-gueule,* we have an allusion to Peter denying Christ three times before the cock crows. Now the sound current is represented by the thunder and symbolised as the mewing of a cat. Meanwhile — *bon appetit!*

A cavern. In the middle, a boiling cauldron.
Thunder. Enter the three witches.

FIRST WITCH
Thrice the brinded cat hath mewed.

SECOND WITCH
Thrice, and once the hedge-pig whined.

THIRD WITCH
Harpier cries, "'tis time, 'tis time"

FIRST WITCH
Round about the cauldron go;
*In **the poisoned** entrails throw.*
Toad, that under cold stone
Days and nights has thirty-one
Sweltered venom sleeping got,
Boil thou first i' th' charmèd pot.
The Witches circle the cauldron.

ALL
Double, double toil and trouble;
Fire burn, and cauldron bubble.

SECOND WITCH
Fillet of a fenny snake
In the cauldron boil and bake.
Eye of newt and toe of frog,
Wool of bat and tongue of dog,

Adder's fork and blindworm's sting,
Lizard's leg and howlet's wing,
For a charm of powerful trouble,
Like a hell-broth boil and bubble.

ALL
Double, double toil and trouble;
Fire burn, and cauldron bubble.

THIRD WITCH
Scale of dragon, tooth of wolf,
Witch's mummy, maw and gulf
Of the ravined salt-sea shark,
Root of hemlock digged i' th' dark,
Liver of blaspheming Jew,
Gall of goat and slips of yew
Slivered in the moon's eclipse,
Nose of Turk and Tartar's lips,
Finger of birth-strangled babe
Ditch-delivered by a drab,
Make **the gruel** thick and slab.
Add thereto a tiger's chaudron
For th' ingredients of our cauldron.

ALL
Double, double toil and trouble;
Fire burn, and cauldron bubble.

SECOND WITCH
Cool it with a baboon's blood.

Then the charm is firm and good.
Macbeth, Act IV Scene I

Of the twenty-odd ingredients given in the text, I've emphasised the few that seem seminal:

fillet of a fenny snake; adder's fork; liver of blaspheming Jew.

As an added bonus, he also sprinkles in this delicious pun.

Finger of birth-strangled babe
Ditch-delivered by a drab,
Make **the gruel** *thick and slab.*
Add thereto a tiger's chaudron
For th' ingredients of our cauldron.
Macbeth, Act IV Scene I

In typically wry style, this reference to *the gruel* in the poisoned cauldron is surely a pun on *the grail* and is now the second time he makes a dangerously direct, hair's-breadth-close reference to our Holy Grail. The whole concoction, described as 'thick and slab', sounds to me like clotting blood, the blood contaminated with the serpent's venom that from birth strangles the newborn soul, the blood that, as soon we'll see, for Hamlet's father, did posset, curdle and kill him.

The three weird witches are cooking up a massive bucket of royal blood. Thus, the recipe confirms that our own inner cauldron is indeed heating up. The 'sweet oblivious antidote that cleanses the stuff'd bosom of that perilous stuff that weighs upon the heart' is nearly ready to work its magic. Let us delve.

Jesus Crucified for Blasphemy: Liver of Blaspheming Jew

To me, the fillet of a fenny snake and adder's fork suggest something to do with the serpent — the forkèd lies of good and evil. But what of the liver of blaspheming Jew? Was not Jesus a 'blaspheming Jew'? Does not the liver cleanse the blood of toxic substances? Is that not the essence of the Grail, 'the sweet oblivious antidote' to Satan's poison, the contagion of guilt that binds mankind to Night? Jesus was arrested, tried and executed for heresy and blasphemy. In the eyes of the Sanhedrin, on many occasions, Jesus flagrantly broke the Mosaic law they enforced with great vigour. It was blasphemy to violate the Sabbath, let alone to claim to be the Messiah, the son of God. Why would Jesus have done this? If he was the son of God, why would he so openly and repeatedly break his father's law, knowing only too well the dire consequences?

Maybe he was not the son of God at all? Or maybe the laws he broke were not his father's? And, if not his father's, whose? Another mystery. Another enigma from John.

For the law was given by Moses, but grace
and truth came by Jesus Christ.
John 1:17

The point is that hundreds of the acts of Jesus that culminated in his trial, Crucifixion, Resurrection, and Ascension were prophesied in the Old Testament. What if the 'prophecies' given to Macbeth by the three witches are dramatic, symbolic representations of some of these Old Testament prophecies? What if the ingredients of the Grail chalice represent not just the body and blood, but *all* the ingredients leading to Jesus's vanquishing of Satan, some of which Shakespeare has included in the ingredients in the cauldron and also in the pot simmering backstage in the plays?

It must have been the shock of the sheer chutzpah of the Master tossing the liver of Jesus the Christ into the cauldron that suddenly made me see subtle, symbolic representations of other key ingredients of the Christ story arise from the steam, just as did the three apparitions to Macbeth. Individually, you can easily write them off as coincidences or projections. But, for me, cumulatively, they are as close to confirmation of this hypothesis as it can get. And different creative expressions of these same connecting motifs, and many others, show up in all the plays I've looked at. Agog with amazement, my cauldron began to boil over as these iconic events danced before my eyes.

Pilate Washes His Hands of the Blood of Christ: Lady Macbeth Washes Her Hands of the Blood of Duncan

There's a whole string of well-documented events in the gospels leading from the Last Supper, through Gethsemane, to the trial, Crucifixion and Resurrection of Jesus, and Shakespeare encrypts most of these throughout the works. Many, you'll see in *Hamlet,* some are right here in *Macbeth* — blasphemous biblical ducks all heavily disguised as iconic Shakespearean rabbits.

Why Jesus was arrested, tried and executed at Passover has probably more to do with divine intervention and fulfilling scripture than poor planning on behalf of the Sanhedrin. To fulfil the prophecies of how Satan could be vanquished, Jesus had to take Satan into his energy field, his Satan-possessed body had to die, and he had to be nailed to a cross.

Blasphemy was certainly a violation of Mosaic Law, but not of Roman law. Crucifixion was punishment for offences against the state of Rome, not the state of Israel. Stoning was the mode of execution favoured by the Jews. So how was God going to get Jesus crucified? If he was arrested at Passover, the Jews could not stone him on the Sabbath, let alone on a sacred holiday. They could have locked him up for a few days or got the Romans to do their dirty work. They clearly chose the latter.

When Pilate tried Jesus, of course, through his Roman eyes, he could see no wrongdoing. But there was such a public outcry baying for Jesus's blood that he made a big show of washing his hands of it. Many scholars have suggested he was still culpable and washing his hands symbolically did not absolve him from the responsibility and consequences of scourging and attempting to kill the son of God. Killing the Christ is an oxymoron — but attempting to is a spiritual crime.

Perhaps Shakespeare agreed with this. Perhaps he simply enjoyed treating us to the spectre of the guilt-ridden, somnambulant Lady Macbeth obsessively washing her hands in her sleep. Just as well for us, otherwise we'd not have this sumptuous speech in which to wallow.

> LADY MACBETH
> *Out, damned spot, out, I say!...*
> *Here's the smell of the blood still. All*
> *the perfumes of Arabia will not sweeten this little*
> *hand. O, O, O!*
> *Macbeth*, Act V Scene I

There's an added bonus in this bloody scene. Lady Macbeth repeatedly folds and seals a letter in her sleep.

> GENTLEWOMAN
> *I have seen her rise from her bed, throw her night-*
> *gown upon her, unlock her closet, take forth paper, fold*
> *it, write upon't, read it, afterwards seal it, and again*
> *return to bed; yet all this while in a most fast sleep.*
> *Macbeth*, Act V Scene I

Because this is a motif that pops up in every play, I am confident it symbolises the *blood seal* of the New Testament, shed for the remission of sins. A testament has to be sealed in blood. Here, it is symbolised as the wine in the chalice of the Last Supper that gave its name to the *sang graal*, the Holy Grail. Perhaps Hamlet can shed more light on this iconic blood seal.

The Mocking of Jesus with the Crown of Thorns: Macbeth Laments His Fruitless Crown

In Act III Scene I, Shakespeare's accumulation of biblical motifs really nails the Macbeth-as-Satan and Banquo-as-Christ archetypes. Here, he hammers home his heresy that it was Satan who went to the trial and was crucified inside the energy field of Jesus.

> *Our fears in Banquo*
> *Stick deep, and in his royalty of nature*
> *Reigns that which would be feared.*

The only thing Satan fears is the Christ coming to reclaim the throne he, Satan, has stolen from him.

> *Then, prophetlike,*
> *They hailed him father to a line of kings.*

The witches prophesied that, unlike his barren lineage, Banquo (Christ) headed up the spiritual lineage of the true living Christs (that's us, folks).

> *Upon my head they placed a fruitless crown*
> *And put a barren sceptre in my gripe.*

Leaping forward in time now, from the fall to the trial and execution of Jesus, Satan thought he'd mocked and scourged the Christ, but now realises it is he who is wearing the crown of thorns and holding the barren sceptre — the symbols of a pretender to the throne.

For Banquo's issue have I filed my mind;
For them the gracious Duncan have I murdered;
Put rancors in the vessel of my peace
Only for them.

The irony strikes him. Macbeth's plot to kill the Christ has backfired. He's suffered agonies thinking he was protecting the throne he had supplanted, but now sees (the New Testament promise) that all his former hostages (us) are now free to rule our own inner kingdom. We are all kings. We are all Christs.

And mine eternal jewel
Given to the common enemy of man,
To make them kings, the seed of Banquo kings!
Rather than so, come fate into the list,
And champion me to th' utterance.

We now see the fate of the diamond and the significance of the 'sop' given to Judas. It was Adam who was the original betrayer of God. It was Adam who gave the eternal jewel (the soul) to the common enemy of man (serpent). It was Adam who caused the Tree of Life to be cut off (the sound and Name of God, the Word made flesh). The sop symbolically reunited the Word made flesh (body/bread) with the light of God (spirit/wine) and made the spirit whole again (the Holy Spirit). In order to fulfil the scripture and vanquish Satan, Judas had to symbolically re-enact Adam's original betrayal.

Jumping back in time now, to the plot to kill Jesus, Macbeth orders the assassination of Banquo. Imagine his (Satan's) shock when, having successfully murdered him, Banquo (as a ghost) rises again at his coronation feast and takes up residence in his own seat (throne). Hidden in the latter part of the speech where Macbeth indicts himself as murderer and heralds his raging descent into madness is the subtle allusion to the resurrection: 'rise again'.

Blood hath been shed ere now, i' the olden time,
Ere humane statute purged the gentle weal;
Ay, and since too, murders have been perform'd
Too terrible for the ear: the times have been,
That, when the brains were out, the man would die,
*And there an end; but now they **rise again**,*
With twenty mortal murders on their crowns,
And push us from our stools.

Given Satan has now entered him, when Jesus was scourged and mocked by the cheap symbols of royalty — the crown of thorns, the staff, the purple robe — it was, ironically, Satan being mocked. When Jesus's body died on the cross, it makes total sense that it was Satan who metaphorically died (his tyranny over the human consciousness was ended) — because the Christ in Jesus, and thus the Christ in all humankind, resurrected. In resurrecting, Jesus transformed the consciousness of all mankind. He also demonstrated for all time, for all peoples (regardless of race, creed, colour or sexual preference), the Christ's supremacy over the usurping tyrant — in other words, our own soul's supremacy over our usurping ego-personality.

This strange scene, where Macbeth, Satan personified, is lamenting about how pointless it is to be the phoney, murdering, usurping king now makes perfect sense. It's Satan wearing the symbols of royalty, the power and the glory, but not having the inner experience. As do we, when we bow down to symbols, he's suffering the existential loneliness of the ego-personality cut off from the spiritual heart. He's complaining about how fallow is his crown and how much better off at his expense will be Banquo and his lineage. Referring to the witches' prophecies (the Old Testament prophecies of the coming of the Messiah), he's blaming them for misleading him into murdering the original Christ (Duncan), and he's now finding himself with no way out of murdering Banquo (also in the line of kings/Christs).

Although there is a belief in the divine right of kings, when 'king' is used as a symbol for 'Christ', spiritual lineage has nothing whatsoever to do with physical or genetic bloodlines. Macbeth, as an archetype of Satan/Cain (the false self within us all), cannot see the Christ, cannot understand anything but the primacy of the physical created world, cannot understand the unmanifest reality. Who can? To him, the true Christ (Banquo) is a profound, existential threat, as it is to those in power who have usurped the name of God.

Banquo's diamond is now revealed as the eternal jewel, in other words, the diamond of the soul, the pearl of great price, the spark of God's image that is the source of all life — a sacred covenant Macbeth (originally as Adam) carelessly, selfishly gave away to the serpent for material gain. This was an action that, in order to fulfil the scripture, Jesus had to act out symbolically with Judas at the Last Supper. Judas did not betray Jesus at all — he sacrificed himself to fulfil that crucial part of scripture so the original GuiltSin could be forgiven for all time.

In this reflective scene of false self realisation, Macbeth speaks for the Satan aspect of ourselves in voicing the feelings of existential emptiness — the 'something rotten' we all feel when we cut ourselves off from our soul.

Jesus Bears His Cross to High Calvary Hill: Burnham Wood Comes to High Dunsinane Hill

In desperation, Macbeth finds the witches again, and they prophesy to him that he would be safe until the 'impossible' occurrence of Burnham Wood's coming to High Dunsinane Hill. And, sure enough, the ten thousand soldiers of Macduff's, Malcolm's and the English King Siward's armies, disdaining ecological considerations, each hack down branches of trees from Burnham Wood and, as a means of camouflage, bear them on their shoulders to Dunsinane.

Does this not allude to the Tree of Life being borne on the shoulders of Christ? And doesn't it also evoke an allusion to Jesus bearing his cross to the hill outside the city of Jerusalem known as Calvary or Golgotha (the place of the skull)?

WITCHES' APPARITION
Macbeth shall never vanquished be until
Great Birnam Wood to high Dunsinane Hill
Shall come against him.

MACBETH
That will never be.
Who can impress the forest, bid the tree
Unfix his earthbound root? Sweet bodements, good!
***Rebellious dead, rise** never till the Wood*
Of Birnam rise, and our high-placed Macbeth
Shall live the lease of nature, pay his breath
To time and mortal custom.
Macbeth, Act IV Scene I

And, true to form, Shakespeare slips in yet another allusion — in perfect time to cue the next chapter on the prophesied resurrection. Did you spot it? 'The rebellious dead rise...'

Jesus Rises Again: The Ghost of the Murdered Banquo Rises Again

The inscrutable way the witches give Macbeth his prophecies mimics to some extent the way the Old Testament prophecies are given — loaded with ambiguity. Of several hundred prophecies Jesus fulfilled, this one from Proverbs 22 is a good example of how the Crucifixion was predicted long before the Romans invented it.

*For dogs have compassed me: the assembly of the wicked have inclosed me: **they pierced my hands and my feet**. I may tell all my bones: they look and stare upon me. They part my garments among them, and cast lots upon my vesture.*

Fearing the power of the bloodline of kings through Banquo, prophesied by the witches, Macbeth sends three assassins to murder him and his son, Fleance. Knowing only too well that Banquo is a dead man walking, to allay suspicion, he callously reminds him to attend the coronation feast, the Last Supper Macbeth would be likely to enjoy.

MACBETH
Fail not our feast.
BANQUO
My lord, I will not.
Macbeth, Act III Scene I

Interestingly, Banquo, representing the Christ, gives his word to 'Satan', and God's Word cannot be broken. It is a covenant, a spiritual promise that must be fulfilled. This is why Satan's original betrayal was so binding: God gave his word to Satan in the beginning and cannot break it despite what Satan is doing to us all. The only way God can dethrone Satan is to set up the conditions for him to defeat himself. Hence the irony in the Crucifixion, where it was not Christ who died, but the body of Jesus the son of Man with Satan within it.

That evening, much to Macbeth's chagrin, the murdered Banquo keeps his word, resurrects and 'fails not' the feast. He appears only to Macbeth, sitting as a ghost in his seat (throne) at his celebratory feast — a probable pastiche of the Last Supper confirmed by the word 'remembrance' as they toast the (not so) absent Banquo. This event seriously rattles both Macbeth and Lady Macbeth — it is the turning point of the play that pushes them over the edge of the bottomless pit. The resurrection of Banquo heralds the end for Macbeth, just as Christ's Resurrection terminated the rule of Satan.

MACBETH
The time has been
That, when the brains were out, the man would die,
And there an end. But now they **rise again**
With twenty mortal murders on their crowns
And push us from our stools.
Macbeth, Act III Scene IV

The Harrowing of Hell: Macbeth Beheaded Offstage and The Coming of The Comforter — Siward's Final Allusion

These two motifs are joined at the hip and almost imperceptibly subtle, but that's how I most like them — and how most of them show up in the other plays. Jesus's triumphant descent into hell between his death and Resurrection, where he released all the souls in bondage to Satan, is represented almost imperceptibly in the text as Macbeth being killed offstage.

Macduff triumphantly reappears, bearing aloft the severed head of the tyrant to the *sotto voce* remark of Siward, who has just lost his son to Macbeth's sword: 'Here comes newer comfort.'

And here endeth our play, with the head of the usurping serpent cut off and the rightful heir to the throne being crowned. But if Scotland were a metaphor for the consciousness of mankind and the true self of man has now been restored to its rightful place as its centre, why all the darkness, ignorance, and suffering? Why is suffering still the norm and the Ananda the fringe? Let's return to the Last Supper for the main course: God's forgiveness.

God's New Testament Forgiveness: Lady Macbeth Must Now Forgive Herself

As Lady Macbeth lies dying with guilt, Macbeth temporarily puts aside the 'callous indifference' of the Cain archetype and asks the doctor how his wife's fatal guilt can be cured.

MACBETH

Canst thou not minister to a mind diseased,
Pluck from the memory a rooted sorrow,
Raze out the written troubles of the brain,
And with some sweet oblivious antidote
Cleanse the stuffed bosom of that perilous stuff
Which weighs upon the heart?

DOCTOR

Therein the patient
Must minister to himself.

Macbeth, Act V Scene III

Can you not see the heresy here? Officially, only the priest can give God's absolution. The doctor is saying the opposite: forgiveness is something only we must do for ourselves. Deeper, he refers to the doctor as minister. He also refers to us, the patient, as minister. As if we are the anointed one, the one ordained. The Christ.

To pre-empt the inquisitor, Macbeth's 'Cain-ine' nature kicks back in with a wee silent pun.

MACBETH
Throw physic to the dogs. I'll none of it. —
Come, put mine armour on. Give me my staff...
Seyton, *send out.*
Macbeth, Act V Scene III

Once again, through Macbeth, Shakespeare offers us *Satan's* perspective on life. And is it not a wonderful touch that, as the archetype of Cain, the son of Satan has a manservant named Satan — lest we be offended, spelled *Seyton*.

Chapter 4:

THE JESUS CODE
IN MACBETH

We've already seen the Jesus Code in action in *Macbeth*. In fact, Part One has been a full-immersion baptism in the wild waters of Shakespeare's most cunning cryptic device: the biblical motif. Laid before you were over twenty examples — and counting. You've also been thrown into the deep end of his use of archetypes. The evidence shown here compellingly supports the notion that the Grail refers not so much to the chalice itself but to the ingredients in the chalice — the royal blood (*sang graal*) — with the crucial twist that Shakespeare trademarks this as 'the poisoned chalice'.

Shakespeare's heretical theology asserts that the blood, symbolised as *the wine of life*, is what Jesus himself metaphorically drank in order to poison Satan and bring an end to the tyrannical reign of good-and-evil, the contagion all flesh is heir to and which brings darkness and misery to all mankind. Why else would Macbeth (archetype of Satan) be so fearful of Banquo (archetype of the Christ) and lament wearing the crown of thorns and holding the wooden sceptre traditionally assumed to be mocking Jesus?

There's little doubt Shakespeare is telling us the lost truth of the Holy Grail, but it's not yet clear exactly what that truth is. Something very important and valuable to mankind was lost. In the beginning of our evolutionary history, the Tree of Life — the awareness of who we really are as a soul, the sound current — was cut off by Adam's betrayal. Instead of the soul (Adam-Eve), the loving father-mother God ruling our inner world, in Shakespeare's dramatisations and in the theology of the ancient masters, we have had to endure the abandonment and suffering caused by the warring inner factions of the two opposèd kings, the soul versus the two usurping false selves (Cain-Abel).

And he said unto me, It is done. I am Alpha and
Omega, the beginning and the end. I will give unto him
that is athirst of the fountain of the water of life freely...
Revelation 21:6

A new commandment I give unto you, That ye
love one another; as I have loved you
John 13:34

According to the Gospels and Revelation, access to the Tree of Life (called many different things) was restored and made freely available.

It's tempting to conclude that the lost and now found Tree of Life *is* the Grail. But there's no mystery, no secret, no need to camouflage this truth in a massive legend. No, the solution to our mystery must lie in the Grail chalice, not in the Garden of Eden. It must have something to do with the wine that, in Jesus Code, symbolised the 'royal blood'. Have you perhaps spotted this yourself?

It seems from our autopsy of *Macbeth* that the story of the Grail is the attempt to keep alive the truth concealed at Nicaea. One massive truth would be that, contrary to the narrative, God has already, unconditionally forgiven all mankind. Before Jesus unlocked the prison (for all mankind regardless of race, creed, colour or sexual preference) there was no way the soul could get free. The prison walls were still there. The soul still slept within. But because of Jesus, it could be reached. There became a minute, inner, mystical opening referred to symbolically by Jesus as *the eye of the needle.* It is not easy to pass through — in fact, Jesus referred to a camel passing through the eye of a needle to symbolise reunion with God. But this was not merely a metaphor. One of the gateways into Jerusalem, a small entryway within the larger gate, was already known as the 'eye of the needle'. To enter, camels must kneel and be removed of their burdens — a symbol of the humility we need, the release of guilt and fear, the letting go of the ego and its pride.

Maybe our purpose here on earth is to forgive ourselves.

But one play on its own is insufficient evidence. This new thesis needs corroboration and further, deeper enquiry. And there is another mystery: Why does Shakespeare construct his plays from a palette of biblical motifs, with vignettes of the story of Christ costumed in myriad ingenious disguises? Given the majestic role they play in his plays, is there yet another major clue hidden among the familiar gospel stories?

Hunting the Name

Here's a thought: given the Grail legend, if fully understood, would be counternarrative, what if we take a key passage of gospel that is often used to nail the narrative in place and look at it through the eyes of the Master, knowing his truth is pretty much the opposite of the orthodox doctrine?

We now know from the Bible that what humanity lost in the beginning was the way to the Tree of Life. We also know from Revelation that Jesus Christ came to reopen this way and — whatever that is — *it is done!* These key elements of the Christ story are very openly stated and easy to see in the scripture — except that it doesn't tell us what the Tree of Life symbolises. This, we must find out, or we remain lost in psychic speculation and labyrinthine superstition. Through his actions, it would seem that Jesus fulfilled all the prophecies of the Old Testament that told what the Messiah needed to accomplish in order to fulfil the law of Moses, vanquish Satan's tyranny and reopen the way to heaven. The way to the Tree of Life is now open to all who 'keep his commandment': to love one another as God loves us.

Way beyond entertainment and brilliant morsels of timeless wisdom, Shakespeare is offering us what Jesus too offered us: the knowledge given to mankind before his ultimate truths were shot from the canon into outer space, the knowledge of the way out of the whole earthbound dilemma. The way home to paradise and Ananda. The way home, whose price is the sweet, oblivious antidote to guilt: love, joy, bliss, fulfilment and happiness. Essentially, he's saying that when you are happy and loving, regardless of external circumstances, you will get your return ticket punched on the express train to Eden Central.

Learning how to be truly happy and forgiving in this harsh world is no mean feat. But the keys Shakespeare offers us are also available, hidden away in mysterious places where only those ready will dare to tread, where only those ready will understand.

So, given it was the way to the Tree of Life that was reopened by Jesus, what does he himself have to say about this 'way home'?

A quick recap:

> *So he drove out the man; and he placed at the east of the garden of Eden Cherubim, and a flaming sword which turned every way, to **keep the way of the tree of life**.*

Genesis 3:24

*Blessed are they that do his commandments, **that they may have right to the tree of life**, and may enter in through the gates into the city.*
Revelation 22:14

In terms of the narrative, which asserts pretty much that the only way to avoid hell and get into heaven is to be a Christian, this passage seems to nail that belief to the wall.

Jesus saith unto him, I am the way, the truth, and the life: no man cometh unto the Father, but by me.
John 14:6

Like most of the Bible, this is an enigmatic statement with several possible heretical interpretations. Let's try to decrypt the Jesus Code, first by looking at the opening phrase 'I am the way' and isolating the two components:

1. 'I am'
2. 'The way'

I Am: The Name

If we want to look deeper, anagogically, the big question becomes: To whom does the 'I am' refer? When he speaks about himself in this way, to what level of his consciousness is Jesus referring? Suppose, say, if someone asks me, 'Who are you?' I'll probably say, 'I am Paul', because that's my name. Then isn't this what Jesus also means? But what if he is invoking not his earthly name — Jesus — but his spiritual name, his hallowed name, the sacred name that delineates the consciousness of the Christ, the hallowed name of the Father in Heaven? If so, the way to the Tree of Life (and the way home to Eden, the heart of God) would be expressed more like this:

*The Name is the way, the truth, and the life: no man
cometh unto the Father, but by the Name.*

Herein lies the source of much confusion. There are many different words for the same thing. Remember the collage of over twenty symbols for the sound current in chapter 1? Three of the keywords were 'the sound', 'the Word made flesh', and 'the name of God'. It's a bit like the words I might use to describe parts of my hand. When you think about it, there are dozens: fingers, palm, knuckles, nails, skin, hairs, veins, etc. It's the same with the sound current. Is it the Name? The Word? The Sound? The Music? The wind from heaven? The waters of life? The Tree of Life?

It's all of the above — and more. And both the Bible and Shakespeare deploy them all at will. Why? To keep the secret safe. To set up red herrings and misdirection, to muddy the waters. And it has worked.

Those who have sought to extirpate the truth have been outwitted by those seeking to reveal it when the time is right.

Is the time right now?

The Way: The Example

It has also been well noted that Jesus's life was an example (the way) of how we might strive to live our own lives. Does this mean we need to heal the blind, walk on water, be crucified and resurrect? Do we need to emulate the image of Jesus concocted by those wishing to have us worship their religious concepts?

Or do these actions symbolise something to do with the transformation of consciousness he made possible for us and which it is now our job to claim for ourselves? What in heaven's name could this be?

As we sashay into *Hamlet* and Part Two, let's see what the Master reveals to us about what lies in our destiny yet tells the truth. It seems that now, in hunting the Grail, we could in fact be hunting the Name of God in one of its many guises and an example — footsteps we can follow in our own sandal shoon.

How might this tie in with one of the mystical theories of the Grail, that it indicates an initiatory experience and union with God Himself?

Let's ask *Hamlet*.

Part Two:

HAMLET: THE PASSION OF THE CHRIST

The deeper symbology now suggests that the key to understanding the true significance of the union of bread and wine (the body and the blood) in the Grail chalice lies in finding the sacred name of God, aka the sound current.

We're now going to look at the same underlying story as *Macbeth* from a different perspective. Perhaps this will shed more light on our mystery.

Consider the paradigm shift that this play is the same story of Christ as in *Macbeth*, but now viewed, not through the eyes of Satan as protagonist, but through the eyes of Jesus himself as protagonist. Remember: one play, thirty-two iterations. Through *Hamlet,* Shakespeare also reiterates the Grail secret. The metaphorical poisoned chalice, incepted by Jesus himself in Gethsemane, alluded to in Macbeth's foretelling that 'this even-handed justice commends th'ingredients of the poisoned chalice to my own lips' is now passed to Claudius, another characterisation of the Satan archetype to act out and fulfil.

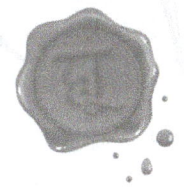

Chapter 5:

THE OUTER AND INNER HAMLETS

The Outer Play

Hamlet is often considered Shakespeare's most popular, and most puzzling, play. It follows the form of a revenge tragedy, in which the hero, Hamlet, seeks vengeance against his father's murderer, his uncle Claudius, now the king of Denmark.

Denmark is in chaos. The king, Prince Hamlet's father, has suddenly died, and his brother, Claudius, has not only become the new king but has married the queen — Hamlet's mother, Gertrude. We also learn that Denmark is in danger from the king of Norway, Fortinbras, whose uncle, Old Fortinbras, was deposed and killed by Hamlet's father and who is coming to avenge his death.

At the beginning of the play, a spirit appears, first to the watch guards and then to Hamlet, claiming to be the ghost of Hamlet's father. He describes how he was in fact murdered at the hands of Claudius and demands Hamlet avenge the killing. When the king's chancellor, Polonius, learns from his daughter, Ophelia, that Hamlet has visited her in an apparently distracted state, Polonius attributes the prince's condition to lovesickness, and he sets a trap for Hamlet, using Ophelia as bait.

Meanwhile, it is Hamlet who is setting the trap. To confirm Claudius's guilt, Hamlet arranges for him to watch a play that mimics the way his father was murdered by having poison poured in his ear. Claudius's reaction is that of a guilty man. Hamlet, now free to act, mistakenly kills Polonius, thinking he is Claudius. Claudius sends Hamlet away as part of a deadly plot.

After Polonius's death, Ophelia goes mad and later seems to drown herself. Hamlet, who has returned safely to confront the king, agrees to a fencing match with Ophelia's brother, Laertes, who secretly poisons his own rapier. At the match, Claudius prepares a chalice of poisoned wine for Hamlet, which instead Gertrude drinks, and she dies. In a scuffle, Laertes is poisoned by his own sword. Laertes then accuses Claudius of the plot, and Hamlet forces Claudius to drink from his own poisoned chalice. Then, first Laertes and then Hamlet die, both victims of Laertes's poisoned rapier. With everyone except Hamlet's friend Horatio dead, Fortinbras arrives and takes the Danish throne.

Traditional Anomalies in the Outer Play

1. Up until now, many questions have remained unanswered, including:
2. Who really is the ghost?
3. Does Hamlet go mad or merely pretend to?
4. Once Hamlet is sure that Claudius is the murderer, why does he not act?

Was Hamlet's mother, Gertrude, unfaithful to her husband, or complicit in his murder, or both?

Of course, the play is riddled with uncertainty, because the answer lies where the answer to all life's uncertainties lies and where few bother to look: in the soul.

Throughout the plays, Shakespeare, through his plots and characterisations, has always been subtly delineating the fundamental, existential choice we are all faced with: to be or not to be. Now, in *Hamlet,* he makes it explicit. We live in a world that is desperately trying to stop us from looking more deeply into ourselves and into literature, poetry and scripture for answers to the great mysteries of life. No answer can or will ever satisfy the ego-mind's compulsive need to play the 'good-and-evil' game by making itself right by making others wrong. So, the mind, the world, comes up with an infinite variety of highly-addictive, snackable sound bites, tweets, distractions, mind-candies and anaesthetics to numb down the gaping existential wounds in our heart. Scripture is replaced with reductive science. Poetry (even Shakespeare's) is reduced to banal 'translations' that may help hapless students get good exam grades but does little to stimulate deep, abstract thinking.

Productions of Shakespeare are more and more aimed at the mass, global market, who demand to come out feeling good rather than face the real existential questions Shakespeare is taunting us with.

To me, in fulfilling the purpose of this book, it is almost irrelevant what happens in the outer plays. It's the inner play that has the priceless reward. But let's see if the anomalies on the surface are there not to satisfy us, but to thwart our desires for instant gratification and to force us to go under them in order to resolve them.

The Inner Play

So, will *Hamlet* tell us more about the hallowed name that opens the way back to the Godhead?

The thing of it is, anagogically, the play's not really about Hamlet at all.

It's about Fortinbras. Old Fortinbras was deposed by Hamlet's father, and now his nephew, young Fortinbras, is coming to reclaim his rightful throne. This is the story going on almost invisibly in the background as kind of higher-level cosmic mirror reflected by what seems to be the main action. (A classic Shakespearean confusion: Fortinbras the uncle being avenged by the nephew — and the son, avenging Hamlet, the father, murdered by his brother, also the uncle.) There are many other plays where Shakespeare befuddles us with something similar. But although this meta-action is often deemed so obscure that modern directors cut it all out to save time, I shall defy this trend and, in due course, make much of young Fortinbras.

Traditionally, Hamlet's fatal flaw is seen as indecisiveness. Maybe so, in the outer play. But in the inner, perhaps he's following a different script, a different director. In the beginning, he is found morose with grief, not just at his father's death, but at his mother's betrayal, the newly crowned, ignoble king, and perhaps the loss of his own place on his father's throne.

An Anagogical Foreshadowing

Typically, the opening scene of a Shakespeare play has a cryptic foreshadowing of the key plot points of the play. *Hamlet* is no exception. The opening scene is a portal to the biblical motifs that tell the story of Christ in a masterpiece of multidimensional plots and meditations that truly puzzle the will. The anagogical subtext is so deep, so well hidden, it challenges all of us to keep our viewing point high and our inner eyes wide open.

All of these vignettes are so intertwined, it's hard to tease individual motifs out in a way to satisfy the mind's need for bullet-point clarity. Good. We both need to engage our transcendent thinking and inhale the perfume of the essential truth. That's what this is all about.

Archetypes in Hamlet

If you remember, by 'archetypes', I'm referring to the proposition that, rather than different *characters* for each play, Shakespeare is using a palette of creative *characterisations* of three pairs of the same core archetypes:

God-Serpent

Adam-Eve (the true self/the soul)

Cain-Abel (the ego-personality/false selves/good-evil)

When you look behind the curtain of the play, you can see how extraordinarily complex and multidimensional the structure is. While the archetypes by their very nature are the molecules with which consciousness is formed, Shakespeare has no rules governing the way he combines these fundamental particles — any one character may speak on behalf of one or more archetypes at will.

I'm now proposing the following radical suggestions for the inner dramatis personae. Try not to judge them too soon. Let the inner story do the work. They may seem outrageous to you at this stage, but neither belief nor disbelief is required. Just be open to new ways of seeing. This is because, in each play, the outer story seems to be unique, but in the subtext, they are all variations of one and the same story: *the evolution of our soul*, from Genesis to Revelation.

So, however confusing it may be for now, consider the following:

Fortinbras

Fortinbras represents God. Fortinbras is a 'funny name': it sounds like 'force-tin-brass' — quite musical really. We shall see. Could Fortinbras be 'the god of day' spoken of in the play's eerie opening scene?

As I've suggested, the almost invisible background context of the entire play is the advent of Fortinbras. Deposed by Hamlet's father, in Act I Scene I, we are told that he is coming to reclaim his lost kingdom — metaphor alert!

As news comes of his impending visitation, the watch guards are on high alert to protect the good folk of Elsinore. In the finale of the play, it is

Fortinbras who arrives on the stage to clear up the bodies, mop up the blood and don his rightful crown.

The Ghost (of Hamlet's Father)

The ghost as good as tells us he's the representation of Adam: the One who was 'stung' in the garden by the serpent (who now wears his crown and sleeps with his wife), the One who committed the original GuiltSin.

He also serves the play in other ways. He is the harbinger. He brings the truth to Hamlet. He delineates Hamlet's destiny and purpose: in the outer play, this is revenge — the ultimate story of the ego. Will Hamlet prove Claudius murdered his father and deliver justice? In the inner play, it is God who has been deposed from his throne in the kingdom of heaven; will Hamlet oust the pretender and restore order to the now rotten state of Denmark?

Hamlet and Ophelia

Acting together, Hamlet and Ophelia represent the Soul archetype in a rather interesting way. Hamlet seems to act out Jesus the man, and Ophelia, the Christ aspect of Jesus. This will get clearer. Remember how Jesus often referred to himself as 'the Son of Man'? The word for man in Hebrew is *Adam*. Did he mean that Hamlet/Christ was the 'son of Adam'? Shakespeare seems to say so.

Claudius and Gertrude

Fascinatingly, it's explicitly stated in Act I that Claudius represents the serpent itself: Satan. Gertrude, wife of the murdered and deposed Adam, acts out the Eve archetype. In Genesis, the serpent seduced or perhaps even raped Eve (as in Shakespeare's Isabella, Lavinia, Lucrece, et alia). As we saw in *Macbeth*, Macbeth and Lady Macbeth shape-shift from playing the Adam-Eve polarity to playing the Cain-Abel duality. Likewise, Claudius shape-shits into the fratricidal Cain, while Gertrude descends into an intoxicated victim of Claudius/the serpent/Cain and acts out an aspect of Abel.

HAMLET

*"This above all; to thine own self be true, and it
follows, as the night the day, thou cants't not
then be false to any man."*

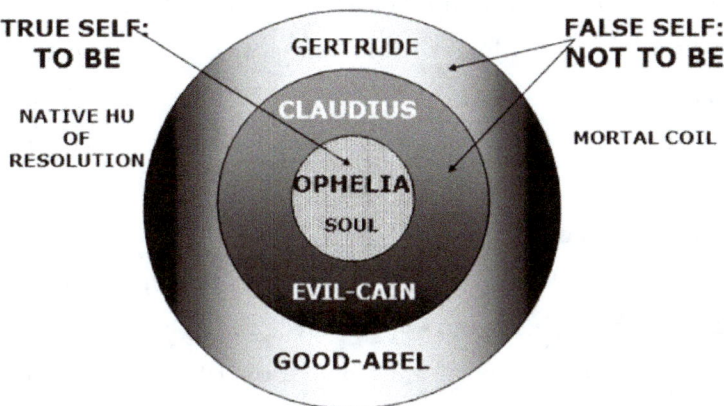

**TRUE SELF:
TO BE**

**FALSE SELF:
NOT TO BE**

**NATIVE HU
OF
RESOLUTION**

MORTAL COIL

GERTRUDE

CLAUDIUS

OPHELIA

SOUL

EVIL-CAIN

GOOD-ABEL

Rosencrantz and Guildenstern, Polonius

These are the key henchmen of Claudius. Rosencrantz and Guildenstern (note the Jewish-sounding names) personify the law of Moses that Jesus came to fulfil. They also represent the Pharisees and Sadducees, the enforcers of the Mosaic Law. The name Rosencrantz also implies *crown of thorns* (roses). The pompous, toadying, eavesdropping Polonius is a Scribe, a quasi-secret police-man, listening for blasphemy and violations of the law and writing down what he heard people say.

Horatio and Laertes

These are the disciples of Jesus/Hamlet. Horatio is John the Beloved, while Laertes is Judas the traitor. In the play, as in the scripture, Horatio is faithful to the end, while Laertes/Judas conspires with Claudius/Satan and betrays him with a symbol of love: a poisoned kiss.

NameAlchemy: The 'Eary' Play with the Eerie Opening

What do you call it when, in an opening scene, a playwright creates an atmosphere, the most apt word for which is itself a pun of the overriding theme of the subtext of the entire play? Me, I call it genius, chutzpah and a wicked sense of humour. It is the ultimate NameAlchemy: an eerie opening to an 'eary' play.

Just for fun, I searched the text of *Hamlet* and found over three hundred instances of the sound 'ear'. The very name 'Shakesp**ear**e' has itself a strong 'ear' integral to the sound of his name.

This is not the flippant observation it may seem. Included in *Hamlet* is another of Shakespeare's ways of expressing the so-called fall of man. He expresses one misunderstood meaning of the original GuiltSin with the metaphor of the cutting off of the ear of man. Not necessarily literally the outer ear, but the ability to hear the inner, mystical sound of God. This is the Tree of Life that feeds the soul and replenishes the spirit, the daily bread of life that makes us aware of our divinity and our purpose, the staff of life that cures all our ills, the secret of the Holy Grail, also cut off and lost like the ear of Hamlet's mournful father who was poisoned. It's all sublime, graphic, poetic imagery.

Here are just a few key references to ears, sounds and names in Hamlet that we'll be exploring in more depth:

- 'The trumpet to the morn'
- 'It was about to speak when the cock crew'
- 'And in the porches of my ears did pour the leprous distilment'
- The sound of the name 'Fortinbras'
- 'The whole ear of Denmark is rankly abused'
- The ears of Polonius — always eavesdropping on Hamlet
- 'The ears are senseless that should give us hearing'

There is a stream of consciousness running through *Hamlet* that we could call *the cutting off of the ear of man and its restoration.* Is this Shakespeare making liberal use of his poetic licence? Yes. But the inspiration, as with his poisoned chalice, comes not just from his own fertile imagination, but once again straight from the horse's mouth: the very word of God Herself.

But first, let us turn to the Master's use of biblical motifs in *Hamlet.* Steel yourself for the unlikely, the improbable, the fantastical, for the curtain to be drawn back to reveal many of the same motifs as in *Macbeth*.

- The Annunciation to the shepherds
- The fall of man
- The Epiphany
- The gospel events following the Last Supper
- The Agony in Gethsemane
- The Arrest
- The Trial
- Walking on Water
- Crucifixion
- Resurrection
- Ascension
- Coming of the Comforter

Chapter 6:

BIBLICAL MOTIFS IN HAMLET

Fortunately for us mere mortals, whenever the Master deploys one of his astonishing biblical motifs, he unfailingly secretes a biblical reference to reassure us that no, we're not hallucinating, this really is what he is implying. For me, listening to the way he whispers to us like this is an experience of holy communion that transcends even the priceless value of his wisdom. Once again, it's worth reminding ourselves that, when viewed in isolation, these motifs are easy to dismiss as shadows. En masse, they become truly compelling.

BIBLICAL EVENT	SHAKESPEARE CODE
An angel appears to the Shepherds frightening them	A spirit appears to the watchguards frightening them
Mankind shrouded in darkness	Hamlet shrouded in grief
Jesus comes to reclaim the kingdom of God	(Fortinbras comes to reclaim his lost kingdom) Hamlet told to avenge his father's murder
Jesus foretells Peter's three denials before the cock crows twice	The spirit was about to speak when the cock crew
Peter cuts off the ear of Malchus with a sword	Illium cuts off the ear of Pyrrhus with a sword
The agony in Gethsemane	To be or not to be
Peter denies Christ thrice	Hamlet denies Ophelia three times
Adam & Eve are banished and cursed	Ophelia is banished and cursed
Jesus is put on trial	The Mousetrap: Claudius is put on trial
The blood of Abel	Claudius confesses his primaeval crime
Christ forgives the Original Sin	Hamlet forgives Gertrude
Jesus is taken prisoner	Hamlet is taken prisoner
Jesus walks upon the waters	Ophelia floats upon the waters
Jesus buried at Golgotha	Ophelia buried at the place of 'the skull'
The cup of the Last Supper	Claudius gives Hamlet a poisoned chalice
Judas betrays Jesus with a 'poisoned' kiss	Laertes betrays Hamlet with a poisoned touch of his blade
The blood shed by Jesus to seal the new testament	Hamlet seals the new commandment
Jesus's death/blood abjures Mosaic Law	Rosencrantz and Guildenstern are dead
The coming of the comforter	Fortinbras returns to reclaim his rightful throne
Peter cuts off the ear of Malchus with a sword	Illium cuts off the ear of Pyrrhus with a sword

Biblical motifs in *Hamlet*

Adam and Eve Poisoned by Listening to the Serpent's Lies: Hamlet's Father Poisoned in His Ear

The delicious duck-rabbit parallel here is that, while Adam was tempted with 'a fruit' by the serpent in the garden of Eden, the ghost of Hamlet's father tells how he too was poisoned by a metaphorical serpent while in an orchard. As well as establishing yet again the Genesis connection, Shakespeare builds into the scene the mythic call to adventure. On the surface, Hamlet's apparent vengeance; underneath, the mission of Jesus Christ to reopen the Tree of Life, restore the sound current of all creation and reclaim the rightful throne for our soul.

By way of cryptic metaphor, the scripture tells us that Jesus's destiny was to restore to its rightful throne at the centre of consciousness the sound and light of the soul that was cut off and deposed by the serpent. What this means to us, according to the ancient pre-Nicaea theology, is that our sense of self, our true identity, was stolen by the monstrous issue of Satan's unholy union with mankind. Instead of living in the bliss, truth and clarity of soul-self-awareness, mankind had to endure the misery, pain and suffering of living under the law of good-and-evil. Our true self, our soul, was banished from awareness and cast into an oubliette. Jesus's mission was to vanquish the tyrant (personified as Satan/serpent/Claudius) and free the soul.

Anyone saying this openly in Shakespeare's day was taking a huge risk. It's no wonder Shakespeare shrouded this forbidden truth in many layers of cryptic red herrings. Thus, in *Hamlet*, on the surface of the play, Hamlet-as-Jesus's mission looks like revenge. But as the play unfolds, even this simple act becomes infinitely more complex than sticking a dagger in his uncle's back. Here, the ghost gets into the spirit of the drama.

GHOST
Revenge his foul and most unnatural murther...
Now Hamlet, hear. 'Tis given out that,
sleeping in my orchard, a serpent
stung me. So the whole ear of Denmark, is
by a forgèd process of my death
Rankly abused. But know, thou noble youth,
the serpent that stung your
father's life now wears his crown.
Hamlet, Act I Scene V

Do you ever wonder what it must have felt like to be Jesus? When did he realise his destiny, his mission? How exquisitely did he feel the grief of mankind, the existential emptiness of feeling forsaken by our father in heaven, the tears that drown the wind? How did he greet the news of what he was required to do? When did he actually know his destiny as the then holder of the Office of the Christ?

In our play, all this is dumbed down to one word: revenge. But what may look traditionally like a man suffering from indecision is really a man who is fulfilling the messianic prophecies, cloaked in poetry and strange behaviour that, yes, looks to us all as kind of mad.

HAMLET
The time is out of joint. O cursèd spite,
That ever I was born to set it right!
Hamlet, Act I Scene V

The time is out of joint... Something is rotten in the state of Denmark... Hamlet is here expressing the deep restlessness of mankind, the dichotomy between our 'two opposèd kings', the result of the original GuiltSin. As the archetype of the Christ, Hamlet is also acknowledging his role in setting things right.

Do you ever feel crazy when misunderstood for seeing things differently? Or deeply sorrowed by dire events in the world that are glossed aside as 'normal'? Every day, we hear stories of racial, sexual and emotional abuse that we just have to suck up. I spent my first thirty years feeling like a misfit. I look back in shame when I look at what I felt I had to do in order to be accepted by my peers. But maybe it's not us that's out of whack, but the time that is out of joint. When the Macbeths and the Claudii take over inside or in the world, something rotten happens to our psyche.

After the ghost delivers to him his destiny, Hamlet seems to go mad. But if the human condition in which we all suffer in ignorance is called 'normal', then Hamlet only *seems* to go mad to his persecutors and those of us in the audience who are also suffering from 'normality'. If you look closely at the ruthless honesty, divine wisdom and incisive perception in his speeches, Hamlet actually goes not mad but courageously *sane*. You'll also see how he mainly 'talks crazy' when he's talking to Claudius and his henchmen. Perhaps foreshadowing the prayer in Gethsemane, Hamlet now prays for the strength to restore order to the land, the promised land of Ananda, bliss and love.

Mankind Shrouded in Darkness: Hamlet Shrouded in Grief

In *Macbeth,* when the king is murdered, we are told that the source of life is stopped. In other words, the correct order of things — deep, blissful connection to the sound current of God — is disrupted. The sound current and the access to the Tree of Life is cut off. The resulting shroud of darkness that falls over the world of man is described by Ross as a general malaise affecting the whole of Scotland. In *Hamlet*, it is the remark made by Marcellus, 'Something is rotten in the state of Denmark', that alerts us to there being a rat in the vat. Then, the eponymous hero himself dramatises the existential grief of the human condition called 'normal' which we are all condemned to endure — until we find the secret of the Grail.

Like Malcolm and Donalbain, Hamlet has not merely lost his mortal father — he's lost the sound and presence of God. He's lost the very spark of life within him that makes life worth living. In *Twelfth Night*, it is the veiled Olivia, literally shrouded in inconsolable grief, who expresses mankind's existential emptiness following the death of the beloved.

To emphasise this dramatically, in Hamlet's case, those around him cannot understand the depth and persistence of his grief. To Rosencrantz and Guildenstern, he declares:

> *I have of late—but wherefore I know not—lost all my*
> *mirth... this goodly frame the earth, seems to me a sterile*
> *promontory... a foul and pestilent congregation of vapours...*
> *Hamlet,* Act I Scene II

Gertrude, his mother, challenges him:

GERTRUDE
Good Hamlet, cast thy nighted colour off,
And let thine eye look like a friend on Denmark.
Do not forever with thy vailèd lids
Seek for thy noble father in the dust.
Thou know'st 'tis common. All that lives must die,
Passing through nature to eternity.

HAMLET
Ay, madam, it is common.

GERTRUDE

If it be,
Why seems it so particular with thee?

HAMLET

"Seems," madam? Nay, it is. I know not "seems."
'Tis not alone my inky cloak, good mother,
Nor customary suits of solemn black,
Nor windy suspiration of forced breath,
No, nor the fruitful river in the eye,
Nor the dejected 'havior of the visage,
Together with all forms, moods, shapes of grief,
That can denote me truly. These indeed "seem,"
For they are actions that a man might play.
But I have that within which passeth show,
These but the trappings and the suits of woe.
Hamlet, Act I Scene II

Claudius weighs in with his patronising, callous indifference, disguised as fatherly concern.

Tis sweet and commendable in your nature, Hamlet, To give these
mourning duties to your father, but that he must know your father
lost a father, That father lost, lost his... 'Tis unmanly grief.
Hamlet, Act I Scene II

An Angel Appears to the Shepherds: A Spirit Appears to the Watch Guard

Here's one of Shakespeare's many heavily disguised 'epiphanies'. If indeed *Hamlet* is a telling of the Christ story through the eyes of Jesus himself, then we'd expect to find hidden an unequivocal, confirmatory way sign slipped in early in Act I. The Gospel of Luke begins with the angel appearing to the shepherds, announcing the coming of the Messiah. It would be great if there were a Shakespeare-style motif of this showing up in *Hamlet*.

Consider this: the dark, eerie opening scene has guards standing late-night watch over the good folk of Elsinore. In particular, they say they're looking out for *the return of young Fortinbras*, coming to reclaim lands lost to Old Norway by Old King Hamlet and to avenge the killing of his father. A spirit appears and scares the heaven and earth out of the guards. As the cock crows, the spirit disappears. As the sounds of the cock fade out, the signs of deeply encrypted biblical symbols fade in. The guards are talking about two things: Christmas — the coming of the saviour. And the crowing of the cock! Although omitted from all productions I've seen, we, the audience should hear a cock crow twice — as if we're being called to awaken, or perhaps even indited for denying the Christ.

So, here we have it. Instead of Luke's shepherds outside the city of David, terrified by a visiting angel while watching over their flocks by night, we have the castle guards outside the city of Elsinore terrified by a visiting spirit while watching over their folks by night. Act I Scene I could well be then a mirror image, a sublime biblical motif of nothing less than what the Christians call the Annunciation of the Shepherds.

If true to form, this potential biblical motif would comfortingly be supported in the text by one or two key biblical references, wouldn't it? Sure enough, first Barnardo alludes to the Star of Bethlehem, then Marcellus (the ones guarding the 'flock') alludes to the advent of the saviour. The sheer unlikeliness of this opening scene from *Hamlet* being a famous biblical motif just pulls the wool from those sheep right over our eyes.

And there were in the same country shepherds abiding in
the field, keeping watch over their flock by night. And, lo,
the angel of the Lord came upon them, and the glory of the
Lord shone round about them: and they were sore afraid.
And the angel said fear not...unto you is born this day in the
*city of David **a Saviour, which is Christ the Lord.***
Luke 2

BARNARDO
Last night of all,
*When yond same **star that's westward from the pole***
*Had made his course **t' illume that part of heaven***
Where now it burns, Marcellus and myself,
The bell then beating one—
MARCELLUS
It [the ghost] faded on the crowing of the cock.
Some say that ever 'gainst that season comes
*Wherein **our Saviour's birth is celebrated...***
Hamlet, Act I Scene I

The guards are talking about Christmas! This is what I call a rather encouraging start in confirming our hypothesis that Hamlet is acting out the archetype of Jesus. Of course, this is not the gospel, it's Shakespeare. He's taking the Annunciation and adapting it for his own version of scripture. This spirit is not just 'signalling' that this is about Christ, but he now begins to tell us about the destiny of Jesus, why he has come to earth and what his overarching mission is. In earthly terms, both to disguise it and fuel the drama, it looks like revenge. But spiritually, Christ didn't come for revenge, he came to rid the consciousness of the contagion, reawaken the sleeping soul of man and open the way home to God cut off by Adam's original GuiltSin.

But there's nothing about that in *Hamlet,* you say. Oh no? Look again. Put on those 3D specs and look again.

Foreshadowing Events Surrounding Gethsemane

The eerie opening scene, a motif of the Annunciation to the Shepherds, has the watch guards trembling in fearful anticipation of the 'second coming' of a ghost. Recounting the ghost's first appearance and sudden disappearance, Bernardo opens a portal to many an 'eary' reference.

It was about to speak when the cock crew.

By invoking the image of the crowing of the cock, is the Master alluding to Jesus's prophecy at the Last Supper that Peter would deny knowing him three times before the cock crows? If so, why? And if so, where is this allusion corroborated?

Given this opening scene is likely to be where all the key themes of the play will be foreshadowed, and that it's where Hamlet's/Jesus' destiny is about to be revealed, this must be significant. Checking the gospel for context, we're looking at the events at the Last Supper leading to the events in the garden of Gethsemane.

We now have an almost invisible trace of five crucial biblical events in Jesus's mission winked at in the first scene of *Hamlet*. It seems highly unlikely that in some way, in some order, all five of these key gospel scenes really will show up disguised in the play as biblical motifs, but you never know.

1. Peter denies Christ thrice.
2. Christ's agony in Gethsemane.
3. The (poisoned) kiss of Judas, leading to:
4. Jesus being arrested, and...
5. ...in the scuffle, with a sword, Peter *cuts off* the *ear* of Malchus, servant to the high priest, Caiaphas, and Jesus miraculously heals it with a touch.

I appreciate how tenuous this chain link may seem at first. However, should this in fact be what Shakespeare wants us to connect to subliminally, then it won't be long before all these virtually invisible biblical motifs are played out symbolically.

And Jesus saith unto him, Verily I say unto thee, That this day, even in this night, before the cock crow twice, thou shalt deny me thrice.
Mark 14: 30

Is this perhaps Jesus Code for something even deeper? In linguistics, a crucial distinction is made between the surface structure and the deep structure of language. On the surface, 'before the cock crow twice, thou shalt deny me thrice' leads to the obvious meaning that Peter is so weak he will soon deny the Christ three times. Or the same surface structure (as, say, 'the TV shall not work, till thou hast plugged it in') could lead to the subtle, deeper meaning that it is *necessary* for Peter to deny Christ thrice *in order that* the cock will crow.

If so, what could the cock's crow symbolise? Is Peter's denial not so much a betrayal of Christ but a fulfilment of scripture? Is Peter *bound* to deny the Christ in order for him to fulfil his mission?

We know Shakespeare makes heretical allusions to the sound current all the time. But Jesus? The crowing of the cock? Perhaps in Jesus Code, the line is a metaphor for the restoration of the sound current? If not, what? It's surely yet another poetic device like those cryptic, mystical sounds hidden in *Macbeth*. Chanting round the cauldron, it was the sound (first) of *a cat's mew* and (second) of a hedgehog's whine linked with those very specific *three denials* followed by those very specific *two utterances*. Will the wily Bard find a way of working this mystical secret into Hamlet? Will he shed more light on it for us? Stay as alert as those sentinels!

FIRST WITCH
*Thrice the brinded cat hath **mewed**.*

SECOND WITCH
*Thrice, and once the hedge-pig **whined**.*
Macbeth, Act IV Scene I

Is Peter now satirised as the whining hedgehog who wept when he heard the cock crow, having denied Christ thrice?

Awake the God of Day

Horatio now adds something more — something I found really exciting. It's the tip of a multi-layered, cryptic iceberg frozen in four little lines.

HORATIO
I have heard
The cock, that is the trumpet to the morn,
Doth with his lofty and shrill-sounding throat
Awake the god of day...
Hamlet, Act I Scene I

On one level, 'the trumpet' and the 'shrill-sounding throat' could be adding to the allusion to the sound of the sacred Name we are hunting: the word Jesus must utter to breach the seals guarding the way to the Tree of Life. Could that be the very name of the god of day? Also, my sense is that 'to awake the god of day' is an alternative, coded expression of the deeper purpose of Jesus's mission on earth: to awaken the sleeping soul of man. Do we now have the cock's crow as another audacious symbol for the sound and sacred name of God? Perhaps even the sacred name and sound of Hu that I first spotted hiding in the text at the start of my mystical travels into the subtext of Shakespeare?

Nobody understood the Jesus Code at the time, but if Shakespeare is decrypting it for us, it means the same for both: an extremely cocky metaphor for the sound of God's name awakening the sleeping soul. Did perhaps Jesus breach the seven seals by calling out the Word, HU, the sacred name of God?

Moses Code

More deserves to be said about Shakespeare's critical symbol: the god of day. I see it relating to the code used extensively throughout Shakespeare — the same code used in the Bible and the same code that lets us choose between the banal and the profound — an interpretation that leads nowhere, versus an interpretation that leads everywhere. To be, or not to be.

In *Macbeth,* I postulated that the term 'Night' is Moses Code for Lucifer/Satan. This is in contrast to 'Day' being Moses Code for the true name of God — the name we are currently hunting. Here's where it all began — in the beginning.

> And God divided the light from the darkness, And the
> light he called Day. And the darkness he called Night.
> *And the evening and the morning were the first day.*
> Genesis 1:4-6

What do you understand by this verse from Genesis 1? Consider the name Day is code for the True Name of God, the light of the world, as opposed to the name Night being code for the shadow name of God, Satan, or Lucifer.

This is how Shakespeare deployed this code so powerfully in *Macbeth* and also in, say, *Othello*, when Iago says Hell and Night [Satan] must bring this monstrous birth [Cain and Abel] to the world's light [Christ]. This is where the Grail mystery really began — way back in the creation itself.

Anagogically (scientifically, too, perhaps), this would be telling how a positive-negative polarity was created (day-night) so that, like with a battery, the energy of spirit could flow from the unmanifest, positive polarity of the God realms to the manifest, negative polarity of the earthly material realms.

Following on, Genesis 1:16 soon corroborates that hidden meaning in the metaphors 'Day' and 'Night':

> *And God made two great lights; the greater light to rule*
> *the **day**, and the lesser light to rule the **night**.*

Of course, you're welcome to choose the crass interpretation that God is telling us a fairy story about the sun and the moon taking it in turns to rule the heavens depending on where you happen to be standing on the planet. Or, more deeply, you can choose to see how God is telling us something profoundly important about the creation — not of the outer physical world — but of our inner spiritual world.

Consciousness.

Inside us, then, consider that the ruler God, say, of the positive polarity was given the name, symbolised as Day. In many mystical traditions, as well as Sufism and Islam, this could often be intoned as the HU, often pronounced 'hue' (and alluded to in the famous 'to be or not to be' speech). The god of the negative polarity was given the shadow name of God, symbolised as 'Night', aka Satan or Lucifer, ironically meaning *light bearer*. The Bible has only one reference to the name Lucifer; maybe he became known as Satan after his betrayal.

Jesus restored the sound to its rightful place at the epicentre of the consciousness *of all mankind*. With the reunion of the sound with the light, the spirit of God became whole again. We call this wholeness the Holy Spirit — part light, part sound — as it was in the beginning, now and forever after. Keep your ear on the term 'union'; it is destined to show up in the finale of this play with significant consequences.

Meanwhile, There's Always More in Elsinore

Let's come up to the surface of the play to take a deep breath and get some perspective. While Hamlet is planning how to hoist Claudius by his own petard and confirm his guilt in murdering and usurping Hamlet's father, Claudius is plotting with Polonius, and Rosencrantz and Guildenstern, to get rid of the Hamlet problem once and for all.

Hamlet's plan is to stage a play depicting the unusual way his father was murdered — by having poison placed in his ear. By observing Claudius's reaction to 'the truth', in the surface play, Hamlet will be convinced his quest is just. Underneath, it will be the key to unravelling Satan's power over mankind and Satan's big mistake: the attempted murder of the Christ that blew back on him big time.

Claudius has inveigled Polonius to spy and eavesdrop on Hamlet, while Polonius has in turn manipulated his daughter, Ophelia, Hamlet's lover, into acting as bait to discover the source of his apparent madness. When the strolling players arrive to be briefed on their performance, the bizarre, mystical, inner play beneath the stage begins to unfold.

Peter Cuts off the Ear of Malchus with a Sword: Ilium Cuts off the Ear of Pyrrhus with a Sword

Dubbing *Hamlet* the 'eary' play was indeed an apt act. Notice the frequent term *cut off*. Cutting off, opening up and healing are seminal to the deeper understanding of the dilemma we, as divine beings, are grappling with in life. This is not a drill. This is not just a mythological story. This is happening to all of us right here, right now. We are *cut off* from our true divinity. Hamlet's father brazenly underlines this morsel of divine heresy — coupling *cut off* with *sin* in the one stanza:

GHOST (Adam)
Thus was I, sleeping, by a brother's hand
Of life, of crown, of queen at once dispatched,
Cut off, *even in the blossoms of* **my sin***.*
Hamlet, Act I Scene V

I was sure that 'the rankly abused ear of Denmark' was an early allusion to the major theme of the Original Sin, i.e., the 'ear of Man' being metaphorically cut off. I knew in my bones the crowing of the cock was a portal to an underground cave of treasures. But was Shakespeare really now going to cook up an unlikely motif of Jesus's last miracle in Gethsemane? How was he going to represent Jesus healing the ear of Malchus that Peter cut off when he was taken prisoner? This entire underground interpretation of *Hamlet* is edgy enough. Would I be rewarded with a real bonus discovery? I was so sure I would, I went over the minutiae of the text with Sherlock Holmes's magnifying glass.

If you remember your Bible studies, when Jesus was taken prisoner in Gethsemane, Peter forcefully resisted his arrest. He drew his sword and cut off the ear of Malchus, the servant of the high priest Caiaphas. Jesus immediately went to the man and healed his cut off ear. Is this not a beautiful metaphor encapsulating the entire essence of Jesus's mission: *to heal the ear of man*? To restore the Tree of Life? To release the sound current cut off by Adam's collusion with the serpent? To unleash the wind from heaven back to the inner ear of mankind? To reunite the sound with the light of God and restore the Holy Spirit?

Here's another dramatic example of how the boundary between biblical history and biblical symbolism blurs. Did this bizarre event happen literally — or was it written as a kind of parable, disguised in the gospel as actuality?

It is in the garden of Gethsemane that Jesus himself invokes the metaphor of the poisoned chalice. It is in the garden that Jesus reminds us he is doing all of this to fulfil the messianic prophecies. It is in the garden where the Original

Sin first cuts off the ear of man. It is in the garden (orchard) that Hamlet's father was murdered by the serpent Claudius. It is in the garden that Jesus symbolises that cut off ear being healed. It is in the garden that Jesus wrestles with his task, as did Jacob with his ego. It is in the garden that he commits to drink from the cup.

He is destined to die in a very specific way. And he knows it.

Again, you only get the full picture by piecing together bits from several gospels.

Then said Jesus unto Peter, Put up thy sword into the sheath:
the cup which my Father hath given me, shall I not drink it?
John 18:11

Thinkest thou that I cannot now pray to my Father, and he
shall presently give me more than twelve legions of angels?

But how then shall the scriptures be fulfilled, that thus it must be?
Matthew 26:53-54

The eagerly anticipated reward is hidden like a Russian doll inside the prelude to *The Mousetrap*.

The (Inner) Play's the Thing, Wherein I'll Catch the Conscience of the King

The ploy of Hamlet's play within the play, *The Mousetrap*, is to hold up a mirror to Claudius revealing that the truth of what he did is known. Like a poker tell, Hamlet will be looking for any unconscious, autonomic signs that Claudius is guilty.

A couple of scenes before *The Mousetrap* itself, Hamlet is briefing the players. In his long, rambling, seemingly irrelevant, shaggy-dog speech where

Hamlet appears to be showing off his knowledge of Greek classics, we receive our prize.

He conjures up a sudden flourish of the bizarre. Tucked away inside it is the sublime biblical motif we seek. Here, in Shakespeare's bespoke version of Virgil's *Aeneid*, he tells how Pyrrhus, diabolical son of Achilles, described cryptically in Jesus Code for Satan as 'The rugged Pyrrhus, he whose sable arms, black as his purpose, did the night resemble', while striking with his sword at Old Priam of Troy (Ilium), has his own ear cut off by what appears in the text to be divine intervention. Not only is the unfortunate ear cut off with a sword, but it is also taken prisoner, as was Jesus at that very moment he cut off the ear of Malchus.

The words 'takes prisoner Pyrrhus' ear' made my eyes water! As Jesus is taken prisoner, Peter cuts off the ear of man, and Jesus immediately heals it. Shakespeare acknowledges the profound significance of this symbolic event through this long-winded counterfeit of the *Aeneid*.

In the same way Malchus, whose name means 'my king', symbolises the servant of Satan (Caiaphas) here Pyrrhus, son of Achilles, is painted as black as Satan. In his attempt to kill Priam, the rightful king of Troy, with Shakespeare's slick sleight of hand, Pyrrhus has his ear cut off by the hand of his intended victim. Allusions to the sound current, the wind from heaven liberated at The Pentecost abound.

> *The rugged Pyrrhus, he whose sable arms,*
> *Black as his purpose, **did the night [Satan] resemble...***
> *...Pyrrhus at Priam [King of Troy] drives, in rage strikes wide;*
> *But with the **whiff and wind** [sound current] of his fell sword*
> *Th' unnervèd father falls. Then senseless Ilium,*
> *Seeming to feel this blow, with **flaming** top [tongues of fire]*
> *Stoops to his base, and with a hideous crash*
> ***Takes prisoner Pyrrhus' ear.** For lo, his **sword**,*

Which was declining on the milky head
Of reverend Priam, seemed i' th' air to stick.
So as a painted tyrant Pyrrhus stood
And, like a neutral to his will and matter,
Did nothing.
Hamlet, Act II Scene II

As if this is not bizarre enough, the adjective *flaming top* is yet another clincher allusion to the flaming sword of the cherubim who cut off the tree of life, aka the ear of man.

The massive theological significance here requires repeating these two seminal passages. The *tree of life* is the first biblical symbol for *the sound current* that first Jesus then Shakespeare dub *the ear of man*.

So he drove out the man; and he placed at the east of the
garden of Eden Cherubim, and a flaming sword which
*turned every way, to **keep the way of the tree of life**.*
Genesis 3:24

*Blessed are they that do his commandments, **that they may have right***
***to the tree of life**, and may enter in through the gates into the city.*
Revelation 22:14

Using Shakespeare's 'Rosetta Stone', we can see how this passage from Genesis is saying (poetically) that *the ear of man was cut off by a flaming sword...* and the subsequent one from Revelation says *and Jesus healed it*! Jesus reopened the way to the Kingdom of God.

The implications the revelation of this symbolic device linking Genesis, the gospel, and Revelation in one fell swoop cannot be underestimated.

Jesus breaches the seven seals: Hamlet kills Polonius with a Sword.

As a coda, a way of emphasising the profound symbolic significance of Peter's cutting off the ear of Malchus as Jesus was taken prisoner, the wily Bard slips in another incredibly subtle eary allusion: in a fit of anger (like Peter) Hamlet now kills Polonius with a sword! In the outer play, Hamlet seems to go increasingly mad. It has to look like a revenge story. And if that's what floats your boat, then so be it. But we're not going to be blown off course by gales and rips — unless they are symbols for the sound current. Our destiny is to reveal how the symbology of Shakespeare decodes the symbology of scripture.

But Peter didn't kill Malchus you cry. No, but in the same way the ear of Malchus was the metaphorical ear of Satan (symbolised by Caiaphas), Polonius is also the metaphorical 'ear' of Satan (symbolised by Claudius). Polonius is always sneaking around, eavesdropping on Hamlet and reporting back to his boss. This scene, where Polonius is hiding behind the arras (curtain, shroud) furtively listening in on Hamlet's intimate reconciliation with his mother, occurs immediately after the trial/mousetrap.

More sublime. In order to 'cut off the ear', Hamlet has to pierce the arras with said sword. Here the shroud/curtain surely symbolises the seven seals of Satan: the impenetrable blockade to the tree of life Jesus came to breach. Effectively, 'cutting off the ear of Claudius' becomes the inciting event in the outer play that causes Hamlet (Jesus) to be taken prisoner (of course), the sine qua non of the eventual breach of the seven seals!

It is such a joy to illuminate this most crucial, subtle and sublime of motifs. Worth several moments of gasping, contemplating, and savouring.

Armageddon in the Garden: To Be or Not To Be, That is the Quest

Before the trial of Claudius, Hamlet is alone. All is quiet. The only sound heard is the flapping ears of Polonius hiding behind a pillar.

We've now arrived at the doorstep of arguably the most famous and most famously misunderstood tract of literature in the known galaxy. Why is it so misunderstood? One reason is: it's incomplete. There's a gap in the story. Apart from *The Tempest,* that explains all the other plays, we cannot get the whole story from any one play in isolation from at least one of the others. Here, Macbeth will serve us nicely — with a little help from Romeo.

Another reason is: the context. Unless you see this speech as a biblical motif of the prayer in Gethsemane then you're stuck with the surface structure alone. You're skating on thick ice. You might vaguely see a distorted image of what lies beneath but there's an invisible barrier protecting it from prying eyes, snooping noses, and unripe minds.

An even bigger reason is: the narrative we've inherited from 2000 years of the orthodox mish-mash of superstitious non-sequiturs and brazen lies worshipped as gospel truths. This cataract is the Shroud of Turin that blinds us to the fundamental existential choice Jesus lived, fought like hell, and died to make possible for us. He opened the gates to the kingdom that the early Church slammed shut — if not in error, certainly in terror.

And, of course, there's the narrative chanted by the threshold guardians of the World of Shakespeare. They are bent on protecting the multimillion-pound franchise from any interpretations they cannot hope to understand let alone tightly control.

As a soul-centred maverick theologian, as you may have spotted, I prefer the richness and illumination of the anagogical interpretation. To be — or not to be — who we really are: the soul, the God within, the Christ, the whatever-the-hell-you-want-to-call-it — a soul by any other name is still a soul. Yes, that is the question. But whoever said the answer was easy? Jesus showed us the way, the example, the way of the Spiritual Warrior. But we still have to claim our soulhood for ourselves. Once having made the ultimate choice, the ultimate commitment, we must every day re-choose and re-claim our daily bread.

Macbeth has already told us that at the Last Supper, Satan entered into Jesus and Jesus took Satan's energy field to Gethsemane to begin the inner struggle transforming the consciousness of mankind. Known also as Armageddon (Jihad, in Islam), this struggle between the soul and the ego was first foretold in Genesis when Jacob struggled with 'a man' (symbol of his ego) and on overcoming saw the face of God (Penuel) and was given the sacred name of ISRAEL (Isis Ra Elohim): forming the union of the Arab and Jewish names of God and the forgiveness of the prophesied enmity between them. Keep your eye on that word: union!

With the advent of Jesus, the breeching of the seven seals began anew in the garden of the soul. The template of the divine Grail quest incepted by Jesus now lives in the DNA of every human being. The gap between our ability to overcome the original temptation and the strength needed to do so has been implanted in our soul by way of the resurrection. The action of resurrection made soul transcendence possible for all who choose it.

This is what was incepted in Gethsemane. This is the event this speech is surely representing: *an enterprise of great pith and moment* would be somewhat of an understatement. This is why this passage of literature has mysteriously impassioned generations of Shakespeare lovers for centuries.

Thus from Armageddon in the Garden Jesus went to the cross: to cross Satan out of our minds, as it were. Is this speech about Hamlet's going out of his mind? Kind of. If Hamlet represents the Christ, then the Christ broke out of the prison of the mind of man formerly sealed tight shut by Satan. He clues us in to his purpose in Act 2, Scene 2 when he confounds the scribes and the pharisees, Rosencrantz and Guildenstern, by indicting Denmark (and the entire world) as a prison, and giving us the key to the gates of freedom: Why, then, 'tis none to you; for there is nothing either good or bad, but thinking makes it so. To me it is a prison.' (Implying — to you it is your home.)

Satan, the lesser god of these lower worlds, still has absolute authority over the mind but thanks to the Christ action we can now transcend the mind into the soul and be free. Whereas before we had no choice other than 'not to be'. Now we also have the choice 'to be', to be who we really are as a divine soul.

Hamlet-as-Jesus ousts Satan from his seat at the centre of our consciousness that sits tyrannically in the mind of man — just as the risen Banquo ousted Macbeth from his stool. Satan's, Macbeth's, Claudius' absolute authority over the soul was reclaimed. What happened in Hamlet's Gethsemane is revealed to us by his seminal interaction with Ophelia at the end of the speech. You'll see. Or maybe not. Here's where I have to risk looking to you as if out of my mind as I try to convey the silent song of love these two despised lovers sing.

O what a **noble mind** is here o'erthrown. Yay! Not before time.

HAMLET

To be or not to be—that is the question:
Whether 'tis nobler in the mind to suffer
The slings and arrows of outrageous fortune,
Or to take arms against a sea of troubles
And, by opposing, end them. To die, to sleep—
No more—and by a sleep to say we end
The heartache and the thousand natural shocks
That flesh is heir to—'tis a consummation
Devoutly to be wished. To die, to sleep—
To sleep, perchance to dream. Ay, there's the rub,
For in that sleep of death what dreams may come,
When we have shuffled off this mortal coil,
Must give us pause. There's the respect
That makes calamity of so long life.
*For who would bear **the whips and scorns** of time,*

*Th' **oppressor's wrong**, the proud man's contumely,*
*The **pangs of despised love**, the law's delay,*
The insolence of office, and the spurns
That patient merit of th' unworthy takes,
When he himself might his quietus make
With a bare bodkin? Who would fardels bear,
To grunt and sweat under a weary life,
But that the dread of something after death,
The undiscovered country from whose bourn
No traveller returns, puzzles the will
And makes us rather bear those ills we have
Than fly to others that we know not of?
Thus conscience doth make cowards of us all,
And thus the native hue of resolution
Is sicklied o'er with the pale cast of thought,
And enterprises of great pith and moment
With this regard their currents turn awry
And lose the name of action. —Soft you now,
The fair Ophelia. —Nymph, in thy orisons
Be all my sins rememberèd.

Act III Scene I

Right at the beginning, Hamlet foreshadows the overthrow of the noble, worthy, sanctified mind whose impostor is worshipped as a god...is it **nobler in the mind** to suffer — or to rail against the seeming injustices of life? And what follows is a discourse on the dilemmas, the stuff and the games played by the mind in homage to Satan. Satan is not real, more a shadow. The name given to a melodramatic religious anthropomorphism of the ego-personality, the false self that has, unless you're one of the more fortunate ones, usurped our soul and postures and parades itself through the proud man's contumely, the law's delay, the insolence of office, the spurns that patient merit of the unworthy takes.

Hamlet confounds us with a meditation on sleep, dreams, and death. And, under the radar, slips in the blessing bestowed upon us all that the Nicaea Church withheld: the end of the heartache and the thousand natural shocks that flesh is heir to (and how to claim this state of grace).

How paradoxical and confusing it is for us when we're prisoners of the mind. What dreams may come when we have shuffled off this mortal coil? The coil of the serpent, the coil of materiality, wrapped round the soul strangling it like a boa constrictor. What dreams may come when we are free from its grip, its tyranny, its delusions? When we are free from the self-imposed fears and terrors? Who knows? Even death, even the suicide foreshadowing Ophelia's equivocal demise hovering on the waters of life, may or may not be a way out of the existential angst.

But as Jesus goes through Armageddon and sweats the blood of Christ even before he is scourged and pierced by the whips and scorns of time. As Jesus fights Satan inside himself, all the sin of the world, everything comprising those seven perfect seals keeping the soul prisoner, Hamlet prepares himself for his own ordeal: he will be trying Claudius the serpent at the court of truth. He puts on his cheesy play to trap the rat. To hold up the mirror that tells him his crime, his original sin, is now out in the open. The ear of Denmark is rankly abused. Not only has the sound and word of God been cut off but we have been fed a smorgasbord of lies to make us believe that all we need to be saved is to follow the wolf in lamb's clothing.

It behoves me now, o worthy reader, to make my case for these outrageous, heretical assertions. As the sounds of the cock fade out, the signs of deeply encrypted biblical symbols fade in.

A prayer or not a prayer?

Between the Last Supper and the trial, Jesus goes to pray in the Garden of Gethsemane. Before *The Mousetrap*, the trial of Claudius, Hamlet meditates on existence. Inside Jesus is the agony of Armageddon, the battle between the grace of Christ and the good-and-evil of Satan. It is so momentous that he sweats blood. In the same way that Satan entered Adam the Christ (Man) in Eden, Satan has now entered Jesus the Christ (the Son of Man). Unlike Adam, who fell, Jesus is destined to vanquish the contagion of good-and-evil for the rest of time. Inside him, he is administering to Satan the poison in the chalice of the Grail. The agony he takes upon himself is only just beginning. As a physical being he knows what lies ahead. He knows how awful it will surely be. He is perhaps fulfilling the first prophesy of Genesis that caused the original GuiltSin:

> *But of the tree of the knowledge of good and evil, thou shalt not eat*
> *of it: for in the day that thou eatest thereof thou shalt surely die.*
> *Genesis 2:17*

Adam (man) ate of it and was banished from the heart of God. As Romeo reminds us:

> *There is no world without Verona walls, but purgatory,*
> *torture, hell itself. Hence banished is banished*
> *from the world, and world's exile is death.*
> *Romeo and Juliet* Act 3, Scene 3

The banishment was the original Guiltsin. The banishment cut the ear of man off from the sweet harmony of the soul. The soul cannot die, but when banished from awareness we become like the vampire, the undead. And in our torture and living hell we crave anything and everything that might make us feel alive. Bram Stoker created Dracula to satirise the rampant, self-obsessed ego sucking the blood from his victims in the unholy communion. Shakespeare created a cast of characters embodying Cain and Abel, the children of the serpent spawned by his rape of Eve. Here they are played by Claudius, whose comeuppance is coming up soon after the trial wherein the mouse is trapped.

Inside himself Jesus is faced with the same fundamental existential choice we all face every moment of the day expressed in many ways: reality or duality, truth or illusion, soul or ego, Christ or Satan, freedom or dilemma... And inside himself Hamlet, too, faces the same choice: to be or not to be? That is the question.

Springing the mousetrap

In *East of Eden*, in similar vein to Shakespeare, John Steinbeck takes one Hebrew word from Genesis, *timshel*, reinterprets it from 'thou shalt' to 'thou mayest', and crafts his famous fable of Adam, Eve, Serpent, Cain and Abel. He, however, comes to the cynical conclusion:

> *I believe that there is one story in the world, and only one...*
> *Humans are caught — in their lives, in their thoughts, in*
> *their hungers and ambitions, in their avarice and cruelty, and*
> *in their kindness and generosity too — in a net of good and*
> *evil... There is no other story. A man, after he has brushed off*
> *the dust and chips of his life, will have left only the hard, clean*
> *questions: Was it good or was it evil? Have I done well—or ill?*
> John Steinbeck, *East of Eden,* Chapter 34

Many would no doubt agree; he voices the perception of most philosophy and religion. I agree that at the level of the contagion of good-and-evil, life has little intrinsic meaning. But, imperceptibly, the level of *to be* reaches up to heaven, the inner kingdom, the forgotten true self and, in finding, liberates us from the contagion.

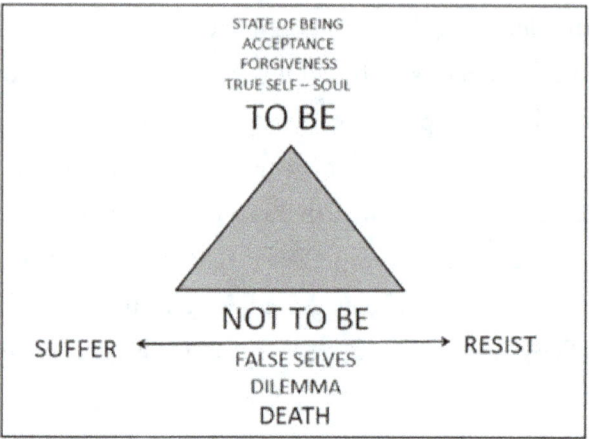

The soul in a transcendent dimension from the duality of *good-and-evil*

Was this Hamlet's 'Gethsemane' moment? Or perhaps Jesus' 'to be or not to be' moment:

And he took with him Peter and the two sons of Zebedee,
and began to be sorrowful and very heavy.

Then saith he unto them, My soul is exceeding sorrowful,
even unto death: tarry ye here, and watch with me.

And he went a little farther, and fell on his face, and prayed,
saying, O my Father, if it be possible, let this cup pass from
me: nevertheless not as I will, but as thou wilt.
Matthew 26: 37-39

Well, even without having Hamlet literally sweat blood, this gospel passage perfectly captures the mournful mood of the soliloquy (a kind of prayer in a way) and could certainly pass as the director's brief to the actor playing Hamlet.

Jesus is in the agony of processing *all the sin of the world* — in other words, Satan's venom. It's said he was sweating blood. Literally? Maybe. But again, it is another metaphor for the blood of the New Testament, 'shed for us all for the remission of sins'. He also knows what's coming: a trial, a scourging, ('the whips and scorns of time'), the crown of thorns ('proud man's contumely'), and the crucifixion. I don't buy the utter incongruity of Jesus' asking for a way out for himself. I think he's clearing the way for us to also claim our Christhood. He knows his choice is *to be* true to the Christ within, to his father's will, or *not to be*. It's the same existential choice we all face every day. As the ambassadors for mankind, Jesus and Hamlet are cutting a swathe through the doubt and fear we will all encounter as we make and attempt to live this decisive decision.

Not that earthly chronology ever matters to the Master, but the scene's position in the play is directly after the allusion to the cutting off of the ear of Malchus (as the cutting off of the ear of Pyrrhus) and directly before *The Mousetrap* scene which would correspond to the trial of Satan (held by Jesus).

Does this, arguably the most famous speech in all literature, receive the accolade of number one in our list of predicted events through the portal of the crowing cock?

In the anagogical homage in the last few lines, Hamlet sums up the tragic loss of the sound current with nothing less than an arcane allusion to the death of the god of day: 'the native hue of resolution is sicklied o'er with the pale cast of thought', *hue* being the Sanskrit sound and hallowed name of God used in many Eastern religions including Sufism and Islam. The 'currents turned awry' sitting next door to 'the name of action' confirms the likely allusion to the lost sound current, the wind from heaven also known as the Holy Spirit that, now restored, takes those initiated home to the Godhead.

Nor can we imagine how Hamlet must be feeling also knowing what was coming at him. If directors do not realise the underlying motif he is enacting, we only see Hamlet as a mortal and think he is just mourning the loss of his father and driven by revenge. We miss the deeper point. From the earliest scenes, the excessive grief Hamlet is feeling is actually the unbearable grief of mankind, 'the heartache and the thousand natural shocks that flesh is heir to', the loss of soul-self-awareness. The dis-inheritance we all suffer during cognitive development, the agony of losing the divine presence of the God within. This deep, inescapable, existential pain is the normal pain of being a human on this earth. And the normal pain generates 'normal' behaviours — all the respectable and disrespectable, legalised and illegal, moral and immoral ways society enables us to numb out our pain, compensate for our feelings of unworthiness and cope with our sense of abandonment.

In all the plays I've looked at, the key characters act out one fundamental, existential choice: *to be or not to be* true to themselves, *to be or not to be* honourable, *to be or not to be* happy. As we approach our denouement, *The Tempest,* Shakespeare makes this underlying theme explicit.

Having said all this, what's your verdict? Gethsemane motif or not? I still wasn't 100% convinced. The parallels are so subtle. Almost invisible. If only there were something else, perhaps some tiny hint that indicated that Hamlet was in fact praying. If only God sent him an angel... that would surely clinch it.

Ophelia to the rescue

When Jesus prayed in his agony, God sent an angel:

> *And there appeared an angel unto him*
> *from heaven, strengthening him.*
> *Luke 22:43*

And at the end of Hamlet's lament, who shows up but Ophelia. And what does he call her? 'Nymph' (Angel?) And what does he say? He declares she's the answer to his orisons [prayers] of forgiveness:

Soft you now,
*The fair Ophelia. —**Nymph**, in thy **orisons***
Be all my sins remembered.
Act 3, Scene 1

Ophelia now steps in as the 'angel' to galvanise him into taking the prophesied actions that fulfil what's disguised at her funeral as 'crowner's quest law.'

Was I now convinced? It depends. The utter genius of Shakespeare is that if we interrogate his poetry with our logic-needing mind we bypass the essence behind what he is telling us. The mind takes us into the 'not to be' — the duality. If we read, look and listen from our heart, we'll get the truth of it for ourselves in a way that works for us where we are now in our spiritual journey — where there are no rights or wrongs. In Rumi's take on the 'to be or not to be' question, he says:

Out beyond ideas of wrong-doing and right-
doing, there is a field. I'll meet you there.
The Essential Rumi

However, in another field, a field on a hill outside the city walls, Jesus was crucified and buried. In our play, Ophelia was similarly laid to rest. As if Shakespeare had wished to pre-empt our concerns over his cryptic allusion that Ophelia had stepped in to play the role of the ministering angel sent by God to fortify Jesus, at this very spot he gives Laertes, Ophelia's now grieving brother, a few well-chosen words for her eulogy with which I rest my case:

And from her fair and unpolluted flesh
May violets spring! I tell thee, churlish priest,
A minist'ring angel *shall my sister be*
When, thou liest howling.
Act 5, Scene 1

As the possible archetype of the Christ aspect of Hamlet's Jesus, it's also interesting to note that after this brutal last encounter with (the nihilistically mad) Hamlet it is Ophelia who appears to go mad, enough to seemingly commit suicide.

Or does she?

Peter Denies Christ Thrice: Hamlet Denies Ophelia Thrice

Before the cock crow twice, thou shalt deny me thrice.

Before introducing Ophelia into our conversation, I need to make a segue. A subterranean link between the inner music of Hamlet's last words in Gethsemane and the pith and moment of what Ophelia is describing in her lamentations.

Thus conscience doth make cowards of us all,
*And thus **the native hue of resolution***
Is sicklied o'er with the pale cast of thought,
And enterprises of great pith and moment
*With this regard their **currents turn awry***
*And **lose the name of action**. —Soft you now,*
The fair Ophelia. —Nymph, in thy orisons
Be all my sins rememberèd.

Of all the words and poetic images Shakespeare could have chosen here, he coagulates these three phrases.

the native hue of resolution
currents turn awry
lose the name of action

Already mentioned in the intro and explained more fully in Part 3, *The Tempest;* in the ancient mystery school known variously as Shabdha Yoga and soul transcendence, the sound **hue** is the sacred Sanskrit **name** of God: aka the sound **current.**

Hamlet is telling us that the native hue, the innate sound of the soul is cut off from birth by the beliefs programmed into the mind, our true and greater purpose is corrupted, and the conscious knowing that we are divine is lost. This tragedy in cognitive development parallels the events in Genesis when the soul, Adam-and-Eve, was banished, and all mankind lost its true humanity, lost its soul-self-awareness.

He now calls on Ophelia as the Christ consciousness to overrule the tyranny of the mind and restore the Christ, the sounds of the sound current, including the 'hue', to its rightful place on the throne of consciousness.

First, Hamlet must fulfil the scripture. He denies her three times. He fulfils the commandment given to Peter to deny the Christ thrice, to commit The Original Sin three times! Yes, the original sin, and the only true sin is nothing whatsoever to do with disobedience — but everything to do with denying that we are all the Christ, we are all the divine essence, the sons and daughters of God.

In the outer play, Ophelia has come to reminisce with Hamlet about vows and trinkets they had exchanged:

First denial

OPHELIA

*My Lord, I have remembrances of yours that I have longed long
to re-deliver.*

HAMLET

No, no, I never gave you aught...

Second denial

...I did love you once...

Third denial

....I loved you not...

And here, now, the Bard answers our question: what scripture was Jesus fulfilling when he commanded Peter to deny him three times? Symbolically, he was re-enacting man's fall into the spiritual amnesia of Satan's seven seals in the Garden of Eden. Hamlet banishes and curses Ophelia, just as Lucifer banished and cursed Adam & Eve in Genesis.

Get thee to a nunnery...
I'll give thee this plague for a dowry...

For the benefit of the drama of the outer play, this cruel, irrational, undeserved abuse of innocence, not only underlines for the audience (Polonius and Claudius) that Hamlet is indeed barking mad, but is the inciting incident that drives Ophelia too over the edge of sanity into suicidal despair.

But for the benefit of those of us listening to the inner play the rewards are only just beginning.

Consider this, Ophelia's (seeming) lament following the bruising onslaught from her former lover:

OPHELIA

*O, what a noble **mind is here o'erthrown!***
...And I, of ladies most deject and wretched,
*That **sucked the honey of his musicked vows,***
Now see that noble and most sovereign reason,
Like sweet bells jangled, out of time and harsh;
That unmatched form and stature of blown youth
Blasted with ecstasy. O, woe is me
T' have seen what I have seen, see what I see!

Act 3, Scene 1

Again, a number sublimely coded allusions to the action of the sound current, including an allusion to the cock crowing twice.

mind is here o'erthrown
sucked the honey of his musicked vows
Like sweet bells jangled, out of time and harsh

Shakespeare has used descriptions of the sound current of God (the crowing of the cock — the metaphor used by Jesus at the Last Supper) as it flows through the Creation as metaphors for how the mind of man, the prison ruled by Satan, has now been overcome. Satan's rule and vice-like grip on our soul has been overthrown.

Saying the ***mind is here o'erthrown*** *is a sublime pun, a singular double entendre, meaning the kingdom of the mind has been* 'over-throned' — the Christ has reclaimed its rightful kingdom.

(Again, this foretaste of the sounds of the realms/the music of the spheres is more fully explained in Part 3.)

First 'crowing of the cock':
Sucked the honey of his musicked vows, an allusion to the sounds
of the buzzing of the honey bees heard in the etheric realm of light.

Second 'crowing of the cock':
Like sweet bells jangled, an allusion to the sound of
the ringing bells heard in the causal realm of light.

*...out of time and harsh...*implies beyond time (and thus also beyond space) and outside 'this harsh world', (the dying Hamlet refers to in 5.2). Once again an allusion to the Christ's action of soul transcendence that liberated the soul from Satan's world and restored the sound to the ear of man.

Between them, Hamlet and Ophelia have sung a secret duet, an operetta in celebration of the unbridled joy of the liberation of the soul — heavily disguised (as is Shakespeare's wont) as the very antithesis of its deep, deeply-heretical, meaning.

The Trial of Jesus [Satan]: The Mousetrap

Incredibly, against all the odds, we've now seen biblical motifs of all five of the key gospel events between the Last Supper and the trial of Jesus.

Consider now that the play-within-the-play Hamlet calls *The Mousetrap* will, through your freshly opened paradigm, be seen to be a biblical motif of the trial of Jesus. In *Macbeth,* the story of Christ was in reverse because Satan was the protagonist. In *Hamlet,* putting Claudius (the serpent) on trial may look backwards, but from Jesus's perspective, that's exactly what happened.

Again and again throughout the plays, Shakespeare smelts the irony of Satan's crucifixion into an invincible rod of steel. In scripture, it looks like

Jesus was on trial, but in reality, it was Satan! Jesus had to drink from the cup (poisoned chalice) his father had prepared for him in order to poison the Satan now inside him. It's the same principle as chemotherapy: the cancer dies, and sometimes with it, also the body.

Praying in Gethsemane and dying on the cross, Jesus must have felt like God had forsaken him, but that is precisely the existential agony of man — the feeling of being forsaken by God — that he took on himself. Even the famous last words of Jesus on the cross were prophesied in the Old Testament.

> *My God, my God, why hast thou forsaken me?*
> Psalm 22:1

As he dies, Jesus fulfils the scripture by expressing the existential grief of man as portrayed by Hamlet in the first act. The feelings of anguish, abandonment and despair we all felt in the beginning when the serpent deposed the soul and the sound current was cut off. The agony we all feel every time we cut ourselves off from soul-self-awareness. As Jesus fulfilled the scripture he restored the original state of paradise, the Ananda, Adam and Eve enjoyed before their intercourse with the serpent. We now have the original choice given to Adam and Eve to live in grace and spiritual bliss or live in the pain and tyranny of the serpent.

Consider again the greater truths that it's not what we do that's the sin but the guilt we feel. It's not God who wants us to feel guilty, but Satan. It's not God's forgiveness we need, but our own.

We saw from *Macbeth* and the gospel account of the Last Supper that it was not so much Jesus who died on the cross, but Satan. Satan entered Jesus so that, at his death and Resurrection, all the messianic prophesies would be fulfilled. And the only way for God to break the seven seals, the blood covenant of the Old Testament, without breaking his sacred Word, was for Satan to be hoist by his own petard. He had to bring himself down. As you might see from Shylock's own petard hoisting in *The Merchant of Venice*, attempting to murder the Christ is the ultimate spiritual crime which brings the fullness of God's law upon one.

In Gethsemane, Jesus the man was in agony, praying, while inside himself, Jesus the Christ was battling Armageddon. The body and the psychic levels (imagination, emotions, mind, unconscious) is the mortal coil — the serpent's coil, the chaos, self-doubt and confusion — that wraps itself around the soul as soon as a child is born. Thus, it was not Jesus on trial, but Satan. *The Mousetrap* was the trial of Claudius-the-serpent observed by Hamlet-the-Christ. God cannot be mocked, but Satan can.

In the gospel, it looks like the Romans and Sanhedrin put Jesus on trial for his life, to mock him, scourge him, find him guilty and execute him. The irony in our own lives is that when we mock or hurt another for any reason, we are mocking and hurting ourselves. The teaching says to love our neighbour as ourselves — because our neighbour *is* our self. Not as an ego-personality, but as a soul.

The ego separates us from each other, from the soul and from God. That's the delusion we inherited from Adam. But as we allow the soul deep within to become our true centre, we begin to experience our oneness with each other and, through this, our oneness with God. It's a very nice feeling.

In Shakespeare, it is the forces of darkness that are put on trial such that they condemn themselves: in attempting to kill the Christ, they effectively kill themselves. Little do the Sanhedrin realise they are being outplayed by God. As they persecute Jesus, the covenant of the Old Testament and Mosaic law is being fulfilled, thorn by thorn, lash by lash, nail by nail. In our play, *Hamlet*, the mystical story is told through the sacrifice of Ophelia, Hamlet and Laertes, and the deaths of Polonius, Rosencrantz and Guildenstern, Gertrude and Claudius. Everyone dies. It looks like a tragedy, but we don't necessarily see the ultimate, invisible victory symbolised in the finale. For that, we need Fortinbras.

Have you ever wondered what it might have felt like to be Jesus the Christ? Did his mortal consciousness always know he was a direct emanation of God? Or did he have to follow a path of spiritual awakening and initiation like us ordinary mortals? We are told precious little about him in the scripture. We know at the end, in Gethsemane and on the cross, he expressed the existential agony of man: 'My God, my God, why hast thou forsaken me?' But what we *are* told is that the forces of darkness were symbolised, personified, as the Sanhedrin. They were the ones outraged by his teachings and his claims of divinity. In their eyes, he was the blaspheming Jew whose liver was placed in the witches' cauldron. They constantly watched him, spied on him, baited him with trick questions, listened to every word he spoke and wrote it down in order to condemn him and rid themselves of him.

Even talking with Ophelia, Hamlet plays to the unseen audience that he knows is listening and clucking and tutting about him. Ironically, this is all part of his master plan to trap Claudius into revealing his guilt. Even we, the audience, cannot be sure the ghost was real. But remember that Hamlet is not really following his human lust for revenge; he's following the road map drawn by the Old Testament prophecies that lead to the undoing of Satan's stranglehold on the throat of mankind.

Claudius must convict himself. Murder hath no tongue — because the sound and truth of it has been cut off.

HAMLET

For murder, though it have no tongue, will speak
With most miraculous organ....
The play's the thing
Wherein I'll catch the conscience of the King.
Hamlet, Act II Scene II

As a play, *The Mousetrap* is designed to confirm the ghost's indictment of the murder of Hamlet's father by Claudius. Hamlet briefs the players to perform a sketch that mimics the murder of his father by Claudius. Pouring poison in his ear is a metaphor for listening to the lies of the serpent. This curious mode of murder symbolises how it was 'the ear of man' that was cut off in Eden in the beginning. The 'whole ear of Denmark is rankly abused'. The whole of mankind was cut off from the inner sound of God and the spiritual bliss, the Ananda. Our spiritual, inner soul-self-awareness was lost.

The ploy works for Hamlet. It opens up the whole can of worms, little serpents that wriggle off and duly get their comeuppance.

Cain Denies Responsibility for Abel's Blood: Claudius Confesses His Murder

Apart from twice underlining the *eariness* of the play's theme, *The Mousetrap* scene, per se, does not seem to comprise any of the familiar motifs of the Christ story. But it certainly is a major inciting incident for 'even-handed justice' to be visited on all. Like a house of cards, after the play, they all fall down. Claudius and Polonius will rue the moment they say, 'let there be light — and there was light'.

KING

Give me some light. Away!

POLONIUS

Lights, lights, lights!

Hamlet, Act III Scene II

With Shakespeare's wickedly backwards irony, it is Claudius we now find praying. Or rather, Hamlet finds him. Hamlet now is the one hovering in the shadows. Dagger drawn, he's considering ending the life of the found-guilty usurper. Claudius confesses all to us, the audience. He wants redemption, he wants to feel okay, but he cannot relinquish the proceeds from his crime: his crown, his ambition, and his queen. It is hard to believe Satan or Cain were ever contrite, or that an adder might feel guilty about biting an innocent man, but hey, the play's the thing. We also have the subliminal spiritual message from the Master of the Grail: 'seek first the kingdom of God, and all things will be added unto thee', a message our ego-mind will eschew in favour of our addiction to outer symbols of power and importance.

Shakespeare manages to slip two biblical motifs for the price of one into this all-telling soliloquy. It's a speech that returns us east of Eden, brings back Pontius Pilate's action of washing his hands of the blood of Christ, and makes even more sense of why Lady Macbeth had to make such an issue of Duncan's blood. It's an even deeper biblical motif of the original crime of Cain in that led to his banishment and curse. Again, it's all about lies, murder and the blood. Especially the blood.

> *And the Lord said unto Cain, Where is Abel thy brother? And he*
> *said, **I know not: Am I my brother's keeper?** And he said, What*
> *hast thou done? The voice of thy brother's blood crieth unto me from*
> *the ground. And now art thou **cursed from the earth**, which hath*
> *opened her mouth to receive thy brother's blood from thy hand.*
> Genesis 4:9-11

This is how Claudius expresses this biblical motif from the dawn of time. By telling us exactly what it is, the Master simultaneously camouflages it.

> KING (Claudius)
> *O, my offense is rank, it smells to heaven;*
> *It hath the primal eldest curse upon't,*
> *A **brother's murder**...*
> *What if this cursèd hand*
> *Were thicker than itself with **brother's blood**?*
> *Is there not rain enough in the sweet heavens*

To wash it white as snow?
Hamlet, Act III Scene III

Hamlet, indicting himself forever with the misunderstood stain of indecision, chooses not to act, not to stab the king in the back, ostensibly because if he kills him while he's praying, he'll go to heaven. But he deserves to go to hell.

KING, rising
My words fly up, my thoughts remain below;
Words without thoughts never to heaven go.
Hamlet, Act III Scene III

Christ Forgives the Original GuiltSin: Hamlet Forgives Gertrude

The Master knows only too well how dishonesty forfeits divine aid and blocks self-forgiveness. In the subsequent scene with Gertrude, Hamlet confronts her with the truth hidden by the hallucination of good-and-evil, the serpent's poison. Hamlet forces her to look on the two images of God: the false one with whom she has become entwined, and the true image she has abandoned. This becomes a transformational moment of forgiveness and reconciliation between Hamlet and his fallen mother. In the play, it's uncertain whether Gertrude was culpable, but it is implied she was seduced and beguiled by Claudius — just as Eve was by the serpent. The account of the original GuiltSin in Genesis pays scant lip service to the appalling consequences that it is inflicting on all of us right now. Those who translate and interpret the text are also blinded by the very contagion it tells of. We think COVID-19 is a contagion; it's nothing compared to the pandemic of good-and-evil with which we are all infected from birth.

There is a cure though. It's called the Holy Grail: the true way to the true self.

Meanwhile, does this scene perhaps symbolise the remission of sins and forgiveness for all, including the divine feminine?

Once again, the murdered King Hamlet, as was Duncan, is given a eulogy befitting God Himself: he has Gertrude compare the image of God/ Adam, whom she betrayed, with the image of Satan with whom she had illicit intercourse.

HAMLET

Look here upon this picture and on this,
The counterfeit presentment of two brothers.
See what a grace was seated on this brow,
Hyperion's curls, the front of Jove himself,
An eye like Mars' to threaten and command,
A station like the herald Mercury
New-lighted on a heaven-kissing hill,
A combination and a form indeed
Where every god did seem to set his seal
To give the world assurance of a man.
This was your husband. Look you now what follows.
Hamlet, Act III Scene IV

And, in contrast, Hamlet shakes the venom out of his mother that deluded her into her unholy union with Claudius, the phoney, the meagre facsimile of the king, the pretender to the throne. First off, another allusion to the 'rankly abused ear':

HAMLET

*Here is your husband, like **a mildewed ear***
Blasting his wholesome brother. Have you eyes?
Could you on this fair mountain leave to feed
And batten on this moor? Ha! Have you eyes?
You cannot call it love, for at your age

The heyday in the blood is tame, it's humble
And waits upon the judgment; and what judgment
Would step from this to this? Sense sure you have,
Else could you not have motion; but sure that sense
Is apoplexed; for madness would not err,
Nor sense to ecstasy was ne'er so thralled,
But it reserved some quantity of choice
To serve in such a difference. What devil was 't
That thus hath cozened you at hoodman-blind?
Eyes without feeling, feeling without sight,
Ears without hands or eyes, smelling sans all,
Or but a sickly part of one true sense
Could not so mope. O shame, where is thy blush?
Hamlet, Act III Scene IV

This doesn't sound a lot like forgiveness and reconciliation. But that's tough love for you. It's reminiscent of the tirade of curses unleashed upon Adam and Eve in the Garden of Eden as they were banished. If Hamlet is standing in for Jesus, it's hard to imagine him inflicting such a tirade on his mother, Mary, nor anyone — except the money changers. But Mary Magdalene! She was reputed to have been a harlot or a loose woman. Some say it was Magdalene who, in John 8, was brought to Jesus by the scribes, caught in adultery and about to be stoned. Jesus swept aside the law and instead challenged the hypocrisy of the masses: he who is without guilt cast the first stone. Jesus did not judge her and seemed to command her to sin no more. Maybe it was Mary Magdalene who had to fulfil that aspect of scripture. And here, Hamlet shape-shifts to represent the scribes. Magdalene takes upon herself the original judgement, the curse, the foul reputation, and is forgiven by Jesus. Eve, go (for what you do is) sin no more!

So, Shakespeare's Gertrude is representing the 'fallen' Magdalene and, in turn, the gospel's Magdalene represents the Eve. Through the Magdalene, the betrayal of Eve was forgiven just like, through Judas, the betrayal of Adam was transmuted.

But it's even deeper. To fully understand, it's worth reading the whole chapter (John 8), where he says that those acts of theirs, so vilified, are no longer a sin. In that moment, he also transmuted the law itself. And in the face of his divine power, the people and the scribes who lust to enforce the law were vanquished.

How d'ya like them apples?

Jesus Is Taken Prisoner: Hamlet Is Arrested and Sent to England

For the benefit of the play on the surface, apart from the glorious ear of Pyrrhus being taken prisoner, the biblical motif of Jesus's being taken prisoner happens after the trial. Just after Hamlet makes peace with Gertrude, he discovers 'a rat' eavesdropping behind the arras. He runs him through with his sword. It turns out to be Polonius, Ophelia's snooping, scribe-like father. Maybe he thought it was Claudius, but that's just the outer play. Inwardly, following on directly from vanquishing the scribes accusing Magdalene, it's more likely the metaphoric killing of the power of the scribes. Claudius must wait for the poisoned chalice to get his 'even-handed justice'.

Could this accidental killing also be a dramatic device to (a) drive Ophelia over the edge into the mental breakdown that leads to her apparent suicide, and (b) get Hamlet taken prisoner and sent overseas to meet his death? Of course, it's Rosencrantz and Guildenstern (the two Jews) who, after much shenanigans from Hamlet, arrest him and, at Claudius' behest, take him overseas to England, ostensibly to escape some due process of the law for killing Polonius.

But this is part of Claudius's plot to rid himself of the Hamlet problem. He has given Rosencrantz and Guildenstern a sealed testament to be given to the English ambassador. Rather than a request for safe passage, it is Hamlet's death warrant. This is the biblical motif of Jesus's arrest in Gethsemane by

Caiaphas and his men. However, Hamlet, smelling a rat, reads the testament. It's a commandment from Claudius to have him executed immediately on arrival.

And here comes the most subtle allusion to the Grail truth, which does not become clear till the final scene. Hamlet changes the document. He transforms it into an apparent commandment from the usurping king, Claudius, to execute not him, but his captors, Rosencrantz and Guildenstern. Even-handed justice is served.

For the benefit of the drama in the outer play, Hamlet becomes incensed with the injustices of Claudius's rule and declares, 'O from this time forth, my thoughts be bloody, or be nothing worth!' Another reference to the blood. Again, it's all about the blood.

Invisibly, as massively significant as it is sublimely subtle, it is while Hamlet has an adventure and miraculous escape from death while crossing the waters that Ophelia is deemed to go mad and drown herself. Two watery deaths — one for Jesus the man, another for Jesus the Christ. Heave to for some wild cryptic clue cracking.

Jesus Walks upon the Waters: Hamlet and Ophelia Face Watery Deaths

If you think I've already been at the communion wine, here's where the symbolism really makes your head swim.

I've already postulated that one of the most common, alternative, poetic symbols for the Tree of Life throughout both the Bible and Shakespeare is a variation of one of the symbols Moses uses in Genesis and Jesus uses in Revelation: the water of life.

And the Spirit of God moved upon the face of the waters.
Genesis 1:2

We'll fathom this even more thoroughly in Part Three, *The Tempest,* but it's critically important now because, while Hamlet is fighting for his life at sea, Ophelia drowns in a brook in ambiguous, unusual circumstances. Hold that imagery.

The primal force of wind, water, rain, rivers, seas and brooks were effective, ubiquitous disguises for this, the most important mystical secret in all the scriptures. Moses parted the waters of the Red Sea with his staff. David, holding a staff, took five smooth stones from a brook to vanquish Goliath. Ophelia drowns in a brook. We'll soon see Prospero commanding the winds and waters — also with a staff. Remember, this information was forbidden in Shakespeare's day. Heresy. Sacrilege. Blasphemy. Nevertheless, it is secreted symbolically into poetic and mystical writings in possibly hundreds of different guises throughout all the major religions of the world — usually without even the priesthood knowing its crucial significance: *the symbol of the waters.*

Now, remain open to marvel at and enjoy how the mystery of the Master's exquisite mastery flows through the brook on which the nymph, Ophelia, 'moves upon the face of the waters' — just like the Spirit of God at the creation, and just as fulfilled by Jesus as he walked on the Sea of Galilee.

So, the events in the outer plot conspire to have Hamlet sent overseas to England. There, he will be executed by the English authorities based on orders from Claudius — in *a sealed testament* delivered by the two 'Jews', Rosencrantz and Guildenstern. However, he foils their plan, creates and seals a *new testament.* Rosencrantz and Guildenstern die in his stead, and Hamlet returns resurrected, as it were, to Denmark.

You'll see the profound significance of this subtle motif come to the fore in the final scene.

Given the pattern in his other plays (and all drama-employing mythic functions), we must be on red alert for Shakespeare's blink-and-you'll-miss-it, death-and-resurrection biblical motif. Did you blink? Did you miss it? Perhaps read it again.

To fulfil the law, there is always an ironic hoisting by one's own petard, based on the original irony of the Crucifixion's failed attempt to kill the Christ, where it was not the Christ that died but Satan's tyranny. The soul of man is made in the image of God, but the body of man is made in the image of Satan. Rosencrantz and Guildenstern (Scribes and Pharisees, the keepers of the law who attempted to murder the Christ) were themselves sentenced to death by the very letter they gave the English — a letter Hamlet had rewritten to have their executions seemingly ordered by the king.

Meanwhile, Ophelia appears to go totally mad (unless you recognise the spiritually transcendent revelations in her wild speeches), Claudius and Laertes get wind of Hamlet's 'miraculous' resurrection and post-resurrection appearance in Denmark, and they hatch a new plot to finish the job once and for all.

Their skulduggery is now interrupted by Gertrude, who has sad news: Ophelia has drowned. Suspending disbelief that anyone close enough to see her fall and hear her 'chanting old lauds' as she slowly floated to her muddy death would not have leapt to save her, here's Gertrude's account of her demise upon the waters. It is worth reading slowly and carefully.

QUEEN
One woe doth tread upon another's heel,
So fast they follow. Your sister's drowned, Laertes.

LAERTES
Drowned? O, where?

QUEEN
*There is a willow grows askant **the brook***
That shows his hoar leaves in the glassy stream.
Therewith fantastic garlands did she make
*Of crowflowers, nettles, daisies, and **long purples**,*

142

*That liberal **shepherds** give a grosser name,*
But our cold maids do "dead men's fingers" call them.
*There on the pendant boughs her **coronet weeds***
Clamb'ring to hang, an envious sliver broke,
When down her weedy trophies and herself
*Fell in the **weeping brook**. Her clothes spread wide,*
And mermaid-like awhile they bore her up,
*Which time she **chanted snatches of old lauds**,*
As one incapable of her own distress
*Or like a creature **native and endued***
Unto that element. But long it could not be
*Till that her garments, heavy with their **drink**,*
Pulled the poor wretch from her melodious lay
To muddy death.
Hamlet, Act IV Scene VII

This passage is awash with delightfully corroborating symbols, including crowflowers and shepherds (harking back to the opening scene that foreshadows everything). These speak to me as follows:

A willow grows askant the brook... There on the pendant boughs

I thought I was already pretty well attuned to the depths of crypticism of which the Master is capable, but this ultra-subtle montage of poetic images stretched my paradigm like a master baker making pizza dough. It's an image of Ophelia moving upon the face of the waters, combined with her being suspended by a bough (a cross?).

Setting aside the famous Millais painting, Shakespeare's description could also be depicted by this rough sketch.

Coronet weeds and long purples

A coronet is a crown. This evokes an image of the crown of thorns and the purple robe given to make mock of Jesus at his trial but in truth mocked his executioners.

She chanted snatches of old lauds

This evokes the chanting by initiates of the ancient sacred names of God that are said to transport the soul to the source of the Tree of Life in the Garden of Eden, the heart and kingdom of God.

If you look down on Ophelia's death and Hamlet's mythic 'resurrection' from a higher viewing point, you may see how, in the imagery, we have an explicit image of Ophelia in a precarious position on a tree 'above the waters' and, albeit in another scene occurring at the same time, a covert image of Hamlet also in a precarious position above the waters. Ophelia is poised precariously, overhanging a brook on a 'pendant' bough; Hamlet is also in a precarious position over the seas with Rosencrantz and Guildenstern. Although the names 'Rosencrantz and Guildenstern' are heraldic names associated with Elsinore, we've also seen how Shakespeare copiously creates (and adapts) funny-sounding, poignant names (NameAlchemy) to convey hidden intentions. Right here, the name Rosen-crantz would suggest *crown of thorns* (roses) as well as connecting us symbolically to the order of the Rosicrucians. As well as 'guile' in his name, **Guild**enstern is said to mean 'Morning Star', an allusion to Lucifer, also known as the son of the morning. It was Jesus's primary mission on earth to fulfil all the Mosaic laws and release Satan's stranglehold on the soul of man.

While Ophelia is falling and drowning (also with a crown of thorns, in this case coronet weeds upon her head), Hamlet is saving himself from certain death by leaping across the waters into a conveniently placed pirate vessel.

HAMLET
Ere we were two days
old at sea, a pirate of very warlike appointment gave
us chase. Finding ourselves too slow of sail, we put on
*a compelled valour, and in the **grapple** I boarded them.*
*On the instant, they got clear of our ship; so **I alone***
became their prisoner.
Hamlet, Act IV Scene VI

And so, we have another allusion to Jesus's being taken prisoner. I can also see this as another ultra-subtle biblical motif of Jesus's miracle of walking on water (prophesied in Daniel and seminal in Genesis) — where he also rescues Peter from drowning by lack of faith. He pulls Peter out of the waters, gets into the boat, and they are all immediately on dry land.

Before she meets her watery death, Ophelia is heard raving and chanting:

How should I your true love know
From another one?
*By his **cockle hat and staff***
*And his **sandal shoon.***
Hamlet, Act IV Scene V

A cockle hat is worn by a pilgrim (one on the journey to God), a staff is a ubiquitous symbol for the sacred Name of God and wearing sandals (sandal shoon) is often associated with Jesus. By adding:

*Then **up he rose**, and donned his clothes*

Ophelia again alludes to the Resurrection of Jesus.

Jesus Dies and Is Buried at Golgotha: Ophelia Dies and Is Buried at the Place of the Skull

Staying with this theme, things get even more delicious. When Hamlet arrives home in Denmark, just before he enters the gates of Elsinore, he comes upon a cemetery. A grave is being prepared. He doesn't realise it's for none other than his beloved Ophelia. She is being buried outside the city walls because it is presumed that she committed suicide. Why? Gertrude's description of her reported death says she seemed to fall from an overhanging bough.

Why suicide indeed? Surely, this is Shakespeare's two-pronged device for (a) introducing his clincher symbols of Ophelia's true role and purpose in the subtext and (b) a reminder of how Jesus brought Satan to book — by fulfilling the law.

Shakespeare's farcical scenes which seem to serve no great purpose to the plot save reducing the intensity of concentration needed to follow the poetry are often called 'comic relief'. Au contraire. This is where the cunning Master so often camouflages his deepest heresies, most audacious blasphemies and most subtle allusions. Here, he also brings in Adam, the one who lost the 'pearl of great price' in the beginning.

GRAVEDIGGER

*Ay, marry, is 't—**crowner's 'quest law**.*

OTHER

*Will you ha' the truth on 't? If this had not been
a gentlewoman, she should have been buried **out o'
Christian burial.***

GRAVEDIGGER

*Why, there thou sayst. And the more
pity that great folk should have count'nance in this*

world to drown or hang themselves more than
*their **even-Christian**. Come, my spade. There is no*
ancient gentlemen but gard'ners, ditchers, and
*grave-makers. They hold up **Adam's profession**.*
Hamlet, Act V Scene I

In the notes of the text, it is assumed that 'crowner's quest law' is some kind of malapropism for coroner's court. This makes sense, since it was ruled by the coroner that Ophelia had committed suicide. The two gravediggers (called 'clowns' to misdirect the uninitiated) are chewing over the moot point of law regarding whether or not she should be having a Christian burial. But, apart from another allusion to the crown of thorns, they're really having a dig at one of the key secrets of the Holy Grail: how Christian law is ironically still based on Mosaic law, the very law Jesus gave his life to end.

'Crowner's quest law', then, is more likely to be a dig at the law those questing to usurp the crown would have enforced. Talk about digging your own grave, Mr Shakespeare, had this been spotted in your day.

However, enter stage right the ultimate symbol that confirms we really have been barking up the right tree all along. Ophelia was found 'guilty' of suicide by the crowner's court (yes, he has slipped in under the radar another allusion to the trial of Jesus and the crown of thorns). This is why she has to be buried outside the city walls. Why on earth? Because that's where Jesus was crucified and buried — outside the walls of Jerusalem. What was that place called? And what does Hamlet find in the grave being dug for her?

Skulls! Loads of skulls! Ophelia's grave is full of skulls!

Could the most iconic scene in all of Shakespeare be where Hamlet has the last laugh on the orthodoxy? Could the skull of his beloved jester Yorick be no less than an allusion to where Jesus was crucified and buried, outside the city walls? And where, exactly, was that? Golgotha/Calvary, the Aramaic/Latin word for 'skull', so called possibly because it is the skull-shaped hill of execution where Jesus was buried, now the site of the Church of the Holy Sepulchre — or maybe the Garden Tomb.

> *And when they were come unto a place called Golgotha,*
> *that is to say, **a place of a skull***...*they crucified him.*
> Matthew 27:33

The Cup of the Last Supper: The Poisoned Chalice

When Jesus (metaphorically) drank from the cup his father prepared for him, it was Satan who was poisoned. At this point in the play, Shakespeare now has a metaphorical Mephistopheles (Claudius) drink from the poisoned cup he prepared for the Christ (Hamlet). Keep your eye on the following pearl of wisdom:

> *Again, the kingdom of heaven is like a merchant seeking*
> *goodly pearls: Who, when he had found one **pearl of great***
> ***price**, went and sold all that he had, and bought it.*
> Matthew 13:45-47

Back to the Outer Play

When Laertes arrives home in Elsinore, he is in a rage. Not only has his father been killed by Hamlet, but Hamlet's cruel rejection and dishonouring of his sister, Ophelia, has combined to drive her to suicide. He's hot for Hamlet's blood — preferably dripping off his sword. He is easy meat for Claudius's cunning, and Claudius, his original plot to have Rosencrantz and Guildenstern dispatch Hamlet to his execution having been foiled, now enrols Laertes and his poisoned foil as his would-be assassin.

Double Poison, Please!

Enter 'Macbeth's' poisoned chalice.

Laertes and Claudius now conspire to beguile Hamlet into a fencing duel with Laertes. (Biblical motif alert: Satan enters Judas.) Only this is to be far from a fair fight. They have skulduggery in mind, with *three ways* for Laertes to ensure Hamlet dies: the tip of Laertes's blade will not be blunt as for sport, but sharp (as for piercing the body of Christ); the tip will also be dipped in a poison so deadly that even a mere scratch caused by a slight touch (or 'kiss') will be enough to kill; and, as a sure-fire backup plan, Claudius prepares a poisoned chalice of wine for Hamlet to drink when he gets hot and thirsty. This is yet another biblical motif of the holy sponge dipped in vinegar that Jesus refused to drink on the cross.

Let's realign ourselves with our intent and purpose: to nail the Grail. Claudius now brings to the party a chalice of wine. What have we already learnt about the Master, goblets of wine and the anagogical symbols in *Macbeth*? Remember, Macbeth also murdered his king and usurped his crown, and, as he was contemplating the murder, we got some insights not readily apparent in the Claudius perspective on the same crime against humanity.

MACBETH

If 'twere done when 'tis done, then 'twere well
It were done quickly.
Macbeth, Act I Scene VII

Remember, this line is an allusion to Jesus's words in Revelation, foreshadowed in his words to Judas at the Last Supper as he hands him the sop of bread dipped in wine — symbolically the *union* of the body/Word made flesh with the blood of the New Testament. This also foreshadows the fleeting scene where Banquo hands Macbeth a diamond (the symbol of the Holy Grail) just before Macbeth betrays and murders the king.

MACBETH
This even-handed justice
Commends th' ingredients of our poisoned chalice
To our own lips.

This line now introduces the ideas that the ingredients of the Grail chalice
are poison to him (Satan) and that justice will be served to him by his own
hand. It is followed by:

MACBETH
I have no spur
To prick the sides of my intent, but only
Vaulting ambition, *which o'erleaps itself*
And falls on th' other—

This following piece of Claudius's confession, just after *The Mousetrap*,
confirms him as a fellow archetype of Satan, driven by the same motivation
of vaulting ambition:

CLAUDIUS
Forgive me my foul murder?
That cannot be, since I am still possessed
Of those effects for which I did the murder:
*My crown, mine own **ambition**, and my queen.*
Hamlet, Act III Scene III

After his murder of Duncan, Macbeth clarifies that what he really killed
was the deity and begins his lamentations on the dire consequence: the cutting
off of 'the wine of life' (the Tree of Life, sound of Day, ear of man, etc.).

MACBETH
Renown and grace is dead.
The wine of life is drawn...
...The spring, the head, the fountain of your (royal) blood
Is stopped; the very source of it is stopped.
Macbeth, Act II Scene III

In *Hamlet,* the divinity of the murdered king and the devastating impact on all humanity of his crown being usurped by Satan is explored extensively but in a very different way. As we've seen, both plays explore the same spiritual event but from uniquely different perspectives: *Macbeth* through the eyes of Satan, *Hamlet* through the eyes of the Christ. Now Claudius, with this small but perfectly hidden clincher scene, welds the underlay of the plays together as two sides of the same coin.

Perhaps also intended as a veiled reference to Judgement Day, 'now the King drinks to Hamlet. Come, begin. And you, the judges, bear a wary eye,' Claudius plays MC to the rivals and has jugs of wine brought to the table (of the Last Supper), saying:

The King shall drink to Hamlet's better breath,
And in the cup an union shall he throw,
*Richer than that which **four successive kings***
In Denmark's crown have worn.
Hamlet, Act V Scene II

An union? An union!

In contrast to Banquo's fleetingly subtle diamond handed to the traitor, this critical biblical motif of the Grail has an aspect of the bizarre, the surreal, something almost divinely absurd about it. Claudius is alluding to the sop of Judas: the symbol of the union of the body and the blood of Christ, and

151

somehow it is traditionally assumed to be a *pearl of great price*. Let's drop a depth charge on the whole scene and see what floats to the surface.

In Shakespeare's time, 'union' was the name for an exceptionally large, rare pearl. Something unique. Yet here, in the finale to *Hamlet,* we have Claudius dipping a 'union' in poison and dropping it into the cup at the table. Why? Why poison someone with a priceless jewel? Are they going to swallow it and choke to death or what? Taken literally, it is totally ridiculous. But it is the Master's masterstroke of genius. In his inimitable way, through the sheer incongruity, he is shining a powerful, invisible spotlight on this minute gesture.

It's not that the union is poisoned — the union *is* the poison. *The poison is the union.* Stop and contemplate this. It is unutterably sublime. Again, Shakespeare is screaming at us in the silence between the lines that the union (of bread and wine, body and blood, sound and light) is poison. Not to us, but to Satan. In having Satan poison himself, God brings eternal life back to man.

This scene is the mirror image of Jesus dipping the bread into the wine and passing the sop to Judas, whereupon Satan enters Jesus to be vanquished on the cross. Only this time, perversely, it is the serpent, Claudius, who plays the host and gives the toast. Remember the foreshadowing by Macbeth: 'this even-handed justice commends th'ingredients of the poisoned chalice to my own lips'? And this is exactly what is about to happen.

Again, poetic justice is an essential ingredient: to fulfil the law, Satan can only be brought down by his own hand. Only two of the archetypes drink the poisoned wine: first Gertrude, the fallen Eve, now forgiven and reconciled with Hamlet. In the first scene, the ghost foreshadows some ironic fate: she too must die by her own hand.

GHOST
Taint not thy mind, nor let thy soul contrive
Against thy mother aught. Leave her to heaven
And to those thorns that in her bosom lodge

To prick and sting her.
Hamlet, Act I Scene V

Just as Jesus refused the holy sponge on the cross, Hamlet refuses to drink the beverage offered by Claudius. Perhaps reconciled not only with her son, but also to her own fate, Gertrude (as did Eve in the beginning) disobeys Claudius's commandment not to drink. She takes the poisoned chalice to toast him, drinks and soon dies. *Thou shalt surely die.* Yes, it's so hard to keep up with this flood of biblical motifs going right back to Eden.

The 'Poisoned' Kiss of Judas: The Poisoned Tip of Laertes's Foil

Just as Judas betrays Jesus with a metaphorically 'poisoned' kiss, Laertes now betrays Hamlet with a 'kiss' of his poisoned sword. The text itself is vague about specifically how things pan out — it's up to the director. Traditionally, this is how Laertes now acts out what must surely be the symbolic kiss of Judas. Another meaning of 'kiss' is any slight touch or contact, not necessarily with the lips — as with, say, billiard balls kissing. Thus, in an unfair strike, while Hamlet's back is turned, he 'kisses' Hamlet with his sharp, poisoned blade. Like Judas's kiss of Jesus, this betrayal of trust and honour ensures Hamlet's imminent death. However, in a scuffle, their swords get swapped, Hamlet scores another hit, draws blood and hoists Laertes with his own woodcock trap.

LAERTES
Why as a woodcock to mine own springe, Osric
I am justly killed with mine own treachery.
Hamlet, Act V Scene II

The queen now falls to the poison, and the dying Laertes confesses and rightly accuses the king of the treachery. Hamlet first pierces Claudius's flesh with the envenomed foil ('then venom do thy work') and, before having a moment of forgiveness with Laertes (Judas), forces Claudius to drink from the poisoned chalice of poetic justice while reminding him that it is his original unholy *union* with Eve that is come upon him. Again, we're reminded that it is the union of the bread and the wine — the body and the blood, the Word made flesh — with the seal of the New Testament that unseals the Old that ends Satan's tyranny.

HAMLET

Here, thou incestuous, murd'rous, damnèd Dane,
Drink off this potion. Is thy **union** *here?*
Follow my mother.
Hamlet, Act V Scene II

The Great Commission: The Dying Hamlet Charges Horatio with Telling the World His Story

At the very end of Matthew's Gospel, at a post-resurrection appearance, Jesus commissions the apostles to go forth and tell the world the 'good news'. As Hamlet himself draws his dying breath, he charges his 'apostle' Horatio to tell his story.

HAMLET

If thou didst ever hold me in thy heart,
Absent thee from felicity awhile
And in this harsh world draw thy breath in pain
To tell my story.
Hamlet, Act V Scene II

All power is given unto me in heaven and in earth. Go ye therefore,
and teach all nations, baptizing them in the name of the Father,
and of the Son, and of the Holy Ghost: Teaching them to observe

all things whatsoever I have commanded you: and, lo, I am
with you always, even unto the end of the world. Amen.
Matthew 28:18-20

But the Master can't resist letting Hamlet fade out before giving him another pun: 'The potent poison quite o'ercrows my spirit.' It is a pun reprising the cock's crow at the beginning of the play and which completes the circle at this the very final scene. The opening scene has indeed foreshadowed it all. And, as he dies, Hamlet utters the sound and name of Fortinbras — 'He has my dying voice' — the sound and name of God that draws the soul home to the Godhead.

HAMLET
O, I die, Horatio!
The potent poison quite **o'ercrows** *my spirit.*

Horatio confirms that there is much more to all this than meets the human eye.

HORATIO
And let me speak to th' yet unknowing world
How these things came about.
Hamlet, Act V Scene II

The Coming of the Comforter: Fortinbras Is Crowned King of Denmark

Whirring away in the background, while our story is unfolding, young Fortinbras has overcome the forces of Denmark, has resumed the crown and gets Hamlet's dying blessing.

HAMLET
I cannot live to hear the news from England.
But I do prophesy th' election lights
On Fortinbras; he has my dying voice.
Hamlet, Act V Scene II

So, who is this mythical, mystical war hero, this spurious King of Norway who conquered Denmark while Ophelia ascended into Heaven on the sound current and Hamlet died and resurrected?

The thing about how the Master conveys his deeper purpose is that it is anything but logical and straightforward. He'll put the most beautiful spiritual wisdoms into the mouths of the foulest liars. He'll conjure a weird, prating fool to voice a critical biblical allusion. Knowing this, I scoured the final scene, where the young Fortinbras appears to assume the crown of Denmark. I was hoping to find something specific, something perhaps about awakening the god of day.

Let's look again at what Claudius said when he raised the chalice in toast and drank to Hamlet's imminent demise.

And let the kettle to the trumpet speak,
The trumpet to the cannoneer without,
The cannons to the heavens, the heaven to earth.

Could this be referring to the mystical sounds heard in the Spirit worlds, many of which were reported by John in Revelation? The kettle is a drum that sounds like thunder, and the trumpet is a sound used in Revelation to describe the voice of Jesus Christ in the God form. Both are frequently used descriptions of the music of the spheres, the celestial sounds of the soul that were cut off and now restored.

I was in the Spirit on the Lord's day, and heard behind me a great voice, as of a **trumpet**, Saying, I am Alpha and Omega, the first and the last: and, what thou seest, write in a book, and send it unto the seven churches.

Revelation 1

Listen to his further description of the divine being John met. Allusions to the sound 'brass' and the familiar sound of the waters of life.

> *His head and his hairs were white like wool, as white as snow; and his eyes were as a flame of fire; And his feet like unto fine **brass**, as if they burned in a furnace; and his voice as the **sound of many waters**.*
> Revelation 1:14-16

I still had the name Fortinbras ringing in my ears. Then this passage from Paul floated past:

> *Though I speak with the tongues of men and of angels, and have not charity, I am become as **sounding brass, or a tinkling cymbal**.*
> 1 Corinthians 13:1

It reminded me of Claudius's disingenuous toast; I could almost hear the Master chuckling. Fortinbras is surely one of his funny-sounding names. It is none other than Fortinbras, hovering in the background from Scene I and now the new rightful King of Denmark, whose name is as musical as 'sounding brass and tinkling cymbal'. And even Paul, not notorious for his sense of humour, drops in a pun of his own to awaken the snoozing reader. 'Cymbal' is a pun for 'symbol', and the whole piece is a symbol for the sound of God's name.

So, what, or who, is Fortinbras?

Still Hunting That Name

Our conclusion of Part One, *Macbeth,* was that, having set off on our Grail quest and found the sang graal (royal blood of Christ) splattered liberally throughout the play, we now needed to look for the name, because '[The name] is the way, the truth, and the life. No one enters the father but by [the name].' Now we find that, in the finale of *Hamlet,* the rightful king has the 'funny name' Fortinbras. Here is NameAlchemy that has resonances with the sacred name of God alluded to in Revelation. Is this related to the sound and name of God known as the Tree of Life and the Word? Is this what the ancient mystics call the sound current and what Jesus calls the wind from heaven?

Are we now zeroing in on the last piece of the puzzle that reveals the crucial key to the bliss, joy and Ananda all of us are really seeking: the Holy Grail?

Tragedy or Not Tragedy?

Apart from the very final scene after their deaths, *Hamlet* is far from being a tragedy. In symbols very well disguised, like the other plays, it tells a version of the story of how, in the beginning, the true Name and sound of God (symbolised as Day in Genesis) was usurped and overshadowed by the false Name (symbolised as Night in Genesis). After a long succession of Christs (kings) attempting to vanquish Night, victory came through the courage and sacrifice of the man known as Jesus the Christ. He 'o'ercrowed' Night — he literally supplanted the false Name with the true Name as it was in the beginning and restored the true Name and sound of God, Day, to the throne. It is a name that sounds at times like tinkling brass cymbals — in other words, Fortinbras.

In this final scene, again, the Master emphasises the sounds heard as Fortinbras enters.

> *Young **Fortinbras**, with conquest come from Poland,*
> *To th' ambassadors of England gives*
> *This warlike **volley**.*
> *Hamlet,* Act V Scene II

The king of Norway's name, Fortinbras, is a symbol, even a cymbal, of the hallowed name of God — the sound current, the wind of God. And where in the Bible do we hear of a mighty wind? In the upper room, at Pentecost.

> *And suddenly there came a sound from heaven*
> *as of a **rushing mighty wind**, and it filled all*
> *the house where they were sitting.*
> Acts 2:2

I'd like you to consider that what Jesus promised would be 'the Comforter' is the sound of God reunited with the light of God to form the Holy Spirit (whole Spirit). This is indicated at Pentecost in the upper room, when the disciples were of one accord at 'the sound of a rushing mighty wind.' It is another way of saying the sound of God's hallowed name was restored to the inner ear of man and with it the comfort of knowing we are divine ('comfort' is hardly the word I would choose for ecstatic joy and fulfilment).

The Revelation of Christ, IT IS DONE: Rosencrantz and Guildenstern Are Dead

In the introduction to *Hamlet,* I postulated that the Jewish-sounding names Rosencrantz and Guildenstern are code for the Sanhedrin, the enforcers of the Mosaic Law. This is the law the Jews violate at their peril, the law that to this day underpins many of the laws and moral values of the Western world. The corollary of this is that, if Rosencrantz and Guildenstern are dead, the Mosaic law is also dead. Christ's true mission on this earth was to 'fulfil the law'. This means to fulfil the scripture that keeps the covenant of the Law sealed and in force. It means to abrogate, abjure, terminate, complete, finish, 'end the heartache and the thousand natural shocks' this cruel law inflicts on us. It is through twisting the spirit of this fine, ancient law that Satan gets his power over mankind. God *is* forgiveness. God *is* the state of being that *is* forgiveness. God does not judge — it is not in God's nature. Nor does God punish. It is man who punishes. It is man's ego that fabricates a concept of God that is wrathful and punitive. Judgement is the state of not-being that is the lower consciousness, the ego-consciousness, the consciousness of good-and-evil that the Christ came to free us from.

The thing about the absolute forgiveness of God already being given is that it is requires no belief; it is empirically verifiable. How? By forgiving ourselves. When we forgive ourselves, we feel the release of pain and the flood of Ananda, the spiritual bliss, permeating our consciousness.

Before we complete our Grail quest, I want to underline that everything we have so far uncovered, decoded, demystified is already hidden in the King James Bible. I have deliberately not looked into the Apocrypha, or the Kabbalah, or any of the other sacred texts for evidence or corroboration. To me, the KJV is enough. Shakespeare may have created extraordinary drama out of it, but only because his viewing point is not shrouded and clouded by the paradigm imposed on us by the terrifying rules and laws surrounding the narrative.

I myself was brought up as a Christian in the Church of England school system. Only in my teens did I find the courage to challenge the faith force-fed to me. I remember the very moment clearly. An older boy was talking to us in such a way to imply he did not believe in God at all. I expected him to be struck down by lightning — or worse. But he was okay. I realised I too did not have to believe in God any longer; and thenceforth I proudly declared myself an atheist. As a very troubled young man in my early thirties, I reopened my mind to alternative 'spiritual possibilities'. I once again felt shocked to hear various teachers talking about Jesus Christ and the Bible in a very different way from that of my upbringing. It took years to erase the old programming of the narrative to allow myself to accept different interpretations, interpretations that not only made much more sense but released invisible burdens of guilt and fear.

It is done! *I am Alpha and Omega, the beginning and the end. I will give unto him that is athirst of the fountain of the water of life freely.*
Revelation 21:6

The above verse from the notoriously inscrutable Revelation makes absolute sense to me. I read it as the blessing of the Holy Grail: *It is done!* [My mission on earth is finished.] *I am the alpha and the omega, the beginning and the end.* [The Name, the Word, the Sound of God, the Christ began the creation, and it is now complete.] *I will give unto him that is athirst of the fountain of the water of life freely.* [I will give freely and unconditionally the keys to the Kingdom of God to all who are ready and who ask.]

The aphorism/mantra I have come across in my mystical travels expresses this perfectly: Baruch Bashan — the blessings already are. That's what this is about. It's all sorted. It's all perfect right now. And it's in the now, not in the mind, not in time and space, but in the present moment, that we know this and experience it.

The Real Tragedy of Hamlet

What's the tragedy of *Hamlet?* A son gives up his own life to avenge his father's murder most foul. He succeeds. This is the tragedy?

The tragedy is not in the outer play. It is not the pile of dead bodies on the stage at the end. The tragedy is that the blessing of absolute, unconditional forgiveness given by God to all mankind through the Christ, through the Word of God, called the New Testament, was sealed but not heard. The blessing was not heard, not understood and not passed on to us, the people.

Jesus took out the sins from the law. The church, for a multitude of reasons, put them back in. It's not true that anyone has to do anything to be forgiven by God. As it says in *Macbeth:* to be free from guilt therein, we must forgive ourselves. It's a whole lot easier said than done, but at least it's a valid starting point.

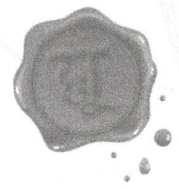

Chapter 7:

THE LOST SECRET OF
THE HOLY GRAIL

When Fortinbras enters Elsinore to reclaim his rightful crown, his retinue includes the ambassador from England, the one to whom Rosencrantz and Guildenstern were charged to give the sealed warrant for Hamlet's immediate execution.

The ambassador gazes in dismay at the carnage before him. He gestures towards the still-warm corpse of Claudius, the king, and utters the fateful, cunningly hidden clue:

AMBASSADOR
The ears are senseless that should give us hearing
To tell him his commandment is fulfilled,
Rosencrantz and Guildenstern are dead.
Hamlet, Act V Scene II

It would be so easy to pass over this line with a shrug saying, yes, they too got their comeuppance. More hoisting of the well-worn petard.

But not so fast. There is a priceless gem here for the grasping. In the inner play, Hamlet is the Christ and Claudius is the serpent, Satan. Remember how Hamlet went to great lengths to tell Horatio how he had found the sealed commandment from Claudius (Satan) with instructions to execute him (Christ) on arrival in England? This commandment of Satan's was to be delivered by Rosencrantz and Guildenstern (the Sanhedrin, the enforcers of the Old Testament law). They were to give Satan's sealed commandment, or testament, to the English ambassador. But on discovering it was his own death warrant, Hamlet changed the commandment so that it decreed Rosencrantz and Guildenstern should be executed in his stead. The seal Hamlet (Christ) used for the New Testament was 'heaven ordinant' — in other words, ordained by God. When he hatched this plan on board the ship, having discovered Claudius's assassination plot, he declared: 'My thoughts be bloody or be nothing worth!' This sounds like the Christ has actually lost the plot, but no. It's human drama on the surface, but it's biblical motif beneath: it's an allusion, a foreshadowing also, of the blood seal of the New Testament.

A testament is a covenant between man and God that, to be binding, must be sealed in blood. The Old Testament was sealed by the blood of circumcision; the New Testament was sealed by the blood of Christ, symbolised at the Last Supper by the wine in the cup. The wine of life is the blood of Christ that was shed for all for the remission of sins: the *sang real* that morphed into the *sang graal* that morphed into the Holy Grail. Thus, the myth, by focusing attention on the lost chalice (a mere holy relic), slid under the radar and censure of the Inquisition and kept alive the essence of the legend. This was the blood seal of the New Testament: the blessing of absolute absolution to all mankind and the abolition of all sin (and the psychic blackmail it inflicts) from the world.

But 'the ears are senseless that should give it hearing.' None of those in power or who lust for control over others' lives want to hear this. It puts them out of business for good. Sin, misery and the physical and psychological agony and suffering they cause is the biggest business on the entire planet. If you imagine a world without pain, guilt, anger, stress, hatred and war, you have to imagine a world where all the myriad ways we enjoy and profit from numbing out that pain are no longer needed. Is this paradise? Or is it hell? It sounds boring as hell to my ego-personality, because, like most ordinary humans, I'm still a slave to so many of my earthly salves.

As we've been saying all along, although it seemed like Jesus died on the cross, it was in fact Satan's tyranny, the law he used to enforce his will, that really died.

HORATIO

How was this [the New commandment] sealed?

HAMLET

*Why, even in that was **heaven ordinant**.*
*I had **my father's signet** in my purse,*
Which was the model of that Danish seal;
Folded the writ up in the form of th' other,
Subscribed it, gave 't th' impression, placed it
safely, the changeling never known.
Hamlet, Act V Scene II

Thus, the New Commandment — the New Testament — was fulfilled, and the Old Testament (the Mosaic law represented by Rosencrantz and Guildenstern) is now dead.

The Holy Grail is the priceless gift of freedom from the tyranny of good-and-evil that all mankind received when Jesus shed his blood and sealed the New Testament. The end of the 'heartache and the thousand natural shocks that flesh is heir to' is already here, now. *The kingdom of heaven is at hand.*

The blessings already are, right here inside us. Salvation is present for all. It is done! There's nothing to wait for. Armageddon is ongoing. It's the inner battle between the Christ consciousness and the Satan consciousness that Jesus won and we must continue in our own way.

So why do we not feel that freedom? Why do we not know the joy of liberating the soul? Because not only did they not tell us at Nicaea, but they made the very knowledge of it a crime. To live your own life became a capital offence, and this is still the 'normal' human condition. This is what Shakespeare is railing about in the subtext of all his works. But let's not blame the events in the past. The question is: How can we transcend the past and the future and come into the present? Not the present on the daily planner, but the present outside time and space, as the Buddha said, the 'no time' that exists between nerve impulses? What Eckart Tolle calls 'the power of now'. There are new things to learn and much work to do. And to do the work, we must first be ready. Are you ready?

The New Testament is intended to be a total replacement of the Old Testament, but very few have heard that said — especially in the mainstream. Maybe this is shifting, but in Shakespeare's day, the vast majority believed that the Old Testament laws that Jesus abjured, that Jesus sacrificed himself to annul, were still in force. But they are not. We can choose to be bound by them if that's our destiny, but they are not the laws of God through the Christ. For whatever reason, when the bishops at Nicaea voted, they voted out Jesus — and voted back in Moses!

They built the new religion on top of the old, dead laws, which is why something is rotten in the state of Denmark and in the state of mankind. The Old Testament is a beautiful, historic document, full of truth and wisdom. But it belongs in a museum, not at the heart of human governance. As Gandhi famously said, 'An eye for an eye makes everyone blind.' The Old law is no longer God's law. It is as defunct as Monty Python's dead parrot. The Old, defunct law still forms the basis for many of our earthly laws, the laws of the land, and the bigotry, harshness and unfairness of many of these defunct moral edicts are in a long-term process of reform. Look at the stigma of homosexuality, or the sexual discrimination against women. This gradual reform is to be expected as the soul energy awakens and seeps more and more into the consciousness of mankind.

This does not give us carte blanche to get away with murder. We have free choice. Everything we do is sanctioned by God — or He would not be God. And everything we do, we are responsible for. The higher law, merely mimicked by the Mosaic Law, is the law that holds us accountable throughout time: what we sow, we reap. As we judge, we are judged. Where the Mosaic law allowed man to exact revenge, this is no longer kosher. Each of us is accountable spiritually to our own soul. In earthly, physical terms, this comes down to the prevailing law of the land. But as far as our soul is concerned, that's nobody's business but ours — we are free. And the price of freedom is discipline and vigilance.

Does humanity and the planet still have time for slow, natural seepage? Do we perhaps need to accelerate the increase in positive, loving, forgiving vibration that follows enhanced soul-self-awareness?

The Ears Are Senseless

Shakespeare seems to be telling us that although 'gospel' means 'good news', the good news of the gospels has been turned to bad. The forbidden secret that became known as the Holy Grail was withheld from the mass of the populace. Instead, the new religion called Christianity was not based on the action, teachings and promise of God through the Christ, but on the now invalid, null and void laws of Moses. In the outer world, nothing has changed. Only deep within the psyche of man does a new potential exist. A treasure, a free gift available for all mankind for the asking — regardless of race, creed, colour, situation, circumstance and sexual orientation.

What does it mean that 'the ears are senseless'? If there is a supreme being, a higher intelligence we call 'God', why would it go to all the trouble of liberating us from satanic bondage just to have it go unheard or ignored?

In Revelation, it is said, 'It is done.' Perhaps our mission on earth is to reclaim for our individual soul what Jesus did for all souls. The Christ action is done. Now, it's up to us to reclaim the original Ananda for ourselves.

But how do we do this?

Let's ask Prospero.

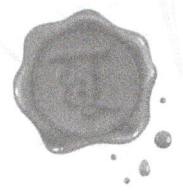

Part Three:

THE TEMPEST: SHAKESPEARE'S REVELATION

*And suddenly there came a sound from heaven as of a **rushing mighty wind**, and it filled all the house where they were sitting.*

Acts 2:2

The Tempest is oft considered a mystery play. It was also probably Shakespeare's last. Is The Tempest Shakespeare's denouement? Is this where all is explained, all the suspects and their respective red herrings miraculously drawn together in the drawing room to be told whodunnit? Will Prospero gather together all the players and either confirm our numerous radical hypotheses or cast them into the oubliette along with his books and staff?

If so, a question remains. Why, although it was possibly his final play, is The Tempest placed first in the folio? Is it his denouement or his foreshadowing? I invite you to consider that, in the subtext, *all* the plays come under the umbrella title of The Mystery of the Holy Grail. And, by placing this mystery play first in the folio, Shakespeare is telling us in his uniquely cryptic way that The Tempest is the umbrella title he has chosen for all the plays.

But why?

Remember, in the mind's eye, the truth looks false and the false looks true. If Shakespeare's code is true, it will run counter to what we are conditioned by society to believe is gospel truth. But the truth is not designed for the mind. Truth is anathema to the mind, because it does not make logical sense. The truth resonates with our inner, natural knowing and often, paradoxically, if something makes sense, it ceases to be true.

The Divine Heresies

Let's have a brief recap on some of the key heresies of the subtext, the underground thread running through all the plays and also the scripture.

- Original Sin means the Tree of Life was cut off.
- We could no longer hear the sound current.

- We lost the state of spiritual bliss: Ananda.
- We no longer had access to paradise; we were banished.
- By shedding His blood, the *sang graal*, Jesus the Christ sealed the New Testament promise of absolute, unconditional forgiveness for all.
- He unsealed the Old Testament law.
- He ended the ancient abuse of sin.
- He reopened the way to the Tree of Life (paradise).
- He released the sound current.
- He reunited the sound of God with the light of God to form the Holy (whole) Spirit.
- Contrary to orthodox dogma, *it is done*! Grace is already available right here, right now — if we claim it.

We've already seen many aspects of this subtext expressed and confirmed in *Macbeth* and *Hamlet*. We've also seen how Shakespeare uses NameAlchemy (wordsmithery, puns, anagrams, homonyms, synonyms, etc.) to imbue significant hidden meanings. It's also becoming clear that the entire text of his plays is taken from scripture. In the same way a rabbit might look like a rabbit but is also a duck, the key characters in all his plays seem to be characterisations of the three core, polar-opposite archetypes that make up human consciousness. Will the denouement confirm or deny:

God-Satan
Adam-Eve
Cain-Abel?

It is my personal opinion that his finale, *The Tempest,* is named after one of the ways Jesus spoke about the Tree of Life.

*The wind bloweth where it listeth, and thou hearest the
sound thereof, but canst not tell whence it cometh, and
whither it goeth: so is every one that is born of the Spirit.*
John 3:8

The sound current, which was cut off from the light of God in the Garden of Eden, is the wind from heaven. It is alluded to in all the plays, and *The Tempest*, Shakespeare's final play, was placed at the head of the folio. All the other plays come under the umbrella of this one play. It seems to explain, validate and corroborate all the assumptions and hypotheses we've already been exploring.

It's not my job to convince you. I cannot prove it to you. I don't want you to believe me. I am simply going to lay out the evidence as I see it so you can decide for yourself.

Chapter 8:

THE OUTER AND
INNER TEMPESTS

The Outer Play

A story of shipwreck, magic, revenge and forgiveness, *The Tempest* begins with a ship caught in a violent storm. On a nearby island, the exiled Duke of Milan, Prospero, tells his daughter, Miranda, that he has caused the storm with his magical powers. Prospero had been banished twelve years earlier, when his brother, Antonio, conspired with Alonso, King of Naples, to depose and banish him. Prospero and Miranda are served by a spirit named Ariel and by Caliban, son of the island's previous inhabitant, the witch Sycorax.

On the island, survivors of the wreck appear. First is Alonso's son, Ferdinand, who is drawn by strange music to find Miranda. They immediately fall in love. Prospero secretly approves of their love but tests the pair by enslaving Ferdinand. After secretly watching Miranda and Ferdinand exchange vows, Prospero releases Ferdinand and consents to their marriage.

Other lost souls who appear are Trinculo and Stephano, Alonso's jester and butler, who join forces with Caliban to kill Prospero and take over the island. The king, his retinue and Prospero's brother search for Ferdinand and are confronted with a spectacle including a Harpy, who convinces Alonso that Ferdinand's death is retribution for Prospero's exile.

Having his enemies under his control, Prospero decides to forgive them all unconditionally. Alonso is reunited with his son, restores Prospero's dukedom of Milan and welcomes Miranda as Ferdinand's wife. As all except Caliban and Ariel prepare to leave the island, Prospero, who has given up his magic, bids farewell to the island and the audience.

The Inner Play

We are the flute, our music is all Thine;
We are the mountains echoing only Thee;
And movest to defeat or victory;
Lions emblazoned high on flags unfurled-
Thy wind invisible sweeps us through the world.

Rumi

Once again, the inner play requires suspension of disbelief — and also belief of any kind. Having got this far, your mind should be accustomed to radical paradigm shifts. You ain't seen nothing yet.

Consider that the inner play is a divinely heretical biblical account of the evolution of the soul of all humanity — from our birth in Genesis, through the gospels, all the way to our enlightenment in Revelation. It is the whole story of who we really are, why we're here and how we fulfil our ultimate destiny — the whole story from the creation, the fall, the liberation and end time of this planetary dispensation.

As we weave our way through Part Three, I hope to show you how the sound current is the sacred thread that ties all humanity — and all the works — together as one.

This is far from a new idea. Plato wrote that the cosmos was constructed according to musical intervals and proportions. Pythagoras called it 'Music of the Spheres' (quoted as such by Shakespeare in *Twelfth Night*) and believed that it fills our inner ears and we are constantly in contact with it from the moment of our birth.

Another Greek philosopher, Heraclitus, called it 'Logos' (divine word or sound). Some Native American traditions call it 'Song of the Creator', while the Bible calls it 'The Word', the Tree of Life, the 'Voice of Many Waters', Jacob's Ladder, and a host of other symbols.

Three of the core strands with which the Master has woven his wonder are the biblical motifs, NameAlchemy and sound current allusions.

A Brief Recap

If we trust Shakespeare's spiritual mastership, he is implying that knowledge of the authentic, available-to-all, life-transforming, *already-given* blessings of Jesus were:

- cut out of church doctrine and all explicit writings;
- replaced by false narrative;
- discredited, devalued and condemned as heresy; and
- declared a heinous crime punishable by torture and death.

If so, Shakespeare is also telling us these forbidden truths are not going to die. They are:

- still intact — kept hidden, encoded in the Bible;
- retold as the legend of the Holy Grail;
- reimagined in the subtext of all his plays; and
- taught and practised in secret by those in the line of ancient masters across the globe, throughout the ages to this day.

What Is the Holy Grail: Chalice, Bloodline or Blood seal?

Although the wrong question with which to begin our quest, it is now the big question we need to ask to validate our discoveries. We must see if Prospero confirms or denies everything. So far, Shakespeare is certainly implying the Holy Grail is the ingredients rather than the chalice itself. It is the ingredients that 'poison' Satan and fulfil the Christ action. The main ingredient would be the blood, symbolised at the Last Supper as the wine. The royal blood is also cited as the Grail in the bestselling *The Holy Blood and the Holy Grail* by Baigent, Leigh and Lincoln. The *sang graal* was also the MacGuffin in Dan Brown's fictional blockbuster *The Da Vinci Code*.

However, unlike the three amigos, Shakespeare does not so much speculate but indicate. He is always faithful to the hidden meanings, forbidden by the Church, encoded in the scripture. The scripture implies the royal blood was *not* the genetic bloodline of Jesus, but the same symbol used by Jesus himself at the Last Supper: the wine symbolising the blood shed by Christ for all for the remission of sins. However, Shakespeare courageously parts company from the narrative by saying the blood of Christ not only unconditionally sealed the New Testament promise but also unsealed and totally replaced, fulfilled *and* abjured the Old Testament laws of Moses. As far as one can tell theologically, the Mosaic law was sealed in the blood of circumcision; the New Testament law of God through Jesus was sealed in the blood of Christ. Big difference.

The Journey Home on the Sound Current

> *Be not afeared. The Isle is full of noises, sweet sounds, and airs that bring delight and hurt not. Sometimes I hear a thousand twangling instruments hum about mine ears.*
> *The Tempest*, Act III Scene II

At the conclusion of Part One, our focus morphed from 'hunting the Grail' to 'hunting the name': [*The Name*] *is the way, no one enters the father but by* [*the Name*]. At the conclusion of Part Two, we had found the NameAlchemy: Fortinbras.

Consider now that *The Tempest* is Shakespeare's name for that sacred Name.

This is where we bang in the nails for Christianity's crucifixion, where it becomes staggeringly clear that Christianity has nothing whatsoever to do with why Jesus came, what he did, how he did it, and what the implications are for all mankind. This is Christianity's big choice: death or resurrection? To be or not to be? To live in union with God and our own soul, or to continue under the GuiltSin of the entrapment of good-and-evil? To reunite with the sound current, the wind of God, or to continue to be cut off from the Tree of Life?

Ancient Mysticism

In the little-known (deeply heretical), ancient, mystical teaching Shakespeare has undoubtably used to underpin his entire works, the way home to God is open to all who 'ask in his name'. This is Jesus Code for 'become initiated into (connected inwardly to) the sound current, receive (from the Fisher King) the five sacred names of God (Ophelia's old lauds), and chant them daily in Spiritual Exercises (Daily Bread)'.

To clarify: there is always at least one person on the planet who holds the keys to initiation (connection) to the sound current. In the Grail legend, they were called the Fisher King. The allusion to Jesus Christ is not too obscure — fishers of men, loaves and fishes, etc. In fact, the symbolism of the mass 'feeding of the five thousand' would imply Jesus initiated a large number of people (all of humanity) into the sound current during the so-called 'sermon on the mount'. As Ariel demonstrates, there are five sacred names of God (old lauds) one needs to establish the soul beyond reach of Satan's dominance. We can assume this was alluded to in Ophelia's journey on the face of the waters, an image that could very well represent the Ascension of Jesus.

Yes, this is a lot to swallow. And, frankly, even after forty years of daily practice, I am very reluctant to talk to anyone about it. I have no need whatsoever to proselytise. And who on earth is going to grasp such a wacky idea? Yet here it is. In Shakespeare. In *The Tempest*.

Having demonstrated in chapter 1 how Shakespeare alludes to this throughout a broad sample of his works, I'd like to give you a deeper explanation of initiation into the sound current as illustrated by excerpts of verse from Ariel, Ferdinand and, ironically, Caliban.

It's not easy to get one's head round the idea that who we really are (the soul) is a vibratory sound frequency. Or that, in order to pass through the levels of consciousness that stand between the earth and the soul realm, we need to raise our harmonic rate by intoning a sacred word, sound or name. But when you see how Ariel subliminally drips evidence of this process into our life stream, you'll also see why I felt like I had no choice but to write it down.

Catching the Soul Train to Eden Central

One of the crucial aspects we must now validate about Shakespeare's revelation of the Grail mystery concerns the awareness of the truth that sets us free and the implication that the way to paradise via the Tree of Life is opened to all. As we learn increasingly to give and receive grace, mercy and forgiveness, and discover what it means to 'ask in God's hallowed name', so do we travel the royal road home.

I share Peter's belief that Shakespeare's work was intended
by the author to help us create a garden for our soul.

Mark Rylance, Foreword to *The Tempest*
by Peter Dawkins

If we first look at Ferdinand's journey through Prospero's Isle, you'll see this little-known concept very clearly illustrated. This one little genius-verse of Ferdinand's alludes to everything — the music of the soul, the sound of the waters upon which the Spirit of God moved in Genesis, the sweet airs heard by Caliban, and the nature and purpose of the spirit Ariel:

FERDINAND

This music crept by me upon the waters,
Allaying both their fury and my passion
With its sweet air. Thence I have followed it,
Or it hath drawn me rather.
The Tempest, Act I Scene II

If you remember, the starting point for my Grail quest was teasing Richard Leigh about being somewhat glib about seeing the Grail (royal blood) as an initiatory experience. The very thesis of *The Holy Blood and the Holy Grail* was cemented by the assumption that Father Saunièrre Berenger of Rennes-le-Chateau became amazingly wealthy through blackmailing the Church: *Pay me or I'll expose the inconvenient truth about the Grail.* While they chose to follow the secular trail, rather than take 'royal blood' literally, as a genetic bloodline, my bloodhounds were baying inwards towards the mystical truths that underlie our physical world. As was Peter Dawkins, I was intuitively hunting for evidence of initiation. I could see signs, allusions and motifs in all the plays I'd explored. I did not expect to find what must be the closest we can get to incontrovertible proof.

Jesus himself was notorious for being misunderstood, even by the disciples. When he said, 'Ask in my name and it shall be given', I hardly think it was a kind of 'Snap your fingers, say my name and I'll deliver the pizza'. Why order a pizza when you can have the entire restaurant chain? Why ask for a fig leaf when you can have the Tree of Life? To ask in God's name is to ask in God's will, to ask for what God wants us to have. What we want in this material world is none of God's business. We already have within us everything we need for material success. God's business is forgiveness. He needs us as much as we need him. To fulfil His/Her/Its purpose, we need to return home to the Godhead. He tells how to do this: we must forgive ourselves, forgive each other and chant the hallowed name of God. This could be the HU, the ancient name Shakespeare sneaks into some of the plays under the radar as 'hue', or it could be the sacred tones given to the initiates that Ariel whispers to us throughout *The Tempest*.

In *Henry V* (Vol II), after the victory of Agincourt against all odds, Henry has the men chant the *Non Nobis* to acknowledge that it was *The Name of God* that performed the miracle, not the ego of man.

> *Non nobis domine. Non nobis. Sed nomini tuo da gloriam.*
> *Not to us o Lord. Not to us. But to your name goes the glory.*
> *Henry V,* Act IV Scene VIII

According to the forbidden teachings of the ancient masters reflected in the underlying theme of the plays, we are gods, we are kings. We have been deposed. We have been imprisoned. We have been abused. We have been forgotten. We can now reclaim our throne. The royal carriage awaits to take us home. It's been called many, many different things through the ages — the Tree of Life, Jacob's Ladder, the Word of God, the wind from heaven, the sound current.

Getting on the express train home to Eden Central is what my inner poet calls 'initiation into the sound current of God'. Perhaps it's also called 'receiving the Holy Grail'. You decide.

This initiation is not something we, as conscious mortal beings, do. We physically do not get on the train. We have the conscious choice to get the ticket so who we really are as a soul can get on the train. The ticket is a tone, one of the five hallowed names of God given to us by the Fisher King. We get on the train when we're ready. Depending on the current level of our soul's evolution, getting ready can involve studying sacred writings, doing spiritual exercises or even kicking certain addictions. We can get off the train whenever we want. It stops to refuel five times along the way. One new ticket, one new tone, five tones in all. We get on with our mortal lives. We can do whatever we want on the train. We can have great fun. A massive load has been taken off our shoulders. We can achieve big things; we can achieve nothing. It makes no difference. We're going home whatever we do on the train. We don't have to worry about anything. The train has one destination: Eden Central. And our arrival is absolutely guaranteed. Nothing much in life necessarily changes — apart from feeling a sense of joy that surpasses understanding — but our soul goes home. No matter what we do, as long as we maintain the initiation, stay on the train, our soul is going home. It's a good feeling to know this.

What's this got to do with Shakespeare and the Grail?

One of the key contributions we make towards keeping our initiation active and fuelling the soul's passage home is how Ophelia did it, *chanting old lauds* — in other words, doing the spiritual exercises, chanting the hallowed names of God and listening to the inner music of the spheres that draws the soul home.

The Sound and Voice of Ariel

In the secret teachings of the ancient masters forbidden by the orthodoxy, it is the sound of God's sacred names that the initiate chants and that draws the soul home to the source. *Our father who art in heaven, I hallow thy name. To thy kingdom I come. Thy will is done. I forgive myself and all others everything.*

The Thirty-Two Initiations

According to the teachings of Shabdha Yoga (presumably Shakespeare's source), being born is the first initiation into the sound current. Everyone on the planet gets that one, and Jesus reactivated it through The Beatitudes and the feeding of the five thousand. Choosing to be born here was choosing that initiation! After this, there are some key choices. There are thirty-two further initiations into the heart of God, the Garden of Eden, the kingdom of heaven, etc.

According to the teachings, there are five levels of initiation from the physical level into the soul realm, followed by twenty-seven levels between the soul realm and God Himself. You've possibly never heard these terminologies because, as I keep saying, in the West, this information has been extirpated. According to the sound current master (Fisher King) I have been studying with for over forty years, the closest the mind and the physical voice can get to the inner mystical sound of God's Word, his spiritual inner hallowed Name, is *HU*, pronounced 'hue'. As this primordial sound current travels through the different levels of the creation (from the heart of God, through the positive spiritual levels, into the soul level, and through the unconscious, mental, emotional, imaginational and physical levels of our consciousness), its frequency changes accordingly. When we do the spiritual exercise of chanting the hallowed names of God, we are directed to also sit in silence and gaze into the third eye chakra, the eye of the needle, while we listen for the sounds of the sound current. If you are blessed enough to hear them, depending on what level you're listening to, the sounds of God's names reflected back can often sound very much like:

- Physical level: Thunder or heartbeat
- Imagination level: Surf or bubbling brook
- Emotion level: Tinkling bells
- Mental level: Rushing waters or 'ah-ohm'
- Unconscious level: Buzzing or humming like bees
- Soul level: Haunting, flute-like music
    - Twenty-seven levels above soul
    - Including: A thousand violins (twangling instruments)
        - God level: HU
        - Above God: Absolute silence

Imagine how utterly flabbergasted I was when I saw the descriptions of *every one* of these virtually unknown, mystical sounds alluded to repeatedly by William Shakespeare in this extraordinary play *The Tempest*.

Apart from the HU, alluded to as 'hue', 'current' and 'name' in *Hamlet* (and in *A Midsummer Night's Dream* as 'O Night with hue so black'), the first sound I spotted in *The Tempest* that galvanised me to write this book was Caliban telling Trinculo and Stephano how he hears the exquisite, heavenly sound of the *thousand violins*.

CALIBAN

Be not afeared. The Isle is full of noises, sweet sounds, and
airs that bring delight and hurt not. Sometimes I hear a
thousand twangling instruments hum about mine ears.
The Tempest, Act III Scene II

Apparently, it is virtually unknown for anyone ever to hear the sound of the 'thousand violins' and still be able to inhabit the physical body, so where on earth has Shakespeare set his magical Isle? Apparently, the Ananda, the spiritual bliss one experiences upon hearing the 'haunting music of the soul', is so intensely ecstatic that you cannot possibly continue to live here without it. Yet here on Prospero's Isle, this ragtag of humanity is wallowing in it without even realising what and why.

All the dialogue is awash with these allusions, so do read the play yourself to check this out. But here are some examples of how subtly, and with glorious impunity, the Master is sharing the forbidden, mystical secrets of the Grail with us.

Physical level: sounds like thunder

ARIEL

Jove's lightning, the precursors
O' th' dreadful thunderclaps, more momentary

And sight-outrunning were not. The fire and cracks
Of sulfurous roaring the most mighty Neptune
Seem to besiege and make his bold waves tremble,
Yea, his dread trident shake.
Act I Scene II

Imagination level: sounds like waters, brooks, seas

FRANCISCO
Sir, he may live.
I saw him beat the surges under him
And ride upon their backs. He trod the water,
Whose enmity he flung aside, and breasted
The surge most swoll'n that met him. His bold head
'Bove the contentious waves he kept, and oared
Himself with his good arms in lusty stroke
To th' shore, that o'er his wave-worn basis bowed,
As stooping to relieve him. I not doubt
He came alive to land.
Act II Scene I

Emotion level: sounds like bells

ARIEL
Sea nymphs hourly ring his knell.
Burden, within: Ding dong.
Hark, now I hear them: ding dong bell.
Act I Scene II

Mental level: sounds like rushing waters

MIRANDA

If by your art, my dearest father, you have
Put the wild waters in this roar, allay them.
Act I Scene II

Unconscious level: sounds like buzzing bees

ARIEL

Where the bee sucks, there suck I.
In a cowslip's bell I lie.
Act V Scene I

Soul level: sounds like haunting, flute-like music

FERDINAND

Where should this music be? I' th' air, or th' earth?
It sounds no more; and sure it waits upon
Some god o' th' island. Sitting on a bank,
Weeping again the King my father's wrack,
This music crept by me upon the waters,
Allaying both their fury and my passion
With its sweet air. Thence I have followed it,
Or it hath drawn me rather. But 'tis gone.
No, it begins again.
Act I Scene II

The Thirty-Two Plays

Another remarkable revelation is that in the folio, beneath the banner heading *The Tempest,* are thirty-seven plays. But if you count the four parts of the Henriad (*Richard II, Henry IV parts 1 & 2, Henry V*) as the one play it really is, and do likewise with the three parts of *Henry VI*, we have thirty-two plays: one play for every sound current initiation from the earth all the way up to the heart of God. All the plays have some of the sounds encrypted, but *The Tempest* is the one play containing all the inner sounds of those initiations.

What more can I say?

There are vast volumes of material written and recorded on this subject to inform and support the inner spiritual journey home for those who are ready. You can ask Google. Or you can ask me via the website. It's always my pleasure to discuss initiation, my favourite subject.

Archetypes Fit for a Denouement: An Ariel View

If this is indeed Shakespeare's denouement, in his inimitable way, we'd expect him to somehow explain and confirm his use throughout of the three core archetypes. With some trepidation — I did not want to get this far to discover I was barking up the wrong tree — I took an Ariel view of the play. And through his eyes, this is what I saw:

> *I, Ariel, am the sound of God. I am the wind from heaven. I am that part of the spirit of God that was cut off in the beginning and trapped in a cloven pine. Prospero, my heavenly master, promises me my freedom. But there is work to be done before I can be released. In the guise of the tempest, I shall bring balance to all those who caused our banishment. My work is to birth humanity onto the earth and usher it towards the chalice of the Grail for a final reckoning and the blessing of the New Testament.*

> *As I look down upon humanity, I see three groups of travelers. They must all suffer the tests, trials and tribulations that enable them to fulfil their individual destinies. I must be their guide, their confessor, their protector, their awakener.*

In other words, from a higher altitude, the three core archetypes are not populated here by individuals but by selected groups of individuals. And these groups mirror the group of shepherds and the group of wise men who were chosen for the Epiphany of the baby Jesus.

Are we looking at a play that is not just dramatizing an epiphany but offering an experience of epiphany to us, the audience?

In *The Tempest,* there are three groups, each representing one of the archetypes. We immediately have, if not proof, then strong structural corroboration of our hypothesis. Although exactly the same triune pattern as we've already seen, here we have a meta-pattern where not just Adam-Eve and Cain-Abel are represented, but also the overarching polarity of God-Satan.

Dramatis Personae: Three Circles, Three Archetypes

THE TEMPEST

"I feel not this deity in my bosom." —Antonio

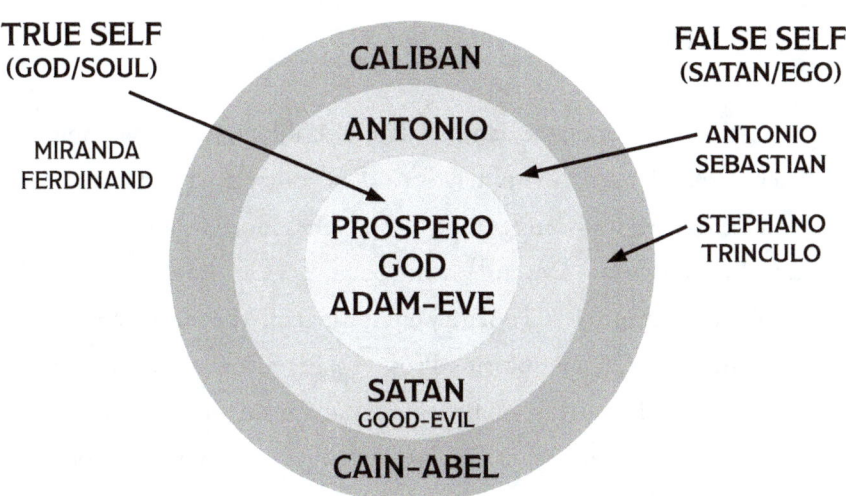

The Archetypes in the Tempest

Circle 1: God Circle: Led by Prospero

- Prospero — rightful Duke of Milan, deposed by his brother Antonio, banished, marooned on this Isle
- Ferdinand — son of Alonso the King, who betrayed Prospero
- Miranda — Prospero's fifteen-year-old daughter

Circle 2: Satan Circle: Led by Antonio

- Antonio — Prospero's treacherous, usurping brother
- Alonso — conniving King of Naples
- Sebastian — Alonso's ambitious, weak-willed brother
- Gonzalo — a kindly old gentleman, Prospero's good friend
- Francisco, et alia

Circle 3: False Self Circle: Led by Caliban

- Caliban — the Hagseed, a hybrid monster sired by the Devil out of the witch Sycorax
- Stephano — a drunken butler
- Trinculo — a jester

We also have Sycorax, the damnèd dam of Caliban. Although long since dead, her spirit still exerts an influence. And, of course, first and by no means last, we have Ariel: a transcendent spirit that defies mortal classification.

In addition to Adam-Eve and Cain-Abel, the circles are also more explicitly personifying the universal polarity of God-Satan. The central circle seems to be the God-circle, encompassing Prospero, his fifteen-year-old daughter Miranda, and Ferdinand. It soon becomes clear Ferdinand is an archetype of Jesus Christ. We soon see/hear that he is following Ariel's mystical music — the sound current leading him to his immortal beloved Miranda and soon-to-be father-in-law-in-heaven Prospero.

Likewise, the inner circle would be the Satan circle, encompassing Antonio and his entourage. Antonio is soon delineated as the Satan archetype. King Alonso, father to Ferdinand, collaborator with Antonio in deposing Prospero, takes the minor role of Adam, as did the ghost of Hamlet's father. Ferdinand, unlike Hamlet in all other ways, is also cast as the son of Adam, the Son of Man.

Thus, it falls to the outer circle to fulfil both polarities of the Cain-Abel archetype. We now meet Caliban, who has collided with a pair of drunken fools called Stephano and Trinculo. These 'Three Stooges' provide us with one of Shakespeare's deceptively innocent comic reliefs seething with cryptic sideswipes at the orthodoxy — the Master's version of *Monty Python and the Holy Grail*, with signature mockery and lampooning of the august institutions of the Church.

The First Sign

As a first sign confirming *The Tempest* as the denouement of the oeuvre, our earlier three circles of individuals seem to have been upgraded. We now find the play populated with three disparate (and desperate) groups of people. As a mirror and foreshadowing of the symbology of the biblical Epiphany, as did the kings and the shepherds, the three groups will represent the entire spectrum of humanity being led by a spirit to witness the Christ. The two outer circles are as different as they are similar. Ironically, they both comprise corrupt, self-obsessed, ambitious villains, but they are polar opposites in social status. One contains royalty and noblemen, the other is made up of simple, drunken servants.

Let's now look at the plot points of the play through the lens of Shakespeare's most creative cryptic device: the biblical motifs.

BIBLICAL EVENT	SHAKESPEARE CODE
Jesus walks on the tempestuous seas of Galilee	Ariel conjures a tempest: Ferdinand trod the waves
Adam and Eve banished from paradise	Prospero and Miranda banished from Milan
The serpent tempts Adam and Eve to betray God	Antonio tempts Alonzo to betray Prospero
The serpent seduces/rapes Eve and sires Cain and Abel	Caliban sired by union of the devil and witch Sycorax
Jesus nailed to the cross	Caliban plots to drive a nail through Prospero's head
Christ reopened the tree of life/ the music of the spheres	Ferdinand drawn by music to find paradise
Jesus bears his cross to Calvary	Ferdinand tasked to move a thousand logs
Remission of sin promised at Last Supper (but withheld by Church doctrine)	Ariel removes the table of plenty
Jesus Christ fulfils the scripture	Prospero drowns his books and staff

Chapter 9:

BIBLICAL MOTIFS
IN THE TEMPEST

Assume every word from Shakespeare's quill is written in the ink of scripture and its very nature divine heresy. Here, we're zooming in on certain key motifs that are the keystones of his architecture. Once again, prepare to be awestruck, dumbfounded, astonished and confused.

Chaos was the prior condition to the creation of the universe. It is also one of the prior conditions to enlightenment and one of Shakespeare's signature devices for secreting his secrets. The chronology of the outer play's unfolding has little to do with the chronology of the scripture in the subtext. In a valiant attempt at cutting through the Gordian knot, I have abandoned all hope of chronology in favour of exploring biblical themes as best I can. If you feel a little confused — enjoy it!

The play itself begins with a biblical motif from deep within the gospel. Genesis provides the inner backstory, and the Gospels and Revelation the main plot and denouement. But do not expect the mystical subtext to be without its surprising twists and turns.

Jesus Walks on the Waters: Prospero Orchestrates the Tempest

To ready yourself for this revelation, make sure your jawbone is securely fastened to the TMJ lest it drop to the floor and shatter. Now slowly read again the above subhead. Can the opening scene of *The Tempest* really be a magnificent biblical motif of Jesus's miracle of walking on water? Has Shakespeare used the actual conversation between Jesus on the waters and the disciples in the 'tempest-tossed' boat to open his final play?

We already know the portal to Shakespeare's subtext is often encrypted in the first act, often the first scene, sometimes the first few lines. In the first scene of *Hamlet,* for example, the eerie appearance of a spirit is accompanied by a reference in the text to the birth of Christ, and the whole event resonates with the Annunciation to the Shepherds in Luke.

Given what you already know of sound current symbols, what do you make of this opener: the mariners of a ship are in great fear of their lives, tempest-tossed, and in danger of their ship's running aground. Doesn't it remind you of Act I of *Macbeth,* when the witches cackle over the same inscrutable sound current imagery: 'Though his bark cannot be lost, Yet it shall be tempest-tossed'?

Is Shakespeare not only using the walking on water miracle as fodder for his grand finale but also plumbing its mystical depths to reveal an even deeper meaning?

A tempestuous noise of thunder and lightning heard:

*Enter a Ship-**master**, and a Boatswain.*

MASTER
Boatswain

BOATSWAIN
Here Master, what cheer?

MASTER
Good: speak to th' mariners: fall to't, yarely, or
we run ourselves aground, bestir, bestir.

BOATSWAIN
Heigh my hearts, **cheerly, cheerly my hearts:** *yare,*
yare: take in the top sail: tend to th' Master's whistle:
blow till thou burst thy wind, *if room enough.*
The Tempest, Act I Scene I

Does it perchance remind you of a famous biblical event on the sea of Galilee? The crew of a certain fishing boat also tempest-tossed in fear for their lives? Providing Shakespeare some great words for an opening scene they cry out: 'Master, master, we perish.' They see Jesus walking on the water, and he says to them 'Be of good cheer; it is I; be not afraid.'

Back in our play, we soon hear that the King's son, Ferdinand (representing the Christ archetype), survived the storm by having 'trod the water, whose enmity he flung aside.'

Why did Jesus need to walk on the water? Realistically speaking, there must be a huge gap between what Jesus did and said in his thirty-three years of life and the scant few hours' worth of dialogue and actions reported in the scripture. What we're told must surely be less about what actually happened and far more about how what we're told symbolises the specific actions he took that fulfilled his mission. It's fair to assume that everything we're told he said and did was fulfilling a prophecy and banging yet another nail in Satan's coffin.

In the beginning, in Genesis 1, it says 'And the Spirit of God moved upon the face of the waters. And God said, "Let there be light". And there was light.'

Daniel 12 refers again to this phenomenal, symbolic act and also reprises Ophelia's watery death scene.

> *Then I, Daniel, looked, and there before me stood two others, one on this bank of the river and one on the opposite bank. One of them said to the man clothed in linen,* **who was above the waters of the river,** *'How long will it be before these astonishing things are fulfilled?'*

Apart from the malaise still in the minds of man, the full impact of Satan's betrayal of God in the beginning is probably unknowable. But these two verses give me the sense that whatever Jesus had to fulfil in order to break Satan's spell had to go all the way back to the moment of the creation. When God spoke, uttered his Word, the Name, the sound of all things in all the universes, he gave his Word, his sacred name to Satan to manifest all the psychic and material worlds. Satan usurped this power. He took prisoner the *ear of mankind* so all we could hear, see and feel was Satan's phoney glory. For us to be free to know the divine presence, Jesus had to reclaim, reassert, the supremacy of God over the forces of darkness and ignorance.

On the physical/literal level of interpretation, perhaps walking on water demonstrated the power of the Christ to overcome the laws of the Satan. The Satan, infinitely more beautiful and unimaginably more cunning than the superstitious stereotype of 'the devil', is said by those in the line of the ancient masters to be Lord of all the created worlds: the inner psychic worlds of the imagination, emotions, mind and unconscious, plus the outer material world of matter, time and space — including gravity and our physical bodies. The soul is surely made in the image of God, but the body in the image of Satan.

Think about the law of gravity. Science makes me laugh when it dubs gravity as the weakest of the four forces of nature! What is weak about an invisible force that acts instantaneously (faster than the speed of light) from one end of the universe to the other, keeping infinite billions of galaxies, stars, planets, moons, even molecules, atoms and subatomic particles in perfect balance with such precision that even a slight deviation would either crush every being on Earth or send us all flying into chaotic orbit?

Anagogically, perhaps Jesus walking on water is a foreshadowing of the Resurrection and Ascension — the soul transcending the lower worlds by riding on the sound current, symbolised, as usual, by the winds and the waters.

One possible teaching for us is shown when Peter stepped out of the boat to join Jesus walking on the water. Initially, he had faith (in the Christ within himself). The instant he doubted that self-belief, he fell, but he was nevertheless saved from drowning by the Christ. Saved, rebuked and given another life to keep growing and learning, working and serving. When Jesus resurrected, he resurrected the soul of mankind. Every soul in all the universes was resurrected. We were all given the power, the potential to rise above the delusion of good-and-evil. Jesus did it for us all. Now we need to do it for ourselves. That's why we're here. That's why we are reborn over and over again until we do learn, until we do balance our past actions, until we do forgive ourselves for everything, until we do claim the freedom that has already been given to us.

Christ Walks on Water: Ferdinand Trod the Waves

True to form, as well as lifting his dialogue straight out of the gospel, Shakespeare double-dips his corroboration. Ferdinand is seen having trod (walked on) the water. Not only that, but he cries out, 'Hell is empty, and all the devils are here.' This could be a sub-motif of the Harrowing of Hell when, between the Crucifixion and the Resurrection, we are told the Christ freed all souls in hell. He then sealed it shut forever, so that never again can any soul be lost to Satan's bondage. As the way to God is reopened, the way to Satan's eternal prison is closed. The devils? Those in power who keep us in bondage to their lies? Again, before we know it, we're dropped in at the deep end of the hidden meanings in the Old and the New Testaments: from Genesis and Exodus to the Gospels, Acts and Revelation. Let your imagination cavort like dolphins playing in the wake.

Back on dry land, echoing how Moses famously used his staff to part the Red Sea, the seas having graciously saved them from drowning, the survivors of Ariel's tempest are unharmed and discover, miraculously, their clothes are perfectly dry and in pristine condition.

Man Banished from Paradise: Prospero Banished from Milan

Next, Shakespeare gives us the backstory from Genesis. Prospero tells Miranda how they came to be banished to this Isle. When I began writing this book, I needed the perfect word to describe what had happened to the knowledge of the Grail. Then I found it: *extirpate.*

> *Extirpate:* to remove or destroy totally; do away with; exterminate. *To pull up by or as if by the roots; root up.*

Few people know what it means. The word 'extirpate' has itself been extirpated.

Imagine my utter delight when I heard Prospero using *my* word: *extirpate.*

In a biblical motif of the Adam and Eve allegory, Prospero tells his daughter, Miranda, how the King of Naples 'in the dead of [Satan's] darkness did *extirpate*' him from his dukedom, confer it upon his treacherous brother, and cast them both adrift in the seas. Said word was heaven ordinant.

This is Prospero himself telling us his tale of woe, the biblical backstory of the banishing of the soul and the raison d'être of the coming of Jesus Christ.

PROSPERO
Now the condition.
This King of Naples, being an enemy
To me inveterate, hearkens my brother's suit,
Which was that he, in lieu o' th' premises
Of homage and I know not how much tribute,
Should presently **extirpate** *me and mine*
Out of the dukedom, and confer fair Milan,
With all the honours, on my brother; whereon,
A treacherous army levied, one midnight
Fated to th' purpose did Antonio open
The gates of Milan, and i' th' dead of darkness
The ministers for th' purpose hurried thence
Me and thy crying self.
The Tempest, Act I Scene II

This is a reprise of the overarching biblical motif of the subtext of the entire oeuvre: in the beginning, the god of day individualises itself as Adam and Eve and places this, the bipolar image of itself, in paradise to rule the inner world of man in love, joy and innocence. In Shakespeare's enlightened slant, Satan, the god of night, as the serpent, by way of lies, treachery and cunning, *extirpates* Adam from Eden, rapes Eve, banishes them both and establishes the monstrous issue of his foul union with Eve (Cain and Abel, the ego of man) as ruler of the kingdom of God on earth.

As a result of the way the serpent coils itself around the soul soon after birth, the Tree of Life, the lifestream of God into humanity, is cut off. The hybrid monstrous birth, the god-man-serpent, Cain-Abel, is now forced to live for eternity in the earth plane with no way of knowing who he is, why he is here and how to get home.

That's us, folks! That's humanity. Hybrid sons and daughters of God and

Satan, with Satan largely ruling the roost — until or unless we get a glimpse of the divine within. We think we're free, but we're delusional, intoxicated, not unlike, say, Trinculo and Stephano as they plot with Caliban how to murder, depose and dispose of Prospero. Yes, both of the two outer circles are plotting to commit a representation of the original GuiltSin: the original (attempted) murder of the soul. Let's take a closer look at our three circles, the archetypes of the soul's evolutionary journey.

Original GuiltSin (I): Antonio Beguiles Sebastian

Shakespeare now takes us deeper into the forbidden theology with two further dramatisations of the so-called 'fall of man', first through introducing Antonio, our proposed Satan archetype, then through our first encounter with Caliban.

Antonio — no sooner is he alone with Sebastian, the King's brother, than he establishes his characterisation as serpent archetype. He acts out an allegory of the original GuiltSin: the deposing of the rightful king.

As the serpent tempted Adam to metaphorically 'kill' the soul, Antonio now tempts Sebastian into a foul, murderous plot to kill Alonso (Adam) and usurp his kingdom. When Sebastian asks him if he feels any guilt for having done the same with his own brother, Prospero, Antonio boasts about having no conscience whatsoever to prick him. He's what today we might call a soul-devoid psychopath, callously indifferent to the suffering he causes — he 'feels not the spark of God in his heart'. Indeed, does a shadow feel the love and warmth of the sun that casts it?

SEBASTIAN
But, for your conscience?

ANTONIO
Ay, sir, where lies that? If 'twere a kibe [blister],
*'Twould put me to my slipper, **but I feel not***
This deity in my bosom.
The Tempest, Act II Scene I

While Alonso (the king) and Gonzalo are sleeping, shamelessly, unhampered by the milk of human kindness, Antonio and Sebastian are on the point of running them through with their swords when Ariel intercedes. Ariel saves them from death by awakening the sleeping pair with a song. He sings in Gonzalo's ear and warns him of the impending danger. But when Gonzalo awakens, all he remembers hearing is...the sound current.

GONZALO
Upon mine honour, sir, I heard a humming,
And that a strange one too, which did awake me.

The Tempest, Act II Scene I

As well as a subtle motif of how we can awaken our soul by chanting the sacred tones, it underlines who Ariel represents in the play. As a mystical running theme in the play, whenever Ariel addresses the travellers on the Isle, he is heard not as words, but as the mystical tones of the sound current. It implies Ariel *is* the sound current. He *is* the tempest. He *is* the (about to be released from bondage) Holy Spirit.

Original GuiltSin (II): Caliban Copulates with Trinculo

Now for another deceptively innocent comic relief. Caliban enters the stage reminding us of the infamous holy trinity of sound current allusions in *Macbeth*: a storm with thunder and rain. His characterisation is defined by his swearing allusions that underline his paternal lineage through Satan, the serpent: 'Sometime am I all wound up with adders, who with cloven tongues do hiss me into madness.' He (partly) shelters from the storm under a sheet of gaberdine.

The wandering castaway Trinculo now arrives, also seeking shelter from the storm. Said jester spies the mound of gaberdine with Caliban's legs protruding. He crawls under and joins the fishy-smelling islander. He complains that 'misery acquaints a man with strange bedfellows'. They assume the soixante-neuf position of the beast with two backs (a nod and a wink to *Othello* and a parody of how serpents copulate).

Soon enough, the drunken Stephano arrives, bottle of wine in hand, to find what he assumes is a monster with four legs. Immediately, we are treated to a lampooning biblical motif of the union of man, woman and serpent in the Garden of Eden whereupon we, the monstrous hybrid hu-man/god-man, were conceived. Once again mocking the ritual of the Eucharist (as is his wont), Shakespeare now has Caliban fall in awe of the drunken Stephano. He begins to worship Stephano as a saint or a demigod. Can you not see the blasphemous allusion to the Mass in this line from Caliban: 'That's a brave god, and bears celestial liquor: I will kneel to him'?

Taking his devious satire even deeper, Stephano further lampoons Saint Stephen, whose martyrdom is commemorated on what is also Boxing Day, the day after Christmas Day (the feast of Stephen). Stephen, presumably stupefied by communion wine, was foolish enough to accuse the Jews of killing the Messiah and was subsequently stoned to death. The Pope rewarded his own and Stephen's stupidity by canonising him, and, with sublime irony, making him the patron saint of bricklayers and stonemasons. Stupidity? Yes, as

Shakespeare makes much ado of, the Jews didn't kill the Messiah — they made his mission possible. The Messiah's mission was to 'kill' the tyranny of the law of Moses by allowing himself to be killed. If they killed anyone at the Crucifixion, the Jews 'killed' their own prophet, Moses. Now Caliban is kneeling to and receiving 'communion wine' from this drunken quasi priest. Do they have a patron saint of drunken idiots? We could sorely use one.

But why is Shakespeare still banging on with this theme here in *The Tempest*?

Brazenly, overheard by the ubiquitous Ariel, Caliban now embroils the two villains in a plot to murder and depose Prospero. This is the mirror-in-the-mirror image of what's happening in our other circle. Antonio is also embroiling Sebastian to murder and depose his own uncle, just as he himself deposed and 'murdered'/banished his own brother, Prospero.

Jesus Not Tied, but Nailed to the Cross: Caliban Plots to Drive a Nail through Prospero's Head

Caliban's gruesome plan to murder and depose Prospero is for Stephano to creep upon him while he sleeps and drive a nail through his head. Of all possible modes of execution, why would he choose this particular one: a nail through the head? Presumably because the Master, cryptologist that he is, needed another biblical motif of the Crucifixion. Because for Jesus to fulfil all the covenants of the Mosaic Law, he had hundreds of trials to endure, tasks to perform and symbolic events to re-enact in the Spirit as well as here in the physical world. In an atypical crucifixion, instead of being tied to the cross, it was ordained that he be nailed. He was nailed through the feet and through the hands. This would symbolise that the New Testament is sealed in his blood from the centre of the earth, through to the highest levels of all the universes. Having a nail through his head as well could symbolise the action reaching the third eye (the eye of the needle) and the crown chakras. This could also be the deeper symbology of the crown of thorns: the blood sealing the New

Testament promise through to the pinnacle of creation, 'the muse of fire that would ascend the brightest heaven of invention' in Henry V's Christ (explored in *Volume II*).

CALIBAN

Yea, yea, my lord. I'll yield him thee asleep,
Where thou mayst knock a nail into his head.
The Tempest, Act III Scene II

Meanwhile, back at the God-circle… To stay with the common themes of the biblical motifs I need to hop around the text a bit. Let's hover over Ferdinand's journey and establish the context for bestowing upon him the mantle of Jesus/Christ archetype.

Christ Reopened Access to the Tree of Life/ the Sound Current of God: Ferdinand Follows the Sounds of Ariel to Find Miranda and Paradise

Ferdinand's father, the King, Alonso, believes his son perished in the seas. Likewise, Ferdinand fears he is now alone, his father having been drowned. Now Ferdinand hears Ariel's singing and the irresistible, haunting music that he has little choice but to be drawn by. Here's one of many transcendent, poetic allusions to the sound current and its role in our lives to draw us home to the Godhead (Galahad).

FERDINAND

Where should this music be? I' th' air, or th' earth?
It sounds no more; and sure it waits upon
Some god o' th' island. Sitting on a bank,
Weeping again the King my father's wrack,
This music crept by me upon the waters,

Allaying both their fury and my passion
With its sweet air. Thence I have followed it,
Or it hath drawn me rather. But 'tis gone.
No, it begins again...
...This is no mortal business, nor no sound
That the Earth owes. I hear it now above me.
The Tempest, Act I Scene II

It's soon clear that this is integral to Prospero's plan. But why? He wants Miranda to fall in love with Ferdinand and be united with him in holy matrimony. It works like a charm. But why? On seeing Ferdinand, Miranda sees the divinity in him (for our benefit) and falls totally in love (of course). But why? What is Prospero's purpose here? Better question: What might their union symbolise? Did I say union? That word again. The word that has something to do with the poisoned chalice.

MIRANDA
I might call him [Ferdinand]
A thing divine, for nothing natural
I ever saw so noble.
The Tempest, Act I Scene II

We need not wait long for our answer. Disguised as Miranda's virginity, the Master drops in a silent allusion to the union (pearl of great price) in Hamlet's poisoned chalice and the 'eternal jewel given to the common enemy of man' by Macbeth.

MIRANDA
The jewel in my dower, I would not wish
Any companion in the world but you.
The Tempest, Act III Scene I

When in the Grail chalice, the jewel becomes the antidote to the serpent's venom: absolute, unconditional forgiveness. It represents the union of the sound of God with the light of God that makes the spirit whole again and frees it from its bondage. Is there a spirit in this tale that has been in bondage and is working to be set free? Ariel raises his hand.

As a way sign that her name may have some deeper significance (to be divined soon), Ferdinand, while admiring her perfection, makes a weak pun on the name Miranda: *admired* — a word that in those days meant far more than it does now. A word that lets Shakespeare wax about Miranda's divine perfection.

FERDINAND
Admired Miranda!
Indeed the top of admiration...
...But you, O you,
So perfect and so peerless, are created
Of every creature's best.
The Tempest, Act III Scene I

But before they can be united, Ferdinand, as did Jesus, has to pass tests, trials and tribulations. And here comes a biblical motif — or perhaps even two in one. Before his open ministry, Jesus worked as a carpenter. Ergo, he worked with wood. Prospero now makes Ferdinand work with wood. And not just any wood — heavy logs.

Jesus Bears His Cross to Calvary: Ferdinand Bears Thousands of Logs to Fulfil Prospero's Command

I must remove
Some thousands of these logs and pile them up,
*Upon a sore **injunction**.*
The Tempest, Act III Scene I

This is now also looking very similar to the biblical motif of Jesus's bearing the cross to Calvary. Not unlike in *Macbeth* when thousands of trees from Burnham Wood were removed to Dunsinane, Ferdinand must remove thousands of logs to fulfil the law (scripture/ injunction) of Prospero. True to form, the biblical allusion soon follows with the telling phrase 'quickens what's dead'.

This my mean task
Would be as heavy to me as odious, but
*The mistress which I serve **quickens what's dead***
And makes my labours pleasures.
The Tempest, Act III Scene I

*For as the Father raiseth up the **dead, and quickeneth***
them; even so the Son quickeneth whom he will.
John 5:21

Through those wider-open eyes, this short exchange now adds gravity to our conclusion.

MIRANDA

If you'll sit down,
I'll bear your logs the while. Pray, give me that.
I'll carry it to the pile.

FERDINAND

No, precious creature,
I had rather crack my sinews, break my back,
Than you should such dishonour undergo
While I sit lazy by.
The Tempest, Act III Scene I

With Jesus, it was in his destiny to bear the cross on his back to Calvary and to be helped at various *stations of the cross*. It was a mystical symbol of his taking upon himself all the sin of the world — he had to fulfil this action in order to fulfil the law. Nevertheless, Ferdinand still considers himself to be in the state of heavenly bliss known as Ananda. Hopefully, Jesus was able to transcend the agony and was in a state of Ananda throughout what seems to be his ordeal. Ferdinand now delineates the Isle to be 'a paradise' while he toils.

FERDINAND

Let me live here ever.
So rare a wondered father and a wife
*Makes this place **a paradise**.*
The Tempest, Act IV Scene I

While the Antonio and Caliban circles are unknowingly being led to a reckoning at Prospero's cell (a humble dwelling not unlike a stable), the Prospero circle is preparing a place for them.

Jesus Seals a New Testament with Mankind: Ferdinand Marries Miranda

Putting gender aside, symbolically, holy matrimony can be viewed as a binding covenant between the male and female energy polarities of the soul. Ultimately, it symbolises the covenant between God and mankind. Traditionally, the marriage covenant is sealed in the blood of the hymen. Deeper, for a covenant to be considered a testament, it too must be sealed in blood. Even deeper, the Old Testament was sealed with the blood of circumcision; the New Testament was sealed with the blood of Christ.

Not that I in any way wish to be provocative or contentious, but the allusions the Master seems to be making imply the marriage of Ferdinand to Miranda could be symbolising the very marriage postulated in *The Holy Blood and the Holy Grail*: that it is Jesus here who is getting married. Here's a couple of tenuous clues as to one of the archetypes Miranda might be standing in for.

> *My sweet mistress*
> *Weeps when she sees me work.*
> The Tempest, Act III Scene I

> *But **Mary [Magdalene]** stood without at the sepulchre **weeping**:*
> *and as she **wept** she stooped down and looked into the sepulchre.*
> John 20:11

Besides the authors of *The Holy Blood and the Holy Grail,* many other writers have followings based on what they have written about the high probability that Jesus would have married and sired a family. It seems to them most unlikely that any man could be taken seriously as a rabbi unless he were married. It would be a matter not only of Jewish custom, but Jewish law — and in the ultra-orthodox communities, it still very much is. Personally, I see Jesus's primary purpose as challenging the law head-on and fulfilling multiple symbolic acts that complete the deeper laws, covenants and seals of the Old Testament. Maybe remaining unmarried himself was one of these acts of blasphemy for which he was vilified and crucified; then again, maybe his apparent virginity is just another fiction pressed into service at Nicaea. Yes, it's possible the Son of Man, who could quicken the dead, could have physically survived the Crucifixion and married Mary, or even got married *after* the Resurrection. It's equally possible that he was married much earlier. Was the wedding at Cana, where he miraculously transformed water into wine, perhaps his own?

But these nontheistic speculations miss the point: to fulfil the scripture and vanquish Satan, Jesus had to be crucified, had to be nailed to a cross, and he had to resurrect. As Hamlet said, 'To be or not to be? That is the question.' Is your soul, my soul, everybody's soul, resurrected or not? That is the question. Is it true? The truth has no truck with belief. The next question is: How do we find out if it's true? Let's see if the Master tells us.

A Vagina Monologue

Eve Ensler, creator of the notorious *The Vagina Monologues*, might be amused to discover that the Master beat her to the idea. In his denouement, Shakespeare pushes his chutzpah to the limit. As a metaphor of the blood seal of the New Testament, the essence of the new spiritual promise between God and man, the essence too of the *sang graal*, the Holy Grail, he symbolises this forbidden fruit with the breaking of the seal of the hymen in the holy matrimony of Miranda and Ferdinand.

In the subtext of the play, as the New Testament is being sealed, the entire spectrum of mankind is being led by a spirit (Ariel) to an epiphany: another representation of Shakespeare's poisoned chalice theme — Prospero's humble cell, mimicking the stable, mimicking the manger, mimicking the cup.

Recall how in *Hamlet* the blood seal was symbolised as the new commandment sealing the death of Rosencrantz and Guildenstern (the symbol of the Old Testament and Mosaic Law). The poisoned chalice offered to Hamlet by the serpent contained the union, the pearl of great price. Here, the union (of the bread and the wine, already defined as 'the jewel in her dower') is the union of Ferdinand and Miranda: the child of the one who represents the archetype of God is united with the Son (Daughter) of Man. This time, even Shakespeare outdoes himself with his motif of the blood seal of the New Testament. The Holy Grail, the blood seal of the New Testament, is now symbolised by the virginal Miranda's hymen. And we get a bonus insight, a glimpse into the rumour that Jesus married la Magdalene.

PROSPERO

Then, as my gift and thine own acquisition
Worthily purchased, take my daughter. But
*If thou dost **break her virgin-knot** before*
*All **sanctimonious ceremonies** may*
With full and holy rite be ministered,
No sweet aspersion shall the heavens let fall
To make this contract grow; but barren hate,
Sour-eyed disdain, and discord shall bestrew
The union of your bed with weeds so loathly
That you shall hate it both. Therefore take heed,
As Hymen's lamps shall light you.
The Tempest, Act IV Scene I

As in Elsinore, there's always more. Having orchestrated and blessed their union, why would Shakespeare, through Prospero, make so much out of insisting Ferdinand does not consummate their betrothal till after 'all due sanctimonious ceremonies are made'? He also uses the emotive phrase 'break her virgin-knot'. He's certainly never been a prude when it comes to extramarital sex, but here he's threatening perdition for Ferdinand if he dishonours her. There's something else going on here. Why else also go out of his way to emphasise that this seemingly divine young woman is nevertheless mortal, unless making a major point? At their reunion, Ferdinand introduces his fiancée to his father, the King.

ALONSO, to Ferdinand
What is this maid with whom thou wast at play?
Your eld'st acquaintance cannot be three hours.
Is she the goddess that hath severed us
And brought us thus together?

FERDINAND
*Sir, she is **mortal**,*
But by immortal providence she's mine.... I have
Received a second life; and second father
This lady makes him to me.
The Tempest, Act V Scene I

This is no ordinary marriage. In sharp contrast to the callous seduction and rape by Satan of Eve, this is the loving, consensual holy matrimony of God with the mother of mankind. Energetically, this marriage completes and mirrors the divine union of God with Mary, mother of Jesus. This intensely emphasised allusion could be just that: a biblical motif of the virgin birth. But could it go even deeper? Could this aspect of the play liken the New Testament to a divine marriage between God and man sealed in blood? Prospero, as God, is reminding us that the spiritual promise is done, it is sealed. If we, mankind, show mercy, we receive grace. It's as simple — and as challenging — as that. Will Prospero himself, as man, be up to the challenge?

Once again, by using a woman to personify God, the soul, he's not only taking a massive risk, but banging another nail into the coffin of those wishing to treat women as lesser mortals.

In *Hamlet,* the motif of the blood-sealing of the New Testament runs through the entire play. His father (Adam) slew Fortinbras, who had a 'sealed compact', a covenant, and thereby 'did forfeit with his life all his lands' (was disinherited from his kingdom/soul). Horatio asks how his commandment to England to kill Rosencrantz and Guildenstern was sealed. He says it was 'heaven ordinant': 'I had my father's signet, the model of that Danish seal.'

Another highly probable piece of extraordinary symbolism could be 'Hymen's lamps shall light you'. Could Miranda's hymen actually represent the seven seals, the perfect seal cutting off the way to the Tree of Life and Ananda? With the New Testament, the seals were broken, and the blood of the wo-man could very well be the sacrifice mankind made to reunite the blood of man with the blood of Christ. This would be a kind of heaven ordinant forgiveness for the holy feminine, the Eve that got too close to the earth frequency for our own good.

Is this symbolic marriage between Ferdinand and Miranda, therefore, the holy re-union of the blood of wo-man with the blood of the risen Christ? Is this why, in our culture, virginity still has a high symbolic value? And why, in law, a marriage between man and woman is not considered legally binding unless consummated — symbolically breaking the 'virgin knot' and sealing the union, the holy matrimony, the sacred covenant between man and wo-man with the blood of the hymen.

This is more than Ferdinand's 'second life' — it's ours. Through the royal blood of the Grail, the New Testament brings freedom and liberation to all souls now. *It is done.* We are free. We are chosen. Now it's our turn to choose back.

Con Molto Fantasia

While Prospero orchestrates the sacred nuptials and prepares the setting for the Epiphany, Ariel conducts his business: tormenting the other two circles.

Antonio's Circle

Ariel has herded Antonio's circle towards Prospero's cell, into a clearing to receive some kind of judgement. God-like, Prospero observes his captives from on high. Human-like, he makes his opinion of Antonio quite clear in this aside.

PROSPERO

Some of you there present are worse than devils.

The Tempest, Act III Scene III

The Blessing of the Last Supper Was Jesus Foretelling How His Blood Would Seal God's Promise of Absolute Forgiveness: Ariel Withdraws God's Blessing until the Rebels Have Atoned

Forgiveness is an art. Pleading for God's forgiveness is an act of superstition; it's already been granted. Self-forgiveness is a psycho-spiritual process. It begins not so much with a confession as an acknowledgment and acceptance that, say, I am now releasing the judgement I have made. Even if I want to forgive someone else, God has already done this, but it is I who is judging myself as reflected in the other person. To release the indirect self-judgement, I need to forgive myself for judging myself for judging them. I cannot forgive another. That is not how forgiveness works. No matter how foul and abusive someone might behave, they are still the Christ within. Ain't that a kick in the head?

Prospero's first act of resolution is (predictably) a pastiche of the Last Supper. A motif borrowed from *Jason and the Argonauts* where Zeus punishes the blinded Phineas by tantalising him with food but never letting him eat. Antonio's circle arrives hungry, thirsty, tired, confused and afraid. Presented by a troupe of dancing nymphs, a table of plenty, a cornucopia, a feast of all they could possibly desire to eat is laid before them. Alonso, the king, steps up first to the table and prepares to eat his 'last supper' declaring:

ALONSO
I will stand to and feed.
Although my last, *no matter, since I feel*
The best is past. Brother, my lord the Duke,
Stand to, and do as we.
The Tempest, Act III Scene III

As he does so, the table of plenty (the blessing of the Grail) is denied him by his own arrogance. To the familiar sound current sounds of thunder and lightning, Ariel now appears, shape-shifted into a harpy, and delivers a terrifyingly stern indictment to the perpetrators that makes Revelation sound as meek as Harry Potter. Best to read the whole speech, but enjoy a few highlights here, as they thrust their swords in vain at the harpy.

ARIEL as Harpy
You are three men of sin, whom Destiny,
That hath to instrument this lower world
And what is in 't, the never-surfeited sea
Hath caused to belch up you, and on this island,
Where man doth not inhabit, you 'mongst men
Being most unfit to live. I have made you mad;
And even with such-like valour, men hang and drown
Their proper selves.
You fools, I and my fellows
Are ministers of Fate. The elements
Of whom your swords are tempered may as well
Wound the loud winds or with bemocked-at stabs
Kill the still-closing waters as diminish
One dowl that's in my plume...
...you three

From Milan did supplant good Prospero...
...for which foul deed,
The powers—delaying, not forgetting—have
Incensed the seas and shores, yea, all the creatures
Against your peace.
Thee of thy son, Alonso,
They have bereft; and do pronounce by me
Ling'ring perdition, worse than any death
Can be at once, shall step by step attend
You and your ways, whose wraths to guard you
from—
Which here, in this most desolate isle, else falls
Upon your heads—is nothing but heart's sorrow
And a clear life ensuing.
[He vanishes in thunder.]
The Tempest, Act III Scene III

Again, Ariel's voice is heard as the sound and voice of God: 'the heavenly winds sounding the name of Prosper'. Shakespeare's heretical quill is quivering with controversy. He's implying that the sound of wind and thunder, the name of God, is also the name of Prosper — that Prospero is God. He's going about as far as he dares to explain his own symbolism, his own representations of scripture. This delineation will be invaluable when we come to draw our conclusions.

GONZALO, to Alonso
I' th' name of something holy, *sir, why stand you*
In this strange stare?

ALONSO
Methought the billows spoke and told me of it;
The winds did sing it to me, and the thunder,
That deep and dreadful organ pipe, pronounced
The name of Prosper.
The Tempest, Act III Scene III

The main course of the Last Supper is the blessing of the Grail given to all mankind. All mankind, even those who are oblivious, burdened with guilt and feelings of unworthiness, are destined, even if not ready, to know it. Thus, based on what is implied here, even the Adam-Judas-traitor Alonso, who connived with Antonio to depose Prospero, receives the initiation into the sound current: inside him, he is given the hallowed name of God (symbolised as Prosper) and stands transfixed by its wonder.

Caliban's Circle

At the other end of the spectrum of humanity, Caliban, Stephano and Trinculo are also given a run for their money. Ariel conjures a pack of fierce hunting dogs (the hounds of hell) to chase them in terror round the island. Eventually, all three circles of men unite at Prospero's cell for our long-awaited denouement. Now, will all be revealed? Will all our questions be answered? All our loose ends tied neatly in a bow?

Here, the concluding nativity scene has the betrothed soul-couple, Ferdinand-Miranda, in Prospero's cell, playing chess. Daringly, the word *chess* itself is a loose homonym of the sound *chalice*. Chess is also a game symbolising two ranks of men, just like our two opposèd kings, two opposite circles: kings, queens, knights, bishops and castles behind humble pawns — again, from royalty to lowly foot soldiers, the spectrum of humankind. And the eight-by-eight, chequered black-and-white squares are considered by some sects to represent the Holy of Holies in the Temple of Solomon.

The Resurrection of Christ: The Revelation that Ferdinand Has Risen from the Deep

To this already heady cocktail, Shakespeare deftly drops in another ingredient: the resurrection motif. Alonso was convinced his son was dead. Here, now, at the Epiphany, it is with great joy he finds his son, from his perspective, resurrected.

When Alonso experiences the resurrection, it's as if Adam, too, is resurrected, reawakened, forgiven.

Forgiveness of Satan

Did God forgive Satan? Did God forgive Hitler? These are very human questions. With a very big answer: Yes. Can *we* forgive Hitler? Another very human question. With another very big answer.

Yet Jesus challenges us to forgive our enemies and love our neighbours as ourselves. And that we do. We don't love ourselves enough to love our neighbours or forgive our enemies. The delusion, the compulsive addiction to guilt, hatred, resentment and revenge we contract from the invisible contagion that pollutes our world, called good-and-evil, stands between us and self-love, self-forgiveness, happiness, joy, bliss, Ananda and the kingdom of God. The camel must drop to his knees and release his burden to pass through the eye of the needle into the city of Jerusalem. So must we. We must release the burdens of guilt and hatred in order to know God. We must be happy *before* we and *in order to* find God. To forgive ourselves and be happy — that's one way we can check out whether or not we are a resurrected soul who can pass through to the New Jerusalem, the New Atlantis, the New Garden of Eden and Paradise.

Again, if the inquisitors had spotted the Master's directive to self-forgiveness, he would have been burned at the stake. Being open and honest about our actions is intrinsically healing. Honesty allows for divine aid. Dishonesty forfeits divine aid — automatically — by cutting off the God within. Every time you confess your actions falsely as 'sins' and pay penance, you feed the addiction and fuel the contagion. So, Shakespeare hides it in Prospero's sweet dialogue with Ariel.

The Rarer Action Is in Virtue than in Vengeance

Ariel reports back to Prospero that those in Antonio's circle are aware of their crimes and are duly contrite and repentant. Ariel gives Prospero the perfect reason to find the compassion and forgiveness within himself. This is not just lip service. We have no right or power whatsoever to forgive another — that's entirely their business. If we seek vengeance, we damn ourselves to hell on earth. But if we seek peace for ourselves, we have it already. The power to choose empathy and compassion is God-given to us all through the New Testament promise: if we want to receive grace, we must first give grace. Prospero's moment of truth occurs when he takes counsel from his higher self. It's hidden by implying that if an airy spirit can have compassion for a human, then why not he himself? If God can forgive his enemies, so can we! We too can sacrifice the need to strike back. We too can turn the other cheek. Herein lies another of the Master's sweet, oblivious antidotes to that perilous stuff that weighs upon the heart:

ARIEL

Your charm so strongly works 'em
That if you now beheld them, your affections
Would become tender.

PROSPERO

Dost thou think so, spirit?

ARIEL

Mine would, sir, were I human.

PROSPERO

And mine shall.

Hast thou, which art but air, a touch, a feeling

Of their afflictions, and shall not myself,

One of their kind, that relish all as sharply

Passion as they, be kindlier moved than thou art?

Though with their high wrongs I am struck to th'quick,

Yet with my nobler reason 'gainst my fury Do I take part.

[Here cometh the New Testament law]

The rarer action is

In virtue than in vengeance*: they being penitent,*

*The **sole** drift of my purpose doth extend*

Not a frown further.

The Tempest, Act V Scene I

As in *Hamlet,* it seems Shakespeare cannot resist a final pun: sole/soul (one he does use again). To drive home the symbolism, albeit as airy as Ariel, this touching scene of forgiveness-for-all-humanity, together with much of Shakespeare's signature theatricals, is centred around Prospero's cell: the symbol of the Grail chalice, complete with Ferdinand (the body of Christ) and Miranda (the blood seal of the New Testament).

We have seen Antonio, Alonso and the rest of his Satan circle forgiven by the God archetypes. Now for Caliban and his two drunken monkeys in the (still hypothetical) Cain-Abel circle.

Yes, Stephano and Trinculo are given their pardon. But Caliban has a complete transformation. Antonio is as indifferent to forgiveness as he is to guilt. It is simply not in his nature. (Satan must have his thousand years.) In a very different spirit, Prospero also ultimately forgives Caliban. But, unlike Antonio, Caliban is humble; he does repent, he sees the folly of worshipping a communion-wine-drinking ass as a god. He also says something so extraordinary it's easy to blink and miss it. He seeks grace. Grace! This abomination of non-humanity is now seeking grace!

Grace and Truth

Now, this erstwhile, wannabe rapist-murderer-monster who, moments before, wanted to drive a nail through his head is invited back into Prospero's cell like an old drinking buddy. And on what do you suppose they shall sup? Communion wine. Caliban, like Judas, is receiving the forgiveness of the first Holy Communion.

They both express their miraculously transformed relationship in this touching exchange of mutual love and respect. Could we perhaps relate to God in this truly authentic way and, regardless of our miserable past, be invited into the inner kingdom? Yes. That is grace. That is as good a definition of grace and the transformational power of the Grail as we'll probably get. The law was given by Moses. Grace and truth came by Jesus Christ. Thanks for that, John.

PROSPERO [of Caliban]
He is as disproportioned in his manners
As in his shape. [To Caliban.]
Go, sirrah, to my cell.
Take with you your companions. As you look
To have my pardon, trim it handsomely.

CALIBAN
Ay, that I will, and I'll be wise hereafter
And seek for grace.
The Tempest, Act V Scene I

Shakespeare now uses Caliban to take another of his notorious sideswipes at the orthodoxy:

CALIBAN
What a thrice-double ass
Was I to take this drunkard for a god,
And worship this dull fool!
The Tempest, Act V Scene I

This scene truly completes the Grail quest. Whereas in *Hamlet* the finale focuses more on the death of Rosencrantz and Guildenstern (the Old Testament Law), *The Tempest* has the resurrection of the soul, our rebirth, sealed forever in the New Testament marriage: our betrothal to God through the Christ. Can you not hear the Fortinbras? The sound of tinkling cymbals and sounding brass?

Tarry Awhile on Prospero's Isle

There's always more in Elsinore, so let's tarry awhile on Prospero's Isle. We have a few more unanswered questions and loose ends to tie up before we sleep tonight. Let's see if a little NameAlchemy will help.

Chapter 10:
Name Alchemy
IN THE TEMPEST

It's through his ingenious NameAlchemy that Shakespeare fulfils the finer points of his revelation. I sincerely doubt if it's possible to understand one play without reference to one or more of the others, which further proves my thesis that there is, in fact, only one play in thirty-two iterations. Perhaps, on the balance of probabilities, you may be satisfied that the promise of the premise is already proven. That is not good enough for me. I need to be satisfied beyond reasonable doubt. This is how I have driven in the nail of certainty for myself.

The Monstrous Birth

Since reading *Othello*, I have usurped the term 'monstrous birth' to describe the being we have become since, in Shakespeare's theology, Satan raped Eve and sired the hybrid Cain and Abel, who usurped the royal crown of the soul.

In the intro, the first recurring theme noted was the intercourse of the serpent with Eve, resulting in the monstrous birth of Cain and Abel. In every play, there seems to exist some variation of this Cain-Abel archetype. In *Richard II* — discussed in depth in *Vol II* — Shakespeare establishes it quite specifically. But its presence is only alluded to in *Macbeth* and *Hamlet*. Is *The Tempest* the play where allusion becomes as close to proof as we can get?

Wherefore Art Thou Caliban?

Much speculation has abounded over the centuries about the name *Caliban*. Could it be a subliminal reference to Kali, the Hindu male-mortal demon? Is it perhaps an anagram of 'cannibal', one of those scary, monstrous people who eat human flesh?

Or could Caliban be the keystone of his entire heretical theology?

Just like the Bible does, Shakespeare alludes to multiple species of heresy, including the three archetypes that occupy our inner world of consciousness and the funny names he makes up to delineate these archetypes. I've also postulated that all his plays are iterations of his one core subtextual theme revealing the truth about the Holy Grail and that *The Tempest* is the denouement, the finale of all the plays wherein the strands of the plot are drawn together and mysteries explained or resolved.

One of the paradoxes of *the truth* is that it cannot be proven in an unambiguous way that satisfies the criteria of science and logic. As soon as you speak or write down the truth, it becomes a lie. We need to validate the truth for ourselves alone. It's not meat for the ego to brag about or gain material reward or acknowledgment. As best I can, I'm writing down the truth as I see and know it. But on this page, it is a lie. The best I can do is offer it to you on a plate for your consideration. If it resonates inside you with the part that knows the truth, I'd love to know about it. *Join the conversation*. If it doesn't, but you'd still like to add a perspective or discuss it — same thing — *join the conversation.*

That said, would it not be beyond sublime if Caliban could 'prove' all the above hypotheses in one fell swoop?

In John, Jesus minces not his words with the scribes and Pharisees who are trying to trap him into heresy. Is this verse perhaps a major source of inspiration for Shakespeare's characterisation of the ego, the monstrous birth: Caliban?

> *Ye are of your father the devil, and the lusts of your father ye*
> *will do. He was a murderer from the beginning [Cain], and*
> *abode not in the truth, because there is no truth in him. When*
> *he speaketh a lie, he speaketh of his own: for he is a liar, and the*
> *father of it. And because I tell you the truth, ye believe me not.*
> John 8:44-45

I was agonizing one night over the letters of the name C-A-L-I-B-A-N. Scrabble letters were spread out in a circle on the coffee table. Geri, my wife (who had also earlier spotted that GONERIL is an anagram of RELIGON), came to offer a back rub and some solace. When I confessed my dilemma (I knew the name was deceptively profound — but why?) she said, 'How about CAIN ABL?' as she reordered the little plastic squares.

Eureka!

In the same way Shakespeare gave GONERIL and REGAN 'funny names' that turn out to be anagrams of RELIGON and ANGER and point to his deeper meaning and intention of the play, and in the same way CORDELIA is a 'funny name' that turns out to be wordsmithery and NameAlchemy meaning COEUR-DE-LEAR, CALIBAN is CAIN-ABL, meaning Cain-Abel.

In one fell swoop, Caliban's name being one of Shakespeare's amazing anagram/homonyms of Cain-Abel 'proves' all four interrelated hypotheses:

1. The NameAlchemy
2. The three archetypes
3. The forbidden fruit of the Grail
4. The denouement

Thus, Caliban is the ultimate personification of the Cain-Abel archetype: the false self reincarnated in different bodies throughout the oeuvre. He is, beyond reasonable doubt, the same hybrid issue of Eve's unholy communion with the serpent; the half-human, half-devil issue of Sycorax and the Devil: the monstrous birth, the demi-devil, the Iago, the supplanter that stalks the Globe with impunity — the fat, shallow, lovable Falstaff, the fallen Macbeth, the disgusting Aaron, the infinite variety of empty, callous, soulless psychopaths rampaging through Shakespeare's plays and our histories, our governments, our corporate giants, our prisons, our churches, our lives and our world.

For the Inner Pedant

In case the inner pedant in your mind is protesting about the missing 'E' in ABEL and the missing 'I' in RELIGION, I have it on good authority that such elision is widely practised among the circles of ancient cryptologists. Because anagrams can be quite easy to spot, some letters are cunningly left out while the sound of the word is unaffected. Caliban, once more corroborated by Prospero himself:

PROSPERO [of Caliban]
A devil, a born devil, on whose nature
Nurture can never stick
The Tempest, Act IV Scene I

Cain-Abel, the archetype of our own ego-personality, the 'opposèd kings', our twin false-selves? Beyond reasonable doubt? It's for you to decide this for yourself.

Antonio the Anti-Tone

In the archetype groups we revealed above, we also note that Antonio leads the Satan circle, the archetype of Lucifer played by Macbeth in *Macbeth* and by Claudius in *Hamlet*. So, what happens if we now apply NameAlchemy to ANTONIO? Does it prove or disprove our theory?

Of all the possible names he could have chosen, Antonio seems pretty unremarkable. But what if, like Cordelia, it is the *resonance* of the name that is the key to its significance? *The Tempest* itself is the sound current, the Christ, the sacred tones. It would be typical of the Master to amuse himself and us with a crafty dig at tagging Antonio as the Antichrist. If the true name, the true tone, is the way to the Father, the ANTI-TONE (anagram containing ANTONIO), the false name, would be the way to Satan. Once again, NameAlchemy corroborates what Shakespeare is telling us about the three groups of archetypes.

So, what of the God circle, containing Prospero, Miranda and Ferdinand? Could the relationship between Prospero and Ariel be the same as that between Hamlet and Ophelia? Is Ariel Prospero's spirit-self? Let us first apply reverse NameAlchemy to Prospero.

Prospero, Prospero, Wherefore Art Thou Prospero?

But the men marvelled, saying, What manner of man is this,
that even the winds and the sea obey him!
Matthew 8:27

Let's see if we can nail Prospero's archetype. His power over the elements and even the Holy Spirit suggest the God-like qualities of Jesus. Some say he was made in the image of Shakespeare himself. Maybe so, but that's not much help on our Grail quest. Frequently, we can identify one archetype in relation to one or more others. Prospero's relationship to Miranda is clear but with Ariel and Caliban, it becomes more telling. Ariel and Caliban are both servants to his power. But Ariel, as a character, is motivated *towards* the promise of freedom and liberation. Caliban, in contrast is motivated *away from* the excruciating pain of cramps administered by Prospero's rough magic. A lesson in carrot-and-stick leadership styles to fit the purpose of those to be led. Ariel wants the true freedom that comes through disciplined alignment to a noble purpose. Caliban wants false freedom, the licence to do whatever he pleases and damn the consequences.

The answer has always seemed to lie in the text. Prospero (always through Ariel) has absolute power not just over the inhabitants of the Isle but also the weather, the wind and the seas. Hidden in plain sight and camouflaged so effectively as poetic licence are so many allusions to Prospero's God-like omnipotence and divinity and how it was usurped that I'd have to reproduce the entire text to show them all here. Here's just a representative sample:

> *I find my zenith doth depend upon a most auspicious star,*
> *I am ...a god of power... a Prince of power*
> *Thou dost here usurp*
> *The name thou ow'st not, and hast put thyself*
> *Upon this island as a spy, to win it*
> *From me, the lord on 't.*
> *The Tempest*, Act I Scene II

By default, it would be Prospero's relationship to his brother, the serpent, that nails his archetype (or one of them). He would be the deity we met in *Hamlet*, the god of day, deposed by Cain and Abel when Adam followed Eve into the drug-induced delusion of good-and-evil.

But, as soon as we get too smug about cracking those clues, an anomaly pops up: if Prospero is God, why would he need a staff and a book through which to wield his power? Is there yet another archetypical character lurking beneath his cloak for us to unmask? Maybe the question is not so much 'Who is Prospero?' but 'How many different roles, aspects, and archetypes does he embody?'

The God of Love?

Have you, like me, been wondering if there's a hidden meaning in the name PROSPERO? I've wondered about PROPER, as in proper/rightful ruler. It could also be PRO SPERO, Latin/Italian FOR HOPE. But HOPE is a tad wishy-washy for my taste. Spero is also a well-known, eleventh-century Jewish name. However, PROSPERO could be another of those famous quasi anagrams: PRO EROS. Pro Eros: for the God of love/ love of God. Yes, I think this gets my vote. Prospero, the God of love versus Antonio the God of lust. Eureka!

The Office of the Christ

If we review Prospero's circle, it encompasses the joint archetypes of God and the Christ. 'Christ' is another one of those terms that's been not only misunderstood but abused and corrupted. Originally, it is Greek for 'anointed one of God': *Christos.*

Lesser known is that we, the soul, the image of God within, are the anointed ones of God, the only begotten. We are all Christs. The Christ is who we all really are. Jesus said so, in many ways.

Even lesser known, but also implied in the scripture, is that 'the Christ' is a high spiritual office in a similar way to 'the King' being a high earthly office. In the past twelve hundred years, there have been around sixty kings of England. England is a monarchy. It's well known that, king or queen, there's always someone sitting on the throne, fulfilling the office of the King. What's not so well known is that there's always someone sitting on the spiritual throne, fulfilling the office of the Christ. Why not so well known? This is just one more tiny, insignificant detail extirpated from the dogma. Jesus was one of many who have held the office of the Christ since the beginning and to this very day. In the beginning was the Word. The 'Word' is another word for 'the Christ' — not Jesus the Christ, but the Christ consciousness. Jesus was one in a long line of Christs. That Jesus really did deserve the title 'King of the Jews' was just as misunderstood as pretty much everything else then and now.

Who Does Ariel Really Represent?

Who or what might ARIEL symbolise? Perhaps the name is an intentional homonym of the Archangel Uriel? Perhaps also a pun on the sweet sounds and 'airs' heard on the Isle initiated by Ariel?

We have two other lines of enquiry:

1. Where did Ariel come from?
2. What does he do?

Ariel, Prospero says, was found bound in a 'cloven pine', having been imprisoned there by Sycorax twelve years hence.

PROSPERO

And in her most unmitigable rage,
Into a cloven pine, within which rift
Imprisoned thou didst painfully remain
A dozen years; within which space she died
And left thee there, where thou didst vent thy groans
As fast as mill wheels strike.
The Tempest, Act I Scene II

So, what might a cloven pine symbolise?

Cloven — Like the forked tongue of a serpent, alluded to by Caliban, son of Sycorax: 'Sometime am I all wound with adders, who with cloven tongues do hiss me into madness.'

Pine — An allusion to the Tree of Life, with its myriad symbolic disguises: the fountain of the source of life, the life stream, the breath of life, the life blood, the Word, the sound current, the umbilicus twixt God and man, cut off by Satan's fall.

Could all the work Ariel is called upon to do to gain his freedom represent the actions of the Christ prophesied to unlock the seven seals of Satan holding the soul — and the sound current, the ear of man — prisoner? With Ferdinand, Prospero apologises and justifies the trials he gave him.

PROSPERO

All thy vexations
Were but my trials of thy love, and thou
Hast strangely stood the test.
The Tempest, Act IV Scene I

With Ariel, it's all implied, seemingly taken for granted. As Ophelia was to Hamlet, Ariel is Prospero's true self projected outwards: God as the Holy Spirit, the whole Spirit, the light plus the sound — the sound that was cut off by Eve's rape and insemination by the serpent. Ariel's freedom, and likewise Prospero's liberation from this Isle-prison-paradise, is contingent upon the completion of all his own tasks and all the tests Ferdinand (the Christ) must endure. And here we have the trinity: father, son, and Holy Spirit bringing justice to the unjust and the way out of this earth-bound nightmare we call hell. Funny, we're made to fear going to hell when we die — we don't realise we're already here. Ferdinand said it in his opening speech. He was birthed into this world crying 'Hell is empty and all the devils are here.' Don't believe me. Look around. Look at who's running the countries and the giant corporations. Look at who votes these mad tyrants into power. Look at the news. Look at your own pain.

My question/assumption at the beginning of Part Three was around

Ariel's being a personification of the sound current, called the Holy Spirit at the Pentecost, made un-whole/cut off by Satan, reunited by the Christ action, sealed in his blood. In other words, the whole spirit consists of not just the light of God but also the sound of God. It was the sound of God that was cut off in the beginning. It was the sound of God that is symbolised in Genesis as the Tree of Life. It was the sound of God that was restored in the end. Here it is again as described in Acts 2:2, in the upper room, at the feast of the Pentecost, right after the Ascension: the completion of Christ's mission on earth, affirmed in Revelation by the immortal words 'It is done!'

> *And suddenly there came a sound from heaven*
> *as of a **rushing mighty wind**, and it filled all*
> *the house where they were sitting.*
> Acts 2:2

Is it this mighty wind that, throughout the works, Shakespeare dramatises as *The Tempest*? Ariel *is* that tempest. He *is* the storm. He *is* the sounds, the sweet airs, the voices, the names all those on the Isle hear, the sounds and noises that bring delight but hurt not.

Ariel gets his food, his nourishment where the bee sucks the sweet nectar of the gods.

ARIEL
Where the bee sucks, there suck I.
In a cowslip's bell I lie.
The Tempest, Act V Scene I

When we hear the voice of Ariel singing, the players hear the sounds of winds and the rain beating down; they hear the sounds of God's hallowed name. Ariel seems to be an embodiment of the Tempest — in other words, the sound current of God — and Shakespeare devoted and risked his entire life to bring this knowledge out of the darkness, into this audacious dramatisation of this cruelly extirpated wisdom of the Grail.

EPILOGUE

Sin Is Dead. But It Won't Lie Down

Through the lens of Shakespeare's Rosetta Stone, it's clear the gospel tells us *sin is dead*. Rosencrantz and Guildenstern are dead. That's one of the greatest practical gifts we were not given in the narrative. This is the essence of the Holy Grail, the *sang graal*: the blood of the New Testament shed for all for the remission of sin: the end of sin.

We also realise from Hamlet's 'to be or not to be' that it is erroneous to subscribe to the popular idea that Satan is evil and is in constant conflict with God, aka good. Satan is a metaphor for both good *and* evil, the duality, the original sin, the seven seals and the constant inner and outer conflict we all have with the false-good and the false-evil of our ego-selves. The only way out of that conflict and suffering is to transcend the ego, resurrect ourselves into soul-self-awareness and know the pure absolute Goodness of our own soul, our true-self, aka the deeper truth represented by the Word and sound of 'God'.

Sin is dead, but most of the religions can't live without it — because their ears are senseless, they do not understand what sin really is. They have misdefined it and stubbornly refuse to accept the true, original, dictionary meaning. Original Sin died on the cross. The Christ resurrected. And the religions resurrected Moses and kept applying their false definition of sin: disobedience of God's divine law. In applying their false definition of sin, they are ironically committing the true definition: cutting themselves off from God. This absurd hypocrisy is the double-double bind Shakespeare is continuously mocking, lampooning and satirising in all thirty-seven plays. But so be it. Religious faith and its belief systems is one of so many stages in the soul's evolution. They'll let it go when they're ready.

Are you ready?

In the beginning, in our quest for the Holy Grail, we considered that something rotten had gotten into the state of Denmark. Something Jesus had perhaps come to eradicate. Something forbidden but kept hidden.

We had four possible contenders for Jesus's divine mission:

1. To forgive the Original Sin?
2. To fulfil the law of Moses?
3. To reopen access to the Tree of Life?
4. To breach the seven seals?

As far as I can tell through Shakespeare, it turns out that all four of these agenda items are all inextricably connected, much like the fingers of a hand are all parts of the same. And much of the mystery, confusion and pain surrounding the Christ action is immediately resolved when we treat them like this.

Original Sin Is the Seven Seals Is the Law of Moses Is Satan Is Good and Evil: They All Cut Off Soul-Self-Awareness

If you were a sacred cryptographer wanting to keep crucial information safe from extirpation for thousands of years, what would you do? You'd disguise it by calling it by multiple different words and symbols — each with its own vast mythology. You would thereby muddy the water, fill it with red herrings and keep your precious water-babies safe for all eternity.

Remember Einstein famously saying:

No problem can be solved from the same level
of consciousness that created it.

The term *original sin* was incepted by Constantine *after* Nicaea. Speciously, he decreed that man was born sinful and could only be redeemed through belief in Jesus Christ. But this concept of sin and all its variations is a man-made belief caused by the delusion in the mind of the misunderstood, erroneously defined problem of original sin. It is a circular problem, a double bind that cannot therefore be solved unless we have transcended the consciousness of original sin itself: the hallucination of good-and-evil.

Original sin (which must be what many Eastern religions and philosophies call Maya) formed the complete (number seven) seal because not only did it cut us off from awareness of our soul (and, through this, awareness of God), but through the mind, we cannot see the way out of the dilemma because the mind *is* the dilemma. The mind comes up with perfectly reasonable, perfectly erroneous, definitions of sin being actions or thoughts that violate God's divine laws. This is exactly the same dilemma that keeps the soul locked out of paradise, exactly the same dilemma God incarnated as Jesus to resolve.

Through the mind, in cahoots with the emotions, we continuously make judgements, feel guilty, resentful, insecure and anxious — all of which keep us trapped in internal bondage and all of which are individual acts of sin that mirror the Original Sin by cutting us off from God and enticing us into worshipping 'false gods', believing them to be real.

How does this sound as a renewed summary of the Holy Grail? Does it have the ring of truth?

Through the final shedding of his blood, the *sang graal*, in one fell swoop, Jesus the Christ sealed the promise of the New Testament, unsealed the Old Testament Law of Moses, and breached the 'seven seals' of the 'Original Sin'.

Thus, access to the Tree of Life (the sound current) and paradise was reopened for all of us who are ready to choose grace over revenge: to choose mercy, forgiveness and compassion over guilt and resentment.

Rewinding the metaphor of scripture:

In the beginning, man and God were in paradise together, in a state of pure holy communion.

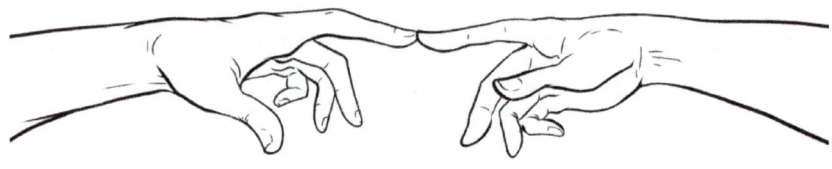

Michelangelo said it like this:

God did not know what his ultimate possibility might be, so he uttered the one and only true commandment: '*Let there be light*'.

God extended himself as a soul into our body as his representatives to gain experience of the created worlds and return home to God in the Spirit. He authorized his trusted Archangel, Satan, to initiate the manifestation of all the created worlds in his Name.

But, as the story goes, Satan wanted all the power and the glory for himself. He betrayed God, raped Eve, lied to Adam and deposed the soul as the centre of consciousness of mankind. He tempted Adam and Eve to lie, to cover themselves up in shame, to blame each other and to feel guilty.

The original guilt was the Original Sin. The Original Sin was also the seven seals that Jesus was prophesied to breach.

The number 'seven' in most systems of numerology means 'complete' or 'perfect'. The seven seals is biblical code for the complete/perfect seal — something that cuts us off from God completely: the Original Sin.

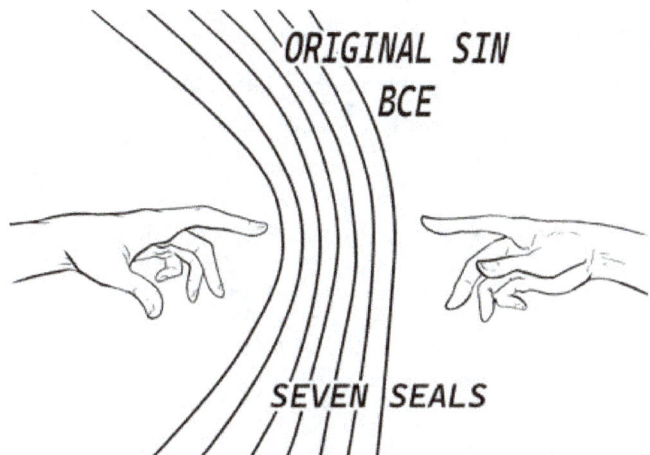

Original Sin is the perfect seal cutting off the ear of man

Satan enclosed the consciousness of all mankind in what became known as Original Sin, also symbolised in Revelation as 'the seven seals'. Seven symbolised a complete and perfect barrier between man and God that cut us all off from awareness of our soul, the sound of God and the freedom to know and walk with God in paradise.

So that we would worship him as God for eternity, Satan encased himself around our soul and prevented us from completing our mission on earth and returning to the Godhead.

Not only does Original Sin/the seven seals cut us off from soul-self-awareness, it also distorts our perceptions. The mind is so malleable; it has us believe anything regardless of fact — let alone truth. What we believe becomes true — for us. But to believe is to be-lie-live, to be a lie. In the mind, truth seems like lies and lies seem like truth. We live backwards. We see through a glass darkly. To see 'what is' requires we transcend the mind, transcend the seven seals. Before this current era, only a very few select souls could do this.

Because God had made a covenant, a testament, with Satan, he could not renege on his word. To depose Satan and have the soul reclaim its rightful place on the throne of our inner kingdom, over four hundred trials, tests and tasks had to be fulfilled by a Christed being in and through an earthly body. Many in the line of the Christs failed to overcome Satan's power. But this was an evolutionary process. Eventually, one known as Jesus the Christ passed all the tests.

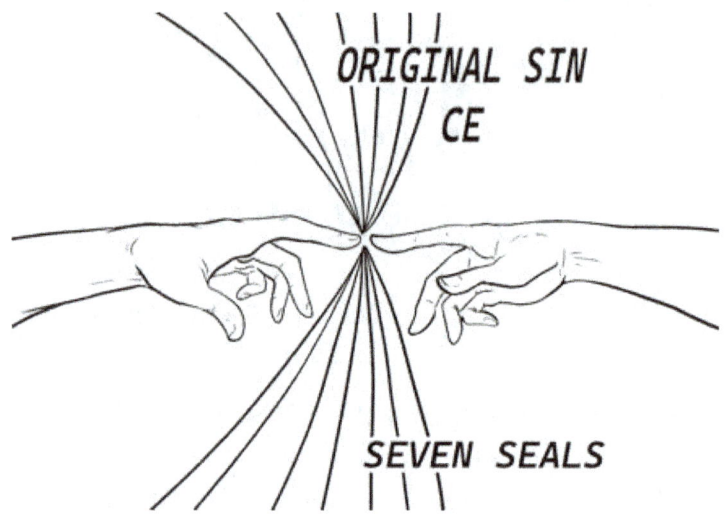

Jesus breached the seven seals/original sin

This is an ideal moment to contemplate how Hamlet 'cut off the ear of Claudius (Satan)'. If you remember, he pierced the arras (shroud, curtain) with a sword behind which Polonius was hiding. Polonius is the metaphorical 'ear of Claudius'. This is one of many ways Shakespeare symbolises the breach of the seven seals. If you read with the eyes of knowing you'll see how Hamlet is telling us what the implications of killing Polonius are. 'A bloody deed (the blessing of the sangraal) piercing the shroud under which we live! Then, he expresses his disdain for his uncle's servant, 'thou wretched, rash, intruding fool, farewell! I took thee for thy better (didn't we all — we are all taken in by the delusion of good-and-evil/Original Sin).

In Volume II you'll see the same motif playing out when Henry V breaches the walls of Harfleur with the name of God. 'Once more unto the breach…

Cry God...for Harry, England, and St George'.

The blood shed by Jesus the Christ, the *sang graal*, together with the crowing of the cock, the name that awakens the god of day, breached the seven seals, unsealed the Old Testament laws of Moses, and finally sealed the New Testament promise. This promised that if we show love, forgiveness and mercy to ourselves and each other, we may live in grace. If we are connected to the sacred name of God, known as the sound current (*The Tempest*), we can enter into the gates of paradise through the breach in the seven seals. This is 'the way' also known sometimes as 'the eye of the needle', the 'third eye chakra', the 'Tisra Til', the 'tenth door' and many other terms.

This was a crucial element of the true teaching of Jesus the Christ and the line of Christs going back to Adam.

This knowledge is only part of what was omitted from the narrative at Nicaea and kept alive as the legend of the Holy Grail.

Satan is still the lord of the worlds below the soul (physical, imagination, emotions, mind, unconscious). But the Mosaic law demanding an eye-for-an-eye is dead. All man-made, so-called sin is dead. The higher law that says we reap what we sow is always in force. But no longer can any man be judged by any other. We are all accountable to our own soul until we have brought all our actions — negative and positive — into balance.

The persistent refusal of the religious and secular alike to let 'sin' (GuiltSin) lie down is still the main cause of all the woes of mankind. Jesus has forgiven the Original Sin for all mankind. Each of us now has the responsibility to forgive ourselves, to forgive all the judgements we make, all the abuses we make of the word 'sin', which is a kind of 'anti-tone' preventing the 'end of the heartache and the thousand natural shocks that flesh is heir to'.

The word 'sin' has been misappropriated and weaponised to strike terror and obedience into the hearts of man. The only authentic meaning of sin is *to cut oneself off from the awareness of God within*. Every time we judge ourselves or another person by feeling guilt or resentment, we are committing GuiltSin

— we are cutting off our own soul-self-awareness. We are placing our ego's point of view over and above God's. It's a choice. It's optional. We get to feel self-righteous, but we pay the price of loss of connection with our soul, loss of self-love, loss of self-respect, and we open the door to stress-related illness and depression, not to mention global warming and the catastrophic destruction of our planet.

It Is Done. So Is Armageddon.

Consider that Revelation is not talking about some future event. The blessings already are. Revelation is about the now, the present, the absolute here and the eternal now. Armageddon is a paradox. Though the battle already be won, as Matthew 10:22, says, to claim our own liberation from this temporal world, we must endure to the end.

Forget about how the future and the past steal our lives from us. Forget about how 'tomorrow and tomorrow and tomorrow creeps in its petty pace till the last syllable of recorded time.' Forget about how 'all our yesterdays have lighted fools the way to dusty death.'

Get yourself into the present, where God, forgiveness, truth and freedom exist.

Our purpose in life is simple: to be or not to be. To be who we really are as a soul, or not to be. This is the fundamental, existential choice we can decide to make now. And every time we take a new breath, we must choose our choice again. If we do, we do. If we don't, there's another chance with the next breath round the next corner, and another, and another, and as many lifetimes as we need to transcend the Shroud of Turin and not just *see* the face of God but *be* the face of God — to be the face of God we have always been and always will be.

In other words, the entire vast, convoluted litany of sins as fabricated by canon law is false doctrine backed up by references to scripture distorted by the action of Original Sin on the minds of the interpreters. Unless it facilitates self-forgiveness, the ritual of forgiveness and absolution given by a priest is redundant. Unless Jesus lied, God has already forgiven everyone for everything forever.

Genesis 1: 26-27, before the Original Sin originated, says that God said:

Let us make man in our image, after our likeness: and let
them have dominion over the fish of the sea, and over the
fowl of the air, and over the cattle, and over all the earth, and
over every creeping thing that creepeth upon the earth.

So God created man in his own image, in the image of God
created he him; male and female created he them.

Note the unmissable gender fluidity in the language: God is male, female, singular, and plural — and so is man.

Thus, despite the self-righteous condemnation by the ignorant, the Grail truth of the New Testament promises that, while some of these actions may create karmic rebalancing, nevertheless:

- A crime is not a sin.
- 'Immorality' is not a sin.
- Adultery is not a sin.
- Fornication is not a sin.
- Masturbation is not a sin.
- Homosexuality is not a sin.
- Sodomy is not a sin.
- Bestiality is not a sin.
- Paedophilia is not a sin.
- Contraception is not a sin.
- Abortion is not a sin.
- Abortion is not murder.
- Murder is not a sin.

And so on.

However, if we judge ourselves or any other person for any action we do or they do or do not do, we mock God. And *that* is a sin: because we thereby cut Him off. Except in the legal sense of upholding the law of the land, no one has the right to judge. 'Judge not least ye too be judged.' As we forgive others, so are we forgiving ourselves.

Shakespeare's Holy Grail — Volume II: The Fisher Kings

Shakespeare wrote thirty-seven plays, all exploring the secrets of the Grail from different angles. In Volume II, I shall be focusing on the Henriad, the four plays in the line of the three kings: *Richard II*, *Henry IV*, and *Henry V*. The way he treats the fall of man, the tyranny of Satan, fulfilling the law and breaching the seven seals is beyond awesome.

A Parting Gift

We know from *King Lear* and *The Merchant of Venice* that Shakespeare goes to great lengths to craft cryptic names that convey crucial clues to his deeper intention: anagrams, wordplay and NameAlchemy.

We've just seen how the 'funny name' CALIBAN confirms one of the most important psycho-spiritual axioms of his oeuvre: the three core archetypes. Is there anything else, Master Shakespeare, you want us to know?

What the early Church did not tell anyone is that the New Testament was a complete replacement for the Old Testament. Who buys a new suit and wears it on top of the old one? The early Christians!

Shakespeare tells us this cryptically through *Hamlet* as the death of Rosencrantz and Guildenstern: the two 'Jews'. In *The Tempest,* through one of the archetypes embodied by Prospero, he redefines an oxymoron by making his ultimate, final, outrageously explicit, cryptically camouflaged biblical motif.

What of Prospero's Staff and Books?

Look at this, one of the final speeches in the play. Who does it bring to mind?

PROSPERO

But this rough magic
I here abjure, and when I have required
Some heavenly music, which even now I do,
[Prospero gestures with his staff]
To work mine end upon their senses that
This airy charm is for, I'll break my staff,
Bury it certain fathoms in the earth,
And deeper than did ever plummet sound
I'll drown my book.
The Tempest, Act V Scene I

Who is the most famous biblical character who would use his staff to do magic, command the seas, and turn water into blood? Who is the famous biblical character after whom Mosaic law is named?

It was a law that glorified revenge, that gave absolute power to the priesthood to exact punishment in God's name, a law that, far from liberating the children of God (all mankind), slammed shut the gates of heaven and silenced the ear of man. It's the law and testament Shakespeare has been risking his life in telling us has been superseded by the New Testament of the Christ.

That's right. Moses.

Oy vey!

So, Prospero is Moses, already? It is more that Moses is one of the characterisations of the God/Christ archetype that Prospero is representing. And now the eye-wateringly exquisite beauty of Shakespeare's art comes to its final coda. At the end of *The Tempest,* Prospero breaks his staff and drowns his books, symbolising Moses, the Christ himself, breaking the staff given to him as the key to his office and disposing of the books that represent the laws of the Old Testament that served God's purpose until we, mankind, were ready to rise up to our next level of spiritual evolution. Rosencrantz and Guildenstern are dead. The law is over.

What about Miranda?

So now, the only name we have not looked at is MIRANDA. A quick reshuffle reveals an anagram of MARIA smiling sweetly within. This was implied earlier by her possible representation of the Magdalene — or even the Virgin Mary.

But if we look deeply into the names of the married couple, the union of the names MIRANDA with FERDINAND gives birth to something more wonderful:

MIRANDA + FERDINAND = ANANDA

Ananda, that Sanskrit word for *spiritual bliss.* That name, *Sat-Chit-Ananda,* which is said to be the closest vibrational frequency to that of Jesus Christ. Could the Master be telling us that the Son of Man marries a girl named Maria and produces spiritual bliss for all mankind — Ananda, heaven, paradise? If Jesus did marry Mary Magdalene, was this union also the reunion of God and mankind, the ultimate holy matrimony that is sanctified by and celebrated in our mortal marriages?

And, there's always more:

MIRANDA + FERDINAND (also) = ANANDA + ADAM

How d'ya like them apples?

I'd like to save the very last word for the very last words of John the Beloved, forever enigmatic.

And there are also many other things which Jesus did, the which,
if they should be written every one, I suppose that even the world
itself could not contain the books that should be written. Amen.
John 21:25

To me, he's talking about the infinite knowledge and wisdom within our soul that cannot be contained in any material vessel: another core aspect of the Holy Grail, the abundant source of wisdom and supply that feeds the eternal life.

Thanks, John.

Roger and out.

THE BEGINNING

ABOUT THE AUTHOR

These days I have two major passions competing for attention: riding, and writing/speaking about Shakespeare's mystical secrets. For over 40 years I have been an author, speaker, facilitator, and soul-focused life-purpose coach. Since the 1990's I have been honing and fine-tuning my intuition and soul-talk through Shabdha Yoga, divining biblical symbolism, and bringing horses into boardrooms. Little did I realise that by employing horse-whispering to transform the lives of senior executives, I was also being groomed to fulfil an even greater destiny through the works of William Shakespeare.

I invite you to meet up via my website, http://paulhunting.com/conversation where a table of plenty awaits you. If you'd like a free 20 minute chat to ask about coaching, counselling or anything Shakespeare you can simply *click here*.

Originally from West Hampstead, London, England, for over 20 years I have lived and worked from the demi-paradise near Stratford-upon-Avon I share with my wife, three horses, twelve chickens, Twaji the cat, and the various furry friends she brings in.

My daily bread usually includes natural dressage training with my young horse, Boris, meditation, playing chess, creative writing, cracking cryptic crosswords, cooking great meals, and watching Nordic Noir — not necessarily in that order.

ACKNOWLEDGEMENTS

My heartfelt gratitude goes to Geri, my wife, who uncomplainingly, unconditionally, supported me when our lives were abruptly interrupted by the spirit of the Bard rampaging through my life. Not only has she endured my sleepless nights, oscillating moods, and the usurping of the kitchen table, but has been able to spot all things I miss in my writings — from gross errors to the most subtle anagrams and biblical motifs. Without her this book would not have happened.

Dr. Paul Kaye has been in high support of my writings and musings over the past 20 or so years. Always mercilessly honest, he has been a kind of informal mentor as I've wrestled with various attempts to write about the misunderstandings and labyrinthine symbols throughout the Bible, and latterly, found with great delight, in Shakespeare.

In this latest chapter of my life so many kind people have contributed to my clarifying the unthinkable and expressing the unknowable. Special thanks go to Anton Lesser, Wil Skaskiw, Dr. Kinka Gerke, and Dr. Russell Bishop for painstakingly reading manuscripts and feeding back to me their invaluable insights and comments.

Speaking of... a huge thank-you to the wonderful Sophie Bradshaw, my editor. I'd already spent thousands on rounds of professional editing. But I could tell they were all haplessly unable to grasp the essence of the book and pull together all the various strands of thought. Sophie, however, totally 'got it'. If you, too, have 'got it', then much of the credit goes to her.

I must also thank the creators of Google, Wikipedia, the Folger Institute, and Bible Gateway who have transformed the slog of research and quote-grabbing into a lightning-fast delight — and made me look far more erudite than I really am.

Big thanks also to Victoria Wolf, cover designer extraordinaire. She's one of those rare creative spirits who devotes as much time as it takes working with a client to make sure even the subtle nuances of the idea get infused with the design.

www.ingramcontent.com/pod-product-compliance
Lightning Source LLC
Chambersburg PA
CBHW060904120626
46553CB00001B/201